Altruistic Reveries:
Perspectives from the Humanities and Social Sciences

Altruistic Reveries:
Perspectives from the Humanities and Social Sciences

edited by

Basant K. Kapur
and
Kim-Chong Chong

National University of Singapore

Springer Science+Business Media, LLC

Library of Congress Cataloging-in-Publication Data

A C.I.P. Catalogue record for this book is available from the Library of Congress.

ISBN 978-1-4613-5250-1 ISBN 978-1-4615-0809-0 (eBook)
DOI 10.1007/978-1-4615-0809-0

Printed on acid-free paper.

Contents

Contributors

Anthony Chang, *Department of Social Work and Psychology, National University of Singapore*

Kim-Chong Chong, *Department of Philosophy, National University of Singapore*

Michael Collins, *Department of English Language and Literature, National University of Singapore*

Vincent C.H. Chua , *Department of Economics, National University of Singapore*

Basant K. Kapur, *Department of Economics, National University of Singapore*

Liew-Geok Leong, *Department of English Language and Literature, National University of Singapore*

Elizabeth Nair, *Department of Social Work and Psychology, National University of Singapore*

A.T. Nuyen, *Department of Philosophy, National University of Singapore*

Antonio L. Rappa, *Department of Political Science, National University of Singapore*

C.L. Ten, *Department of Philosophy, National University of Singapore*

C.M. Wong, *Department of Economics, National University of Singapore*

Wei-Bin Zhang, *Ritsumeikan Asia Pacific University*

Acknowledgements

The papers in this volume arose out of a Conference on "Perspectives on Altruism from the Humanities and Social Sciences" held at the National University of Singapore (NUS) on 29 October 1999. The Conference, initially proposed by Basant Kapur, received strong and valuable support from the then Dean of the NUS Faculty of Arts and Social Sciences Tong Chee Kiong and the Director of the NUS Centre for Advanced Studies (CAS) Brenda Yeoh. It was funded by the CAS and organized by a Committee comprising Ngiam Tee Liang (then Deputy Director CAS), Yong Jong Say and Robbie Goh (both Assistant Directors of CAS at that time). We thank Ngiam Tee Liang and his team for their efforts in organizing the Conference. The process of bringing out the volume based on selected papers from the Conference was left to us, the editors. We thank the contributors for their cooperation in making revisions.

We would also like to take this opportunity to thank Lily Kong, Dean, Faculty of Arts and Social Sciences, National University of Singapore, who has encouraged our efforts in bringing out this volume. We are most grateful for her thoughtful and gracious Foreword. We also thank Allard Winterink of Kluwer for his guidance and support in the process of publication.

CAS was most generous in acceding to our requests for funding toward the publication of this volume. For this, we are grateful to both the Director of CAS Brenda Yeoh and the Deputy Director Tan Ern Ser. One of the main functions of the CAS is to support multidisciplinary research. We are happy to say that this volume brings together the perspectives of people from different disciplines, from both the Humanities and the Social Sciences. It was most appropriate therefore that the philosopher C.L. Ten — Elected

Fellow of both the Australian Humanities Academy and the Australian Social Sciences Academy—gave the Keynote Address at the Conference.

Basant Kapur
Kim-Chong Chong

June 2001

Foreword

It is my great pleasure to pen this Foreword, for a variety of reasons. First, it is an excellent effort on the part of two senior colleagues in the Faculty of Arts and Social Sciences, National University of Singapore, to take the lead in encouraging and developing multidisciplinary and interdisciplinary dialogue. Basant Kapur and Kim-Chong Chong sought out the contributors, including philosophers, psychologists, political scientists, economists and literary scholars, whose papers in this volume attest to the rich diversity of talent and insights in the Faculty. I have always held that academic disciplines are human creations, and to understand particular human and social phenomena in as close to fullness as possible requires that multi- and interdisciplinary approaches be taken. This volume bears testimony to this in its approach to understanding altruism.

Second, this volume is the outcome of a conference held in October 1999. It represents the Faculty's effort to develop research by encouraging and supporting the organization of such opportunities for dialogue and debate. More than that, this volume also represents sustained effort to ensure that there was not just a great deal of talk, but a tangible outcome, so that the thoughts and theses first tested out in the conference room might be shared with a larger audience.

Third, the chosen subject of discussion and debate itself – altruism – speaks to me of the critical importance of humanistic and social scientific understanding in the (post)modern world. The predominance of hard scientific research as we enter the 21st century, what with investigation of the human genome and new media technologies, may cause humanistic and social scientific research to recede in the public imagination, if not in the very real budgetary acts of research grant bodies. Yet, it is in issues such as the ethics of cloning, the morality of prolonging human life, the possibilities of altruism, the universality of filiality and so forth that we engage with issues that reach into the depths of our souls and touch on the meanings and essences of our existence.

I would like to share my congratulations with the editors Basant Kapur and Kim-Chong Chong, as well as all the contributors, for interrogating a meaningful question, and for engaging in multi- and interdisciplinary work.

Assoc Prof Lily Kong
Dean, Faculty of Arts and Social Sciences
National University of Singapore

Chapter 1

Introduction

BASANT K. KAPUR and KIM-CHONG CHONG

'No man is devoid of a heart sensitive to the suffering of others...My reason..is this. Suppose a man were, all of a sudden, to see a young child on the verge of falling into a well. He would certainly be moved to compassion, not because he wanted to get in the good graces of the parents, nor because he wished to win the praise of his fellow villagers or friends, nor yet because he disliked the cry of the child' (Mencius, quoted in Chong, this volume).

The above vivid example aptly encapsulates the central concern of this volume. Are human beings simply atomistic individuals, absorbed in the pursuit of their own interests, and entering into relationships with others only when it serves those interests? (Such, for example, is the basis of Nobel Laureate Gary Becker's theory of marriage.[1]) Or are there fundamental tendencies in human nature that, almost involuntarily as Mencius' example suggests, incline them to a concern for the well-being of others? If so, what are these tendencies, and what are their individual and social implications?

The premise of this volume is that an issue as basic and wide-ranging as this cannot be answered from the stand-point of a single discipline: multiple perspectives are required to shed light on the multi-faceted phenomenon of altruism, and its role in society. Each discipline illuminates important aspects of it, and enriches other disciplines' study of it. This volume certainly does not purport to provide the last word on the subject: indeed, one volume, or more, would be required to fully explore *each* discipline's perspectives on altruism. Nonetheless, selective though our coverage inevitably has to be, the various chapters contained herein 'hang together' very well, illuminating as they do central aspects of the nature and role of altruism. A number of chapters also raise critical questions, illustrating the complexity of the issues involved. Both individually and collectively, the various chapters provide considerable stimulation and food for thought to the interested reader, and by the end of the volume he should have a much richer appreciation of the range and subtlety of the issues involved. It is our belief that this richness derives, in no small measure, to our adoption of an interdisciplinary focus, which distinguishes the volume from the vast majority of past writings on the subject.

A brief discussion of the various chapters in this work follows.

1. PHILOSOPHICAL STUDIES

In his Keynote Address to the Conference, "Altruism and Its Limits", Professor C.L. Ten defines altruism in its broadest sense, as acting to promote the interests of others, even when this may go against some of one's interests. Although Ten talks of "limits," he recognizes that there are individuals who are able to extend their altruism to the whole of humanity. However, most people are confined to the altruistic love of family or groups. In this regard, altruism alone is inadequate, especially when it comes to resolving issues of public life. Some common values have to be found as additional bases for resolving public issues. For example, the values of mutual toleration and justice may nurture a more extensive concern for others' interests. These, together with a wider sense of social and political participation, are ingredients out of which a community-wide altruism may grow.

Ten points out that, paradoxically, within the many contemporary pluralistic societies motivational altruism can lead to serious conflicts. These could be due either to the fact that altruists may have different accounts of what is good, or because altruists have an account of goodness different from that held by their intended beneficiaries. Unfortunately, fanaticism may arise when people think they are acting altruistically. There must be recognition of restraining principles of justice and toleration that can ensure the co-existence of different conceptions of the good. This should be the case, whether we are talking of international relations or of relations within a society. Ten's paper is a good reminder that it is not self-interest alone that can lead to conflicts of interest. Fanatical altruism, or altruism not tempered by a respect for pluralistic accounts of the good, can lead to social conflicts as well. Interestingly, while he refers to the values of mutual toleration and justice as "restraining principles," he also describes them, as indicated above, as belonging to "the likely ingredients of the soil out of which a community-wide altruism grows." Thus, while laying out the limits of altruism, Ten at the same time suggests how they may be extended.

Scepticism about the possibility of altruism is very common, both among laymen and scholars. They question whether there is "really" such a thing as altruistic behaviour. Kim-Chong Chong's "Mencius and the Possibility of Altruism" deals with this perennial scepticism, and shows that we have something to learn from an ancient philosopher here. Chong defines altruism as a concern for the well-being of others, independently of whether one has a particularistic relationship with them. Against the moral sceptics of his age, Mencius (*circa* 4th century B.C.) clarifies the conceptual grounds of altruism with certain hypothetical examples, such as the famous one, given above, of the child in danger of falling into a well, and the spontaneous concern which that elicits. A careful analysis of Mencius' example leads one to see that Mencius differentiates such concern from say, the desire for some pleasurable state. Compassion for the child is outward-directed, such that it makes no sense to say that one should redirect one's desire elsewhere: something that can be said about a desire for some pleasurable state when it is thwarted.

Chong also argues that a concern for those near to one, i.e. particularistic concern, is not necessarily opposed to non-particularistic concern. Instead, the former could serve as the basis for the latter. Any conflict between the two may be resolved in terms of what it is appropriate to do given one's roles and responsibilities, which may well be social ones. Certain virtues such as benevolence, dutifulness, ritual propriety, and wisdom should be cultivated before one can be said to have either form of concern.

The next paper invites us to see the human being as radically situated in an altruistic tendency towards his/her fellow humans. In "Altruism as the Condition of Subjectivity", A.T. Nuyen notes the fact that we sometimes disadvantage ourselves in benefiting others out of a concern for their welfare. The person who does this he calls "the practical altruist." He sets out to explicate and provide support for a moral theory of Emmanuel Levinas, according to which to be a moral subject at all, one has to be a practical altruist. Ordinarily, we may see altruism as a matter of choice. For Levinas, however, this is not the case. As Nuyen explains, "One does not first become a subject and then choose to act in certain ways, altruistically or otherwise. One becomes a subject in acting out of the concern for others, altruistically. Altruism is the condition of subjectivity, not the other way round."

Metaphysically, real separation manifests itself in a desire "to transcend the totality of one's own being and to reach the infinity that lies on the hither side of one's being. The separation that constitutes subjectivity is completed only in the desire for the other." Nuyen illustrates this metaphysic of morals through the feeling of pity. The phenomenology of pity reveals that, typically, pity brings to our cognition the possibility of acting simply for the sake of others. Nuyen's paper not only helps us to regain our faith in humanity, it does so by surprisingly inverting what we normally hold to be the case: the recognition of true separation from our fellow humans is not a basis of egoism, but instead, serves as the basis of altruism.

2. SOCIOLOGICAL STUDIES

In "Altruism, Risk, and Sibling Rivalry", Michael Collins defines altruism as "action, undertaken at some risk to the actor, to save another person's—or a community's—life or hopes." As such, altruism is not to be taken for granted, since there are different levels of risk tolerance. The altruism highlighted by sociobiologists begins with genetic relationships. Even here, we have to contend with the phenomenon of sibling rivalry, where one sibling perceives another in terms of both relatedness and risk, as may be gathered from the study of the sociobiological behaviour of some bird species: "...even full siblings, with half their genes in common, have the option of looking at each other as half identical (a glass half full, as Mock and Parker put it) or half alien (a glass half empty). Sibling X kills sibling Y because he looks at Y as a half-empty glass that wants to fill itself with food X needs for health and survival. The altruistic perspective is the one that sees the glass as half full; the selfish or egoistic perspective sees it as half empty."

At the human, social level, the situation is complicated by shared memes, defined by Dawkins as self-propagating ideas that spread "from brain to brain." Collins cites the recent Elian Gonzalez case to illustrate the lengths to which genetic kin will go in a battle for the survival of their memes and the identities built on those memes. At one level, the conflict is between different altruistic objectives, mixed as it is with choosing and protecting an identity. Thus, even if there are programmed genetic altruistic predispositions, they require the right meme to trigger them. The genetic and risk-taking perspectives provide informative additional dimensions to the study of altruism, although, as Collins and the other authors in this volume recognize, they are not the only possible approaches to the subject.

The subject of empathy is the theme of Anthony Chang's very scholarly chapter. He cites various authorities to the effect that empathy is 'one of the basic human attributes supportive of social life', and has, over the years, evolved through diverse definitions to its current conceptualization as a phenomenon with both cognitive ('the imaginative transposing of oneself into the thinking, feeling, and the acting of another') and affective (the vicarious experiencing or sharing of the observed emotional state of another) dimensions, as well as with elements of concern. Empathy has traditionally been linked to prosocial helping behaviour, although the relationship between the two is probably moderated by other factors (such as costs to oneself, the presence of others, and the salience of cues) which we need to identify and understand better. Chang concludes that 'viewed in the broad, social context of a likely linkage with prosocial helping and reduction of aggression, social and emotional understanding (EQ?), and the capacity to love others, empathy becomes an important socio-psychological phenomenon'.

Elizabeth Nair draws a distinction between prosocial acts that are altruistic (selfless and non-calculative) in nature, and acts motivated by considerations of social exchange (a rewards-costs calculus). In her study, 464 respondents aged between 12 and 23 were asked to complete a questionnaire requiring them to choose between five sets of two, mutually exclusive, alternatives, one altruistic in nature and the other motivated by social exchange. The issues presented were: alternative reasons for taking care of elderly parents; donating towards the cost of training for either a handicapped person or a drug addict; helping someone who was helpful to oneself previously versus helping anyone who needed help; helping one's own community versus any community that needed help; and, finally, selecting between making useful friends versus being kind to everyone. The findings reflected a mixture of social exchange and altruistic motives. Analysis by age categories indicated a possible developmental difference from altruism towards social exchange.

As an original, albeit preliminary, field study, Nair's work is valuable and thought-provoking. As she herself acknowledges, alternative interpretations can be placed on some of her findings, which are somewhat more favourable to the altruism hypothesis, although the result that older respondents tend to be somewhat less altruistic than younger ones appears fairly robust. The issue is further complicated by the fact that she includes 'psychological rewards and costs', including (in contrast to Anthony Chang) 'empathic joy', in the social-exchange domain, while defining altruism as acts whose purpose is '*mainly* to alleviate the situation of the person in distress' (emphasis added). The points this raises are discussed further in Kapur's concluding chapter in this volume.

3. ECONOMIC STUDIES

Turning next to the Economics papers, Wei-Bin Zhang develops an illuminating and insightful 'two-group model of a welfare economy'. The two groups are a well-off class and a poorer class, and it is assumed that a tax-transfer system is in operation to transfer a fraction of the former's income to the latter. Zhang characterizes the steady-state equilibrium of this economy, and then studies the effect on this equilibrium of a state-mandated increase in this fraction. He obtains a number of interesting results: (i) if the marginal savings propensities out of income (positive) and wealth (negative) of the two groups are identical, then an increased transfer has no effect on national income and wealth, and simply re-allocates resources from the well-off to the poorer class; (ii) if the two groups have different marginal savings rates, with the well-off in particular having a higher marginal savings rate out of income, then an increased transfer would reduce their well-being, increase or reduce the well-being of the recipient group, and increase or decrease national income and wealth; and (iii) if the increased transfer is devoted to education and training, which enhances the productivity of the recipient class, then it is possible that *both* groups may become better off. Conversely, if the increased transfer weakens the recipient group's work ethic, then all could become worse off.

Zhang's paper highlights the important consideration that altruism need not be a one-dimensional process, consisting simply of transferring money from one group or person to another. Its effects depend not inconsiderably on the form it takes, and the consequences for savings, education, and work behaviour. One is reminded of an ancient Chinese adage: 'Give a man a fish, and he will eat for a day; teach him to fish, and he will eat every day.'

Vincent Chua and C. M. Wong provide an economic perspective on altruism, focusing in particular on charitable giving by individuals. Most economists have studied altruism as an issue involving interdependent utilities, and have been concerned with determining the degree of pervasiveness of the free-rider problem and finding ways to mitigate its effect. Can the private voluntary contribution system be improved or redesigned to improve the funding for the less fortunate? Is there a need for a more active role by the government? To satisfactorily address these and related issues, there is need for an understanding of the factors that determine the level of charitable giving. Towards this end, they examine the available empirical literature straddling a number of countries, including Singapore, with a view to providing some directions for policy makers. The issues discussed include the price of giving and tax policies to encourage giving, the cost of fund raising and its implications for the organization of fund-raising activities, the sensitivity of donations to changing income levels, and the possible strategic interactions between private voluntary giving and public sector spending. It is also noted that changing the social mindset to encourage giving may be an important consideration in the longer run.

4. LITERARY AND POLITICAL STUDIES

The next paper gives us a concrete illustration of altruism at work, under dangerous circumstances. In "Altruism in Wartime: Self, and Others", Liew-Geok Leong adopts the definition of altruism given by Eisenberg and Miller as "intentional voluntary behaviour that benefits another and is not performed with the expectation of receiving external rewards or avoiding external punishments or aversive stimuli." This is congruent with the definition of Samuel and Pearl Oliner, in their well-known book *The Altruistic Personality: Rescuers of Jews in Nazi Europe*, which characterises altruistic acts as directed towards helping another, involving high risk or sacrifice but without expectation of external reward, and being voluntary in nature.

These definitions make no mention of the religious factor. However, it is in fact crucial to Leong's account, and makes us realize that religious belief is sometimes the basis of strong altruistic behaviour. The true stories of Sybil Kathigasu and Elizabeth Choy, who risked their lives to help others during the period of the Japanese Occupation in Malaya and Singapore illustrate this very well. They show how altruistic behaviour can be motivated by unshakeable religious faith. The religious upbringing of Kathigasu and Choy inculcated in them a commitment to the spiritual, and they interpreted the moral in religious rather than in secular terms. The ethic of care and concern for others practiced by both women was spiritually imbued. Another interesting factor that Leong mentions is the Anglophile loyalty of these women in their resistance against the Japanese. The description of this and the religious factor in the altruism of both women supports the remarks of Amartya Sen quoted in the beginning of the paper, that "We all have many identities, and being 'just me' is not the only way we see ourselves...all [these] identities ...can be, depending on the context, crucial to our view of ourselves, and thus to the way we view our welfare, goals or behavioural obligations."

Antonio Rappa provides an interesting discussion of the Classical origins of modern altruism. Modern altruism argues that there potentially exists an objectively discernible morality enjoining all rational agents to behave altruistically, described as "a willingness to act in consideration of others without the need for ulterior motives" (Nagel). But what is the philosophical basis of modern altruism? Rappa traces its roots to Plato's *Dialogues*.

Plato, he argues, has identified five ingredients that are "jointly necessary" for altruism to exist. These are justice, friendship, temperance, wisdom, and valour. Justice is about equal treatment for all citizens under the law. In historical retrospect, altruism has taken place within unjust political systems yet the seminal *Dialogues* suggest that altruism has a better chance of developing within a just society. Another ingredient of altruism is friendship. As seen in the Dialogue called *Lysis*, a person who is genuinely friendly to strangers and to acquaintances alike is more likely to act altruistically than one who is not. Temperance is about modesty, moderation, and self-control. Wisdom is about increasing one's store of knowledge that leads to a deeper understanding of humanity. The understanding of others' experiences that wisdom brings with it increases the potential for altruistic behaviour because of empathy. Finally, the *Republic* defines valour as bravery in defence of the family and the state. At one extreme, valour results in death in battle. Giving one's life for another is the ultimate form of altruism. All five ingredients are explained in terms of how they might provide for the rise of altruistic behaviour. In the construction of the perfect city, citizens who strive for justice, friendship, temperance, wisdom and valour are simultaneously striving for altruism, and a shared cosmological consciousness. Understanding the Classical basis of modern altruism is one step towards the alleviation of pain and suffering in the modern world.

5. CONCLUSION

The concluding chapter, by Basant Kapur, provides a discussion and interpretation of some of the key issues discussed in the Conference. It is organized around five themes: the definition of altruism; the altruistic personality; the relationship between altruism and self-cultivation; the metaphysical dimension; and a broader view of altruism. Kapur reviews the various papers in this volume, and a fairly wide range of further writings, and concludes that altruism is not simply an adventitious phenomenon: it is integral to the self-cultivation of the individual, and the well-being of society. This, perhaps, is an appropriate note on which to conclude this Introduction.

Notes

1. 'A Theory of Marriage: Part I', *Journal of Political Economy*, 81 (4), July-August 1973, *pp*. 813-846.

Chapter 2

Altruism And Its Limits

C.L.TEN

1. INTRODUCTION

There is a story, probably apocryphal, about two altruists caught in a burning building, with the only exit wide enough to take one person at a time. The first altruist said to the second, "After you", to which the second replied, "No, I insist, after you." And so they went on, each as deeply entrenched in his altruism as the other, until they were both consumed by the flames. Some feminists, noting that I have used the masculine pronoun to describe the two altruists, would no doubt point out that the moral of the story is the stupidity of male rationality. However, my purpose in telling the story is to remind us that it is not only the pursuit of self-interest which leads to conflict, but that altruism as a motivating force can also lead to harmful conflicts. But the situations I have in mind are different from that in the story. They are situations in which altruistic aims must be tempered by a primary social virtue of toleration.

Let me begin by clarifying the terms and the general framework of the debate between egoism and altruism. Then I shall locate one corner of the debate where I shall drop my neutrality and take sides.

2. NOTIONS OF SELF-INTEREST AND ALTRUISM

The terms "self-interest" and "selfishness" are often used as if they were synonymous when in fact there is a difference. If there is abundant food and

I eat as much as I want because I enjoy eating, then I act in a self-interested manner, but not selfishly because I do not adversely affect the interests of others. On the other hand, if I eat as much as I want when there is not enough food for everyone, and I know that my behaviour will adversely affect others, then I act selfishly. Selfish behaviour is self-interested, but self-interested behaviour need not be selfish. The failure to distinguish between self-interest and selfishness makes it more difficult to understand some of the claims made in the debate between egoism and altruism. For example, there is a line of argument, to which I shall return, to the effect that the common good is best promoted by each person acting in a self-interested manner. This is an empirical claim which may be false, but it is not incoherent. However, it may be difficult to even understand the claim if one formulates it in terms of selfish instead of self-interested behaviour.

There is also some ambiguity about the notion of altruism. Sometimes a person is said to be altruistic when she gives equal weight to the interests of others, including total strangers, as she does to her own similar interests. Altruism is equated here with strict impartiality of the kind demanded by utilitarians, who evaluate conduct in terms of the standard of maximizing happiness. At other times a person is said to be altruistic when she gives greater weight to the similar interests of others as she does to her own. For some purposes this distinction is vital, but it does not much affect what I want to say here. It is enough to note that the demands of altruism, in either sense, are great if no restrictions are made with respect to time, or place, or persons. In the broadest sense, altruism is acting to promote the interests of others, even when this goes against some of one's own interests. This sense may be pretty minimal in that it is satisfied even when the relevant interest of others is great while one's own foregone interest is by comparison very slight. Thus if I give you some water in order to save your life when I have plenty of water to spare, then I am, in this broad sense, acting altruistically. The altruism is still minimal even when the interests involved are comparable, but minor. If I give you a glass of water from my ample supply, not in order to save your life, but simply because I know that you are slightly thirsty, then I am still acting with minimal altruism. It is only when the interest sacrificed for the sake of others is substantial that altruism becomes demanding. This can happen both when the interests of others are greater than one's own, and when the interests of others are lesser. Examples of minimal or minor acts of altruism are quite common. However, the more demanding acts of altruism are not so common outside the narrow circle of family and friends, and in ordinary circumstances when there is no emergency. This is particularly so when we consider altruism as a virtuous disposition to act for the sake of others, rather than as the performance of isolated acts.

The scope of altruism may be narrow or extensive. Some are altruistic only to members of their own family, and to a few close friends. Others may be altruistic to a wider group, for example to members of their religious or ethnic group. Not so many are altruistic to the whole of humanity. The strength of altruistic concerns also varies. Even those who are universally altruistic may be more altruistic to some than to others.

Self-interest and altruism are supposed to be contrasting notions. However, the distinction is sometimes blurred by the enlargement of what counts as self-interest. Concern for the interests of others can be generated by the presence of affective bonds or by various commitments. To those who are familiar with the work of Amartya Sen, let me just say that this distinction is similar to his distinction between sympathy and commitment, except that I use my terms more loosely and more broadly (Sen, 1990, 31-4). In the case of affective bonds, there are certain feelings which motivate one's behaviour, e.g. a mother's concern for her children because of her love for them. Is a mother who makes sacrifices for her children acting out of self-interest? Some say that she is because she herself is happier with the sacrifice than without it; her own happiness is closely tied to that of her children. In the case of a commitment, a person makes a sacrifice in accordance with a principle or in order to promote a cause that she believes in. The sacrifice is not motivated by an affective bond as it can be made to benefit total strangers, and the person making the sacrifice is worse-off as a result. The distinction between this type of case and the case in which there is a motivating affective bond may not be as sharp as some, including I think Sen himself, have supposed. For even in the case of a commitment, the person who makes the sacrifice will often say that it gives her satisfaction to do what she did, or that she could not live with herself had she acted otherwise. I regard both types of acts, those based on commitments and those arising out of affective bonds, as altruistic, provided that they were done for the sake of others, and not in order to promote the agents' own happiness or satisfaction, even though the agents in fact derive such happiness or satisfaction from the performance of the acts. But I am not going to worry too much if others disagree, so long as they make plain what they mean so that we will not be bogged down in fruitless verbal disputes.

However, it is important to note that if we extend the notion of self-interest too broadly, then there will be little or nothing with which to contrast it. Thomas Hobbes is usually considered to be an unmitigated psychological egoist, namely someone who believes that human beings are only capable of acting in a self-interested manner. So when Hobbes gave money to a beggar, it was thought that he had falsified his own view. But he replied that he acted not in order to relieve the beggar's distress, but in order to relieve his own distress at the sight of the beggar's distress. Perhaps the content of self-interest can be stretched a little in this Hobbesian manner. But if we go much further down this path, we will end up claiming that every voluntary act, no matter how great the cost to the agent, and no matter what terrible state it left her in, was done because it gave her satisfaction to do it, and so it must in the end be in her self-ineterst. Such an expanded notion of self-interest cannot explain anything, cannot predict anything. It is empirically empty.

3. FACTUAL AND NORMATIVE ISSUES

When we have sorted out our terms, and restricted them appropriately, we find that there are genuine debates about egoism and altruism, which centre on factual or normative issues, or on a combination of both. The main factual issue is whether self-interested motivation best explains various types of behaviour. Economists and others often work with the model of "the rational economic man", who is motivated solely by self-interest. They use this model to explain and predict all kinds of behaviour - consumer choices, patterns of voting, the conduct of public officials, etc. The model has been famously attacked by Amartya Sen. But it survives, and indeed in some quarters the pursuit of self-interest is still considered as the paradigm of rationality. A normative claim is merged with the factual claim. Here I take no sides on the factual claim. Perhaps the persistance of the model of the rational economic man among economists is connected with the evidence suggesting that students of economics are more strongly motivated by self-interest than others.

Factual assumptions about self-interested behaviour have historically been used to support the extension of the franchise to the working classes and to women. It was argued that governments would simply ignore the interests of groups which did not have the vote. Interestingly, some men claimed, on the contrary, that women's interests would be well-looked after by their loving husbands and adult sons. This idea might have played a part in delaying the giving of the vote to women. John Stuart Mill, a passionate defender of the franchise for women, rejected the view that political participation was a burden from which women could be spared, and argued for their involvement in politics, not only on the ground of protecting their interests as they saw them, but also on the grounds that political participation had educative functions, enlarging the knowledge, interests, and perspectives of women.

One important normative issue to-day is the extent to which altruism should feature as a motivating force in public life. This is the issue on which I shall now focus. In formulating the issue in the way I have, I am deliberately limiting my discussion in three dimensions. First, I am interested in altruism in public rather than in private life. It is an important aspect of public life that the demands we make on one another should not be as relaxed, as indefinite, and as open-ended as the demands which arise among friends, lovers, and members of the same closely-knit family. Even in private life things can go wrong, and when they do, we may have to invoke some elements of the public structure, some claims about specific rights and duties.

Secondly, I have posed the issue, not in terms of whether it is appropriate to have self-interested or altruistic motivations, but rather in terms of the extent to which altruism is appropriate in public life. Although I wish to suggest some limits to altruism, I do not want to endorse the view of some conservative thinkers who believe that it is better in the long run if people acted on the basis of self-interest rather than of altruism because Providence, the invisible hand, or some other convenient mechanism, will ensure the harmony of interests, promoting the good of all. Various versions of this view are still current, and are held sometimes by very privileged people, and sometimes by people who want to severely circumscribe the social responsibility of big business. The view is ugly when it is used to withhold the giving of help to those in great need.

Thirdly, and most importantly, I pose the issue in terms of altruistic motivation. We need to distinguish between motivational-altruism, or procedural-altruism, and outcome-altruism or result-altruism. In many areas of our lives we are familiar with the idea that the goal we seek may best be achieved indirectly rather than directly. For example, I have been told that many good strokes in tennis are best perfected by a less conscious effort to achieve them, by playing more spontaneously and naturally, at least for those who have natural talents. Again, some goals in education, such as the cultivation of critical skills, may be best achieved indirectly by not having them consciously before our minds when we study, but instead by treating them as the welcome by-products of our immersion in intrinsically desirable scholarly activities. The various relationships between motivations or procedures on the one hand, and results or outcomes on the other hand, are matters of some complexity on which I shall only touch.

In *A Theory of Justice*, John Rawls distinguishes between imperfect and perfect procedural justice. In both cases we know what the just outcome is independently of the procedure we use for trying to achieve it. Thus we know that in the case of a criminal trial, a just outcome is one in which the guilty are convicted and the innocent acquitted. We devise a procedure, the trial, for reaching the desired goal. But here we are confronted with imperfect procedural justice, and no matter what procedures we adopt, whether it be an adversarial system or a more cooperative system, we cannot guarantee that we will always get the just outcome. On the other hand, in the case of perfect procedural justice, we have a procedure which will, if adopted, guarantee the just outcome. Rawls's example is the cutting of a cake made by many people, each one of whom has made an equal contribution, and each wanting as large a slice as he or she can get. The just outcome is an equal slice for everyone, and the procedure which guarantees this is that in which the cutter of the cake takes the last piece. The largest piece that she can get for herself is one equal to everybody else's, and so she will divide the cake into equal slices. Rawls mentions one other important notion, pure procedural justice, in which the just outcome is any outcome which emerges from the application of a just procedure, there being no conception of a just outcome independent of the procedure. But I am interested in the idea of imperfect procedural justice and its application to motivational-altruism.

4. ALTRUISM AND DIVERSITY

Outcome-altruism is not my concern here, at least not directly. If it is achieved it is obviously a good thing. Certainly the beneficiaries would have no cause for complaint. The interesting questions relate to what counts as its achievement. This raises issues about the content of the goal that is regarded as truly altruistic, and the extent to which it is to be defined in terms of values independent of the subjective interests and perspectives of the beneficiaries. Motivational-altruism also raises these issues of definition and content, but it raises other issues as well. Bertrand Russell refers somewhere to the evil that good men do. He was focussing, as I am, on the mismatch between good motivations, altruistic motivations, and bad outcomes. There are many reasons for this mismatch-human fallibility and lack of knowledge of others' interests are among them. But I want to focus on a pervasive feature of many complex contemporary societies, characterized by a diversity of lifestyles and various, even incompatible, conceptions of what constitutes a worthwhile human life. The sources of this diversity include religious and cultural differences, and the sheer, unavoidable, and irreducible differences between human beings who are born with different genes, who have different experiences and histories, and who assimilate, interpret, remember, and reshape these different influences in different ways. These facts about our individual and social differences are undeniable, and they set certain limits to motivational-altruism.

First, there are problems about how the disposition of motivational-altruism is to be nurtured and sustained. We are familiar with the altruism that grows out of the affective bonds of love and friendship, but there is no such basis for altruism among strangers who lack any face-to-face relationships. Another basis for altruism is the family and blood relationships. But these are either inseparable from love and friendship, or else they depend on some notion of blood that has to be pretty diluted if it is to cover all in a large society. When blood gets as thin as water, it loses its causal power to motivate. Yet another source of altruism is a set of comprehensive shared interests and values, such as that which binds together members of the same church, but this is the very condition that is absent in diverse, plural societies. We cannot now recreate the conditions under which these familiar forms of altruism breed and thrive. We seem to be stuck with small pockets of altruism, with nothing extending to society as a whole. If a new basis of altruism is to be found, it has to be in some notion of unity in diversity. In the case of religion, the more enlightened believers have finally acknowledged that the only proper basis for their relationship with those from other religions is mutual toleration. This common value may in time nurture a more extensive concern for the interests of others. Similarly, we may hope that diverse groups will develop bonds of altruism across their differences if they believe that their relationships are based on justice, which of course must include mutual toleration of their differences. So justice, toleration, and social and political participation, which nurtures a sense that one has shared in building the community to which one belongs - these are the likely ingredients of the soil out of which a community-wide altruism grows.

Furthermore, there is also the possibility that as people with different values and conceptions of the good get a better understanding of the bases of their differences, they may come to acknowledge several things. The first is that some of their differences are merely different ways of expressing or honouring the same fundamental values, in the manner that different rules of etiquette and different rituals embody a fundamental similarity of interests and concerns. Secondly, they may come to acknowledge that their conception of the good is only one among several acceptable conceptions. No doubt it is a conception with which they feel closely identified because of personal and historical circumstances, but they may nonetheless realize that it is a conception which does not preclude an endorsement of the different conceptions with which others are similarly identified. Sometimes it is possible that those who are deeply attached to a small group of persons may find in these particular attachments the security and strength to go on to care for others as well, not quite in the same way, but with sufficient intensity. There may indeed be some truth in Herder's remark, "The savage who loves himself, his wife and his child, and his tribe, can find room in his hut for a stranger: the saturated heart of the idle cosmopolitan is a home for no one ..." (Quoted in Berlin, 1965, 41). Finally, it is also possible that people with a deep attachment to a particular conception of the good may come to acknowledge, not that other conceptions are also acceptably good, but rather that you cannot really promote the interests of others if you act against their own deep-seated conception of what is good. This is an idea, sometimes called the endorsement condition, which drives the theories of some liberal thinkers, such as the legal philosopher, Ronald Dworkin. If it is acknowledged, then we have a sharp limit to altruistic paternalism, for "no one can improve another's life by forcing him to behave differently, against his will and his convictions." (Dworkin, 1995, 304).

These are some of the ways in which we might hope to develop acceptable forms of altruism. I am not optimistic about the rapid spread of altruism in contemporary societies, but I am quite sure that the old and familiar forms of altruism have no growth potential.

5. ALTRUISM AND CONFLICTS

Now I come to another problem posed by plural and diverse societies. Suppose, somehow, we have succeeded in developing a society-wide form of motivational-altruism. Have we arrived at the good society, defined either in terms of outcome-altruism, or in some other terms? Sadly, the answer is no. Motivational-altruism is not the solution, unless it goes at least with the endorsement condition. For no matter how people develop their altruism, once they are already altruistic, then they are likely to conceive of the interests of others in terms of their own conception of the good, their own account of what a worthwhile human life should be. Even those who acknowledge a plurality of conceptions of the good, in the manner suggested earlier, will set limits to this plurality, which will still exclude many other conceptions. For example, religious believers and atheists, if they are driven by benevolence and good-will, might come to accept a plurality of conceptions of the good, of which their own is only one. But belief and atheism are incompatible, inspite of the best efforts of some theologians who have argued that, for example, the essence of Christianity is a certain way of life, the rest is metaphor. Most believers and atheists will not include both religious belief and atheism in the same set of compatible conceptions of the good, however broad that set may otherwise be. Yet there are good, and some very good, men and women in both camps.

So disagreements between different and incompatible conceptions of the good will resurface and lead to harmful conflicts, unless they are regulated in some way. We tend to think of the pursuit of self-interest as generating harmful conflicts. But I return to the point with which I began: there can also be serious conflicts arising out of altruism. These conflicts will be between altruists themselves with different accounts of the good of others, or between altruists and their intended beneficiaries. The conflicts generated by altruism can in fact be even more serious than the conflicts which are the products of self-interest. People are capable of great fanaticism when they think that they are acting altruistically. Self-interested people cannot expect support from others if they openly pursue their own good against the interests of others. But those seeking to promote altruistic goals can openly and passionately pursue their aims, feeling fully justified, and unencumbered by any sense of guilt. That is why differences in altruistic aims can be fought so openly and so fiercely. In the case of some religious conflicts, the introduction of a new dimension of other-wordly interests lifts the conflicts to a higher level of unmitigated violence. The Grand Inquisitor was in his own eyes an altruist seeking the best for an unappreciative people.

Some of the dangers of motivational-altruism are manifest in the international scene, which is in some respects a plural society writ large. At the international level it is perfectly clear that there are very sharp differences between states pursuing very different interests. The distinguished political philosopher, Brian Barry, relates with pride how in 1961 he was thrown out of Henry Kissinger's seminars at Harvard for questioning one of the premises on which he claims the seminars were based, namely that foreign policy was to be conducted solely in order to promote the national interests of the United States (Barry, 1991, 14). Now I have no wish to defend the purported Kissinger approach to foreign policy, for there are many alternatives of a more balanced kind. But the opposite policy of running foreign policy on the basis of pure motivational-altruism can have some undesirable consequences. A small, well-defined state, with a distinctive but non-tyrannical conception of the type of public institutions and way of life it wants, will not welcome the altruism of a powerful state which thinks that, in the best interests of the small state, certain changes must be made. An unrestrained altruism of the powerful will lead to a great deal of unwanted interference with the internal affairs of weaker states. Similarly, within one society there must be something to restrain the dominant group from exercising altruism in the light of a conception of the good which is not shared by the supposed beneficiaries. What the society needs is a restraining principle of justice or toleration which ensures that different conceptions of the good can co-exist, and that individuals can lead their lives in accordance with their own conceptions.

This does not mean that altruism has no place in domestic or international policies. Altruism confined to the provision of what Sen calls the basic capabilities, such as the ability to meet one's nutritional requirements, to be clothed and sheltered, and to have the power to participate in social life, or confined to the provision of Rawls's social primary goods of income, wealth, opportunities, and liberties - altruism of these kinds can help people to better pursue their own conceptions of worthwhile lives (Sen, 1995, 328). These forms of altruism are compatible with the principle of justice or toleration. Furthermore, even in plural societies, we tend to agree much more about what is evil than we do about the highest reaches of the good. Altruism directed towards the removal of agreed evils is different, and more acceptable, to altruism aimed at the promotion of the ultimate good of all.

So it is that sometimes we need to be rescued from the indifference or malevolence of others. A society bereft of extensive altruism is not a good society. But a society brimming with unrestrained altruism can be suffocating, Sometimes we need to be protected from the concern and good intentions of others. When things go wrong, may justice and toleration protect us from the suffocating embrace of good men and women.

References

1. Barry, Brian, *Democracy and Power* (Clarendon Press, Oxford, 1991).
2. Berlin, Isaiah, "J.G. Herder", *Encounter*, July 1965.
3. Dworkin, Ronald, "Foundations of Liberal Equality", in Stephen Darwall (ed.) *Equal Freedom:Selected Tanner Lectures on Human Values* (University of Michigan Press, Ann Arbor, 1995).
4. Rawls, J., *A Theory of Justice* (Harvard University Press, Cambridge, 1971).
5. Sen, Amartya K., "Rational Fools: A Critique of the Behavioural Foundations of Economic Theory", in Jane J. Mansbridge (ed.) *Beyond Self-Interest* (University of Chicago Press, Chicago, 1990).
6. Sen, Amartya, "Equality of What?", in Stephen Darwall (ed.) *Equal Freedom: Selected Tanner Lectures on Human Values* (University of Michigan Press, Ann Arbor, 1995).

Chapter 3

Mencius And The Possibility of Altruism In Early Chinese Philosophy

KIM-CHONG CHONG

1. INTRODUCTION

What has Mencius, a philosopher of the 4th century B.C. in ancient China, to offer to a contemporary discussion on altruism? The answer lies in his reply to moral scepticism, a perennial feature of both ordinary and intellectual thought. According to Mencius, there are certain ethical predispositions which manifest themselves spontaneously in appropriate circumstances. These predispositions constitute a direct moral concern which is to be distinguished from motivated desires. Such concern may either be particularistic, i.e. directed toward those in a personal relation with ourselves, or non-particularistic, i.e. directed toward those who have no personal relation with ourselves. Both types of concern are not mutually exclusive.

I take the term "altruism" to refer to a concern for the well-being of others. Generally, a concern for the well-being of others with whom one has a particularistic relationship is not considered problematic in motivational terms. On the other hand, there may be cases where one is concerned for someone, independently of whether one has a particularistic relationship with him/her or not. In such cases, the issue of motivation is often raised. The thought that there is "really" no such thing as genuinely altruistic concern is fairly common. During the time of Mencius, this scepticism was either prompted or represented by the doctrines of Mo Tzu, Yang Chu, and Kao Tzu.

2. MORAL SCEPTICISM

Mo Tzu[1]

Mo Tzu is not a moral sceptic, and it might seem strange that he is mentioned in the context of moral scepticism. However, his insistence that it is possible to love others as oneself, their parents and friends as one's own, the cities and states of others' as one's own, etc., gives rise to scepticism as to how this is possible. This is the doctrine of *jian ai*, which has been translated as "universal love", "indiscriminate concern", or "concern for everyone".[2] Mo Tzu diagnosed the disorder of his time as due to partiality towards those with whom one has a particularistic relationship. This partiality leads to internecine conflict and war, as well as unjust acts of various kinds. The remedy is for everyone to reject partiality, and to adopt an attitude of equal regard for everyone. Thus, universal love amounts to the rejection of particularistic concern, in favour of non-particularistic concern for everyone.

A possible interpretation of Mo Tzu would be to see him as asserting a modern idea expounded by both the Utilitarians and Kantians, that in the moral scheme of things, each is to count as one. From this perspective, one judges in abstraction from the bias of interests, affections and social positions.[3] However, though Mo Tzu does take as his measure of right action the utilitarian criterion of whether a course of action is to the benefit of all, he constantly harps on the possibility of loving others as oneself, others' friends and parents as one own, etc. The question how this is possible is raised several times, but not convincingly answered. Thus, in response to the point that (trying to adopt) universal love would be like picking up a mountain and leaping over a river with it, i.e. that it would be practically impossible, Mo Tzu denies the relevance of the analogy by claiming that universal love is something which the ancient sage kings had practiced.[4]

Against Mo Tzu, it is unclear whether by ruling beneficently, the ancient sage kings agreed to the practice of universal love in the way Mo Tzu advocates. The same reply can be made to Mo Tzu's charge that the partial-minded man is inconsistent, since he would leave his family in the charge of the universal-minded man when he goes off to war.[5] Given the choice of leaving one's family in the hands of someone who would treat them impartially just like anyone else, or leaving them with one's good friend who would treat them specially, it is doubtful that the partial-minded man would opt for the former.

Mo Tzu seems to realize the unconvincingness of his replies and is ultimately forced to appeal to self-interest. For example, a filial son wishes to ensure his parents' welfare. One way to ensure this is "to make it a point to love and benefit other men's parents, so that they in return will love and benefit my parents." Mo Tzu cites a passage from the Book of Odes:

> "There are no words that are not answered,
> No kindness that is not requited.
> Throw me a peach,
> I'll requite you a plum."

Mo Tzu comments that "The meaning is that one who loves will be loved by others, and one who hates will be hated by others. So I cannot understand how the men of the world can hear about this doctrine of universality and still criticize it!"[6] Thus, we may say that in the final analysis, universal love is a form of investment in the welfare of oneself and particular others.

It is fair to conclude that Mo Tzu's theory of universal love ultimately accentuates moral scepticism, instead of answering it. We should note the following points. Mo Tzu assumes that: (1) Non-particularistic concern must arise out of some motivation. And as we have just noted, the best motivation is that of self-interest. (2) Particularistic concern is both opposed and harmful to the project of non-particularistic concern. As we shall see, Mencius' theory of ethical predispositions addresses these two assumptions.

Yang Chu[7]

Mencius describes Yang Chu as an egoist (*wei wo*, literally, "for myself") to the extent that "Even if he could benefit the Empire by pulling out one hair he would not do it."[8] A.C. Graham has described the Yangist as one who withdraws from politics, preferring to live in private. He does not do so, however, as a result of high-minded moralistic principles, and in protest against a corrupt age. Instead, he believes in the primacy of life and its preservation and nourishment.[9]

It has been argued that Mencius misinterprets the Yangist philosophy, for his own purposes.[10] For there are occasions when the Yangist makes no distinction between his life and the life of others: both are equally valuable. This is the case in the story of King Tan-fu, whose state was invaded by the people of Ti. After failing to get rid of the invaders with various enticements, King Tan-fu decides to leave the state so as to preserve his own life as well as the lives of his subjects. According to him, there is no difference whether he or the men of Ti are the rulers. The principle he cites is that "one must not injure that which he is nourishing for the sake of that by which he nourishes it." This is explained by a commentary:

"The Great King Tan-fu may be said to have known how to respect life. He who knows how to respect life, though he may be rich and honored, will not allow the means of nourishing life to injure his person. Though he may be poor and humble, he will not allow concerns of profit to entangle his body. The men of the present age, if they occupy high office and are honored with titles, all think only of how serious a matter it would be to lose them. Eyes fixed on profit, they make light of the risk to their lives. Are they not deluded indeed?"[11]

It could be argued therefore that Yang Chu's is not an egoism of overriding self-interest. Instead, one is urged not to confuse attachment to material things with life itself. It could also be argued on Yang Chu's behalf that although the cost of pulling out one hair seems trivial, it is a way of emphasizing that the costs of holding office during the social and political disorder of the time outweigh the benefits.[12] On the other hand, there may be circumstances where refusing to take office or to do one's duty could result in dire consequences for the empire as a whole. One can therefore imagine Mencius' concern about the implications of Yang Chu's doctrine, if widely adopted.

Another aspect of the Yangist doctrine is the gratification of the senses and the desires. The character Robber Chih in the *Zhuangzi* brings this out in terms of "man's true form" (*ren zhi qing*): "His eyes yearn to see colors, his ears to hear sound, his mouth to taste flavors, his will and spirit to achieve fulfilment." The gratification of the senses and desires is to be treasured, given the short life-span of man. Robber Chih asserts that "No man who is incapable of gratifying his desires and cherishing the years fate has given him can be called a master of the Way."[13]

Spontaneity is also a value held by the Yangists. In another chapter of the *Zhuangzi* which has been identified as Yangist, "The Old Fisherman", the protagonist tells Confucius what he means by "genuineness" or *zhen* (translated as the "Truth" by Watson):

"I mean purity and sincerity in their highest degree. He who lacks purity and sincerity cannot move others. Therefore he who forces himself to lament, though he may sound sad, will awaken no grief. He who forces himself to be angry, though he may sound fierce, will arouse no awe. And he who forces himself to be affectionate, though he may smile, will create no air of harmony. True sadness need make no sound to awaken grief; true anger need not show itself to arouse awe; true affection need not smile to create harmony. When a man has the Truth within himself, his spirit may move among external things. That is why the Truth is to be prized!"

This is a criticism against the cramping rituals of the Confucians. The passage continues: "In seeking to perform the finest kind of service, one does not always try to go about it in the same way. In assuring comfort in the serving of one's parents, one does not question the means to be employed. In seeking merriment that comes with festive drinking, one does not fuss over what cups and dishes are to be selected. In expressing grief that is appropriate to periods of mourning, one does not quibble over the exact ritual to be followed."[14]

Implicit in all this is an accusation that the ritualistic rules of behaviour set up by Confucianism is unnatural. The Confucians have imposed an artificial morality on natural behaviour, thereby cramping spontaneity. Mencius' response is to argue for the spontaneity of moral behaviour in terms of the ethical predispositions. At the same time, however, the logic of their operation is such that they are different from the gratification of the sensory or appetitive desires.

Kao Tzu[15]

This is in fact the strategy that he adopts against Kao Tzu. Kao Tzu asserts that there is nothing more to human nature than the life process typified by the desires for food and sex. As he says, "Appetite for food and sex is nature."[16] In his debate with Mencius, he likens the construction of morality out of the nature of human beings, to making cups and bowls out of the willow. In another analogy, human nature is said to be like whirling water, which is directionless until it is channeled. In other words, morality is a construct, imposed upon raw human nature, which he defines in terms of biological life.[17] All this is reminiscent of the Yangist philosophy of nurturing and nourishing life, the gratification of desires, and the critique of the artificiality of the Confucian emphasis on ritual behaviour.

3. MOTIVES AND ETHICAL PREDISPOSITIONS

Consider now the famous example of the child about to fall into a well given by Mencius:

"No man is devoid of a heart sensitive to the suffering of others...My reason...is this. Suppose a man were, all of a sudden, to see a young child on the verge of falling into a well. He would certainly be moved to compassion, not because he wanted to get in the good graces of the parents, nor because he wished to win the praise of his fellow villagers or friends, nor yet because he disliked the cry of the child."[18]

This is one example of what Mencius claims to be the four "germs" or predispositions of the heart: compassion; shame and loathing; courtesy, modesty and respect; and (a sense of) right and wrong. If developed, these predispositions give rise respectively to the virtues of benevolence, duty, propriety, and wisdom. There is no guarantee that these will be developed, however, since reflective thought, effort and environmental conditions are all factors which have a role to play in fostering the predispositions.[19]

It could be argued against Mencius that although one may suddenly feel alarmed at the sight of the child on the verge of falling into a well, this does not necessarily amount to compassion. In other words, the example alone does not serve as good or adequate empirical evidence for the existence of the germ of compassion in all persons.

But from the perspective of the sceptical background described earlier, we may construe Mencius to be clarifying the conceptual grounds of altruism and other direct social and moral responses with hypothetical examples like this one. Thus, note that in his description of the example, Mencius is careful to distinguish the feeling of compassion from certain motives: getting in the good graces of the child's parents, winning the praise of others, or stopping the annoying cry of the child. In other words, nothing motivates the concern for the child. The concern is direct, and to be differentiated from these motivations.

The directness of this concern may be reinforced by seeing that the perception of the child on the verge of falling into a well is not a pure cognition. In other words, the compassion is not a concomitant part of the cognition, but may be said to constitute the mode in which the situation is registered or perceived. This point can also be made in terms of another example Mencius gives. Presumably, in ancient times, burial practices did not exist. Some people observed that the bodies of their dead parents were eaten by creatures and flies. Breaking into a sweat, they returned home for baskets and spades to bury them. Mencius states that "The sweating was not put on for others to see. It was an expression of their innermost heart."[20] Once again, Mencius is stating a direct response of concern, and careful to differentiate it from a motivation.

4. THE LOGIC OF CONCERN[21]

Mencius' examples assert the possibility that a direct ethical response is a natural and spontaneous element of human behaviour. Conceptually, they may be seen as an answer to the Yangist criticism of ritualistic artificiality of Confucian morality, and Kao Tzu's claim that morality is constructed or imposed onto human nature. However, this ethical response is of a different logical order from the gratification of the sensory and appetitive desires. This is but a corollary of the earlier distinction between the expression of an ethical predisposition and having a motivation. As we have seen, Mencius is careful to dissociate the compassionate response from various motives. This is another way of saying that the compassion evinces a concern *for* the child. The various motives such as pleasing the child's parents, winning the praise of others, and stopping the annoying cry, etc. may be described as having a desire for certain things. Similarly, one could of course describe the compassionate concern as a desire for the welfare of the child. But one should also note the difference.

It is clear that the desire for the child's welfare is unlike the desire for some pleasurable state, or a desire to get rid of some unpleasurable state. In these latter cases, the focus is on consummating a desire-state. Compassion for the child, on the other hand, is outward-directed. The difference can be accentuated by considering that an unfulfilled desire may yet be gratified by redirecting one's efforts elsewhere. For example, I may be motivated by a sense of pride that I am compassionate, and to gratify my proud conception of myself, I go about looking for suitable occasions where my "compassion" can manifest itself. In such a case, one can truly and non-absurdly be said to be redirecting one's compassion. Suppose we apply this description to the case of the child on the verge of falling into a well. Imagine also that despite my efforts, he drops into the well. What would it mean to recommend that I redirect my effort to save him? If it is agreed that this would be an absurd thing to say, then the sense of absurdity highlights what it means to be concerned about another, as compared with the gratification of a desire. In other words, one is not concerned about the consummation of a desire-state, but about someone.

We should note that Mencius also describes the difference between the ethical predispositions and desires in terms of the the germ of loathing and shame. Consider the contrasting examples of choice which he provides.[22] Suppose I am choosing between two delicacies. If I cannot have both, I might settle for one over the other. Compare this with another case, where the desire to remain alive could be such that a man may resort to any means to keep alive. But Mencius goes on to give a third possibility:

"Yet there are ways of remaining alive and ways of avoiding death to which a man will not resort. In other words, there are things a man wants more than life and there are also things he loathes more than death. This is an attitude not confined to the moral man but common to all men. The moral man simply never loses it."[23]

The germ of shame and loathing is such that a man is capable of resisting the biological urge to live. Instead of being on the same level as any desire, the sense of what is hateful judges the desires. Kao Tzu's definition of human nature as the biological processes of life, and his insistence that there is nothing more to human nature than the appetites for food and sex, are therefore unacceptable.

5. THE TWO KINDS OF CONCERN: A NON-EXCLUSIVE DIVIDE

It was noted earlier that Mo Tzu assumes that, given its partiality, particularistic concern is opposed and also harmful to non-particularistic concern. But paradoxically, he had to appeal to a particularistic concern to motivate non-particularistic concern. Mencius' example of the child about to fall into a well, as we have seen, explains the possibility of a direct, non-particularistic concern. However, Mencius would still insist that normally, and other things being equal, one would give preference to those with whom one has a particularistic concern, especially one's parents.[24]

But although priority is to be given to one's parents, the point of the theory of the ethical predispositions is that they need to be developed into the virtues for one to flourish into a human being. For Mencius, the human being is defined not just by the possession of the four germs alone, but also by the ability to relate to others in terms of the virtues of benevolence, dutifulness, observance of the rites, and wisdom, as opposed to the gratification of desires alone.

Put in general terms, this means that non-particularistic concern is a function of the development of the virtues such as benevolence, dutifulness, ritual propriety, and wisdom. It is these virtues which both define and shape human relationships. Without the overall development of these virtues, as Mencius says, one cannot be in a position even to tend to one's parents, let alone have a regard for others.[25] The parent-child relationship is important not just for the special love which both parties enjoy, but as a basis for the development of feelings of love and concern for others.[26] Non-particularistic love begins with the feelings and the virtues that one develops in a particularistic relationship. It is possible that an overconcern with particularistic relationships would lead to a neglect of a concern for others. But contrary to Mo Tzu, there is nothing inherently wrong with particularistic relationships or the partiality that is due to such relationships. Instead of being a hindrance to non-particularistic concern, one would have to look at the situations and contexts in which partiality may or may not be appropriate. Furthermore, acts of partiality are constrained by the role one occupies.

Here is one example: Mencius is asked by someone called T'ao Ying to consider what the sage emperior Shun would have done, if his father had killed someone. Mencius' reply is that "The only thing to do was to apprehend him." Mencius is then asked whether Shun would not have tried to stop his father's arrest. Mencius replies, "How could Shun stop it? Kao Yao (the judge) had authority for what he did." Pressed further to say what Shun would have done, Mencius replies, "Shun looked upon casting aside the Empire as no more than discarding a worn shoe. He would have secretly carried the old man on his back and fled to the edge of the Sea and lived there happily, never giving a thought to the Empire."[27]

The conflict between particularistic and non-particularistic concern is resolved in this case by being aware of one's roles, and what it would be appropriate or inappropriate to do given these separate roles. In his role as emperor, Shun was morally powerless to prevent the arrest of his father. This role overrode his duty as a son. Shun, however, decided that the Empire was not as important to him as his duty as a son. He therefore relinquished his post, and performed his filial duty.

A doubt could be raised as to whether this is actually a case of conflict between the two kinds of concern? Should it not be described, more accurately instead, as a conflict between two duties: to the state and to one's own father? However, this points to the realization that conflict between the two kinds of concern cannot be resolved purely as a matter of weighing one against the other. The question of roles, duties, proprieties and responsibilities, etc., will have to be considered. Nice questions can arise here, about whether Shun was not taking his duties as emperor too lightly, or being irresponsible. To make a proper judgment, we need to determine specific factors such as how important it was that Shun remained as emperor, what the social and political circumstances were, and whether there were any able successors, etc. But it is interesting that Mencius put Shun's attitude toward his emperorship in terms that a Yangist would appreciate. As he says, "Shun looked upon casting aside the Empire as no more than discarding a worn shoe." This reminds us of the attitude of the King Tan-fu who was described earlier in the discussion on Yangism. King Tan-fu had no qualms about giving up his state to the invaders from Ti. A.C. Graham has pointed out another passage from the "Yangist chapters" of the *Zhuangzi*, where it is commented of another character, "The Empire is the weightiest thing of all, but he would not harm his life for the sake of it, and how much less for any other thing! Only the man who cares nothing for the Empire deserves to be entrusted with the Empire."[28]

Perhaps we can say that because Shun was concerned about his particularistic duty as a son that he manifested an admirable virtue and was as such, worthy to be an emperor who would do his best for non-particular others. He is someone who is benevolent, righteous, mindful of ritual propriety, and wise, and as such, able to do much for non-particular others in his role as emperor. Similarly, the Yangist who cherishes his life above material possessions and social and political office has the kind of virtue that might, say, put him beyond the desire for power and riches. As such, he is someone who might be able to devote himself to the non-particularistic tasks of public service, instead of being concerned about entrenching himself in power, and all the intrigues that involves.

6. CONCLUSION

In sum, there are three insights to be drawn from Mencius' reply to moral scepticism. Firstly, humanity is such that there are certain spontaneous ethical predispositions which manifest themselves in appropriate situations. This allows for, say, compassion, which is just as natural as the desires. Secondly, however, a distinction has to be drawn between the altruistic concern that arises out of these ethical predispositions and other forms of motivational desire. This allows us to appreciate what it is to have altruistic concern.[29] Thirdly, particularistic concern, or a concern that one has for those in a personal relation to ourselves, and non-particularistic concern, or a concern for those with whom one has no such relation, are not mutually exclusive. Both types of concern are related in that there are certain virtues which need to be developed before one can be said to have either kind of concern.

Acknowledgement:
I thank my colleagues A.T. Nuyen, C.L. Ten and Basant Kapur for their incisive comments on an earlier draft of this essay. See note 29 below for some of these comments.
I have followed the authors cited in the use of the Wade-Giles system of romanization, especially with regard to the names of persons. I have, however, resorted to *Hanyu pinyin* for

the use of certain terms, and the names of certain texts, e.g. the *Zhuangzi* instead of Chuang Tzu, *jianai* (universal love), *zhen* (genuineness or Truth), etc. As this paper is addressed to a non-specialist audience, I have kept the Chinese terms to a minimum.

Notes

1. See Burton Watson tr., *Mo Tzu: Basic Writings* (New York: Columbia University Press, 1963. The discussion below is based on the chapter on "Universal Love", pp. 39-49 of Watson.
2. "Universal love" is the term used by Watson, ibid.. Kwong-loi Shun, *Mencius and Early Chinese Thought* (Stanford: Stanford University Press, 1997), uses "indiscriminate concern", while A.C. Graham, *Disputers of the Tao* (La Salle, Illinois: Open Court Publishing Company, 1989), has "concern for everyone".
3. A possibility broached by David Wong though not intentionally, when he discusses the tenets of Western impersonal morality as against particularism before going on to discuss Confucianism versus Mohism in his paper, "Universalism Versus Love With Distinctions: An Ancient Debate Revived" in *Journal of Chinese Philosophy* 16 (1989), p.252. Wong notes the universalistic element in Confucian ethics, but states that "It should warn us against associating universalism too closely with Western, impersonal morality, or with political liberalism or social individualism. The presence of Mo Tzu as a challenger to the Confucian position reinforces this point." See Wong, p.253.
4. Watson, ibid., p.44.
5. Ibid., p.42.
6. Ibid., pp.46-47
7. The doctrines of Yang Chu are to be found in the texts *Lüshi cunqiu* (*Lü shi ch'un ch'iu*) and *Huainanzi* (*Huai-nan-tzu*), and *Liezi* (*Lieh-tzu*). Recent scholarship has also determined that certain chapters in the *Zhuangzi*: "Yielding the Throne" (or "Giving Away a Throne" in Watson tr. - see note 11), "Robber Chih", "Discourse on Swords" or "Discoursing on Swords" in Watson tr.) and "The Old Fisherman", hold Yangist ideas. My discussion of Yang Chu follows the ideas found in these chapters of the *Zhuangzi*. See the discussion by A.C. Graham in pp.53-64 of *Disputers of the Tao*.
8. *Mencius* 7A26. See D.C. Lau tr., *Mencius* (Hong Kong : The Chinese University Press, 1984), Volumes I and II.
9. Graham, ibid., p.53.
10. Ibid., p.59.
11. Burton Watson tr., *The Complete Works of Chuang Tzu* (New York: Columbia University Press, 1968), pp.310-311.
12. See the discussion between Ch'in Ku-li and Meng Sun-yang in the "Yang Chu" chapter of the *Liezi* (*Lieh-tzu*) as quoted in Graham, ibid., pp.60-61. Meng Sun-yang says: "That one hair matters less than skin, and skin less than a limb, is plain enough. However, go on adding to the one hair and it amounts to as much as skin, go on adding more skin and it amounts to as much as one limb. A single hair is certainly one thing among the myriad parts of the body, how can one treat it lightly?"
13. Watson tr., *The Complete Works of Chuang Tzu*, pp.330-331.
14. Ibid., pp.349-350.
15. Kao Tzu appears in the text of the *Mencius*, especially Book 6A.
16. *Mencius* 6A4.
17. *Mencius* 6A3-4.
18. *Mencius* 2A6.

19. See the discussions in *Mencius* 6A6-15. Note that in 2A6, one of the four germs is stated as the heart "courtesy and modesty," whereas in 6A6, this is stated as the heart of "respect". I have joined these "courtesy, modesty and respect" together. I have also rendered ***xiu wu*** more literally as the heart of "loathing and shame" instead of merely "shame", as given by D.C. Lau.
20. *Mencius* 3A5.
21. In this section, I make use of ideas which I have presented in another paper, "Mengzi and Gaozi on *Nei* and *Wai*" in Alan Chan ed., *Mencius: Contexts and Interpretations* (Honolulu: Hawaii University Press, 2002).
22. *Mencius* 6A10.
23. Ibid.
24. See *Mencius* 3A5, 7A35.
25. *Mencius* 2A6: "If a man is able to develop all these four germs that he possesses, it will be like a fire starting up or a spring coming through. When these are fully developed, he can tend the whole realm within the Four Seas, but if he fails to develop them, he will not be able even to serve his parents."
26. See David Wong, "Universalism Versus Love With Distinctions", *Journal of Chinese Philosophy* 16 (1989) 251-272 for a discussion about this development of love and concern.
27. *Mencius* 7A35.
28. From the "Giving Away a Throne" chapter in the *Zhuangzi*. See page 309 of Watson, tr. I have quoted from Graham, ibid., p.59. Watson's translation is slightly different: "The empire is a thing of supreme importance, yet he would not allow it to harm his life. How much less, then, any other thing! Only he who has no use for the empire is fit to be entrusted with it." This is even closer to Mencius' "casting aside the Empire as no more than discarding a worn shoe."
29. In an earlier version of this paper, I had tended to talk as if *nothing* motivates what I have called a "direct concern" for others, in contrast to having a desire for certain things. This comes out as a result of my contrasting having a direct concern, with having a motivation. But we can say that for Mencius, the ethical predisposition of compassion is itself a motivation, albeit, as I have tried to show, having a different logic from the logic of consummating a desire. In this connection, however, another problem arises from the notion of "redirecting a desire." There are certain cases where having a desire for an unique object is not redirectable. Such a desire could also be selfish, e.g. a desire to have sex with one particular person. Nevertheless, these difficulties should not obviate the point that Mencius is concerned to point out the possibility of a direct concern for others, which my example of redirection is meant to emphasize. At the same time, however, these difficulties point to further complexities in the topic of desire and its relationship to the objects of desire that I shall have to take up at a later stage.

Chapter 4

Altruism As The Condition Of Subjectivity

A.T. NUYEN

1. PRACTICAL ALTRUISM

In one sense, the term "altruism" refers to the tendency to act altruistically. In another sense, it refers to an ethical theory that seeks to justify acting altruistically. Clearly, by "altruism as the condition of subjectivity," I mean altruism in the first sense. I call the person who is disposed to act altruistically the "practical altruist," and the philosopher who subscribes to the ethical theory of altruism the "theoretical altruist." Whether to be an altruist of one kind is ipso facto to be an altruist of the other kind is not my concern in this paper. The aim of the paper is firstly to explicate, and secondly to provide some support for, a moral theory, due to Emmanuel Levinas, according to which to be a moral subject at all, one has to be a practical altruist.

We frequently act in such a manner as to benefit others in some significant ways (that is, not trivially such as when we act out of courtesy). In so acting, we disadvantage ourselves relative to others, and sometimes absolutely. If we seek to benefit others significantly (thus disadvantaging ourselves relatively or absolutely) out of a concern for their welfare then we act altruistically, or act as a practical altruist.[1] I take it that the ethical theory of altruism seeks to justify acting in this way, that is, to justify the attempt to benefit others in terms of their welfare. By contrast, egoism, insofar as it is taken as an ethical theory, seeks to justify all actions, including those that happen to benefit others, in terms of the agent's own welfare. Critics of altruism typically ask whether genuinely altruistic behaviour is possible and if so, how it can be regarded as morally superior to other kinds of behaviour, e.g. acting egoistically. Just as typically, defenders of altruism respond to the first question by claiming that the motivation to act altruistically lies in the common vicarious affects of being pleased by others' pleasure and pained by others' suffering. They may be what Hume calls the feelings of sympathy, or what psychologists call empathy. To be sure, those vicarious affects will have to translate themselves into reasons for acting altruistically. Thus, a genuine (practical) altruist is not simply *caused* by vicarious affects to seek to benefit others. As Nicholas Rescher puts it, the motivation operates "in the order of reasons rather than causes."[2] Insofar as Hume merely posits sympathy as the moral motivation that causes moral behaviour, he is not a theoretical altruist (even though he may have been, occasionally, a practical altruist). If the vicarious affects operate on the agent as causes then there is a sense in which the agent acts only "within oneself." It is "in the order of reasons" that the agent may be said to be acting out of a genuine concern for others. This is not to say that altruism is, by necessity, a cognitivist theory, or a theory that posits moral reasons as causes of moral behaviour. It is to say simply that the practical altruist must somehow be cognizant of the fact that he or she is acting out of a concern for the welfare of others. In summary, I take it that an altruistic act is an act performed by an agent who, in so acting, (1) seeks to benefit others significantly in a way that (2) disadvantages him-/herself relatively or absolutely, (3) out of a conscious concern for their welfare.

"In the order of reasons," altruistic acts are a matter of choice. What the theoretical altruist defends is the choice to benefit others based on the concern for the welfare of others, not the behavioural pattern of someone afflicted with vicarious affects. The concern for others is taken as the standard of the moral evaluation of acts freely chosen by an agent. Only acts chosen on the basis of positive concern have moral worth. Acts performed out of a concern to harm others are evil. If I am right in my characterization of altruism as an ethical theory then altruism presupposes that altruistic acts present themselves as choices for a subject. The moral worthiness of a subject then is a function of the frequency of such choices. Mother Teresa is more morally worthy than I am because she chose to act out of a positive concern for others more frequently than I do. This accords with the common view of subjectivity, namely, a self-conscious being, an "I," endowed with the freedom to choose and becoming more or less moral, more or less evil, with the choices that it makes. If there is any miracle of creation, it begins and perhaps ends with the creation of a human subject, complete in itself and endowed, as a gift, with freedom; God is not responsible for the choices, including the moral ones, made by the human subject subsequently. Given this common view of subjectivity, it is a matter of regret that human subjects have not chosen wisely, that there has been so much evil, so much so that we are conditioned to look to the future with pessimism, even despair. This view of subjectivity has been challenged by Emmanuel Levinas. His philosophy affords us a radically different perspective on altruism.

2. LEVINAS AND SUBJECTIVITY

For Levinas, one does not first become a subject and then choose to act in certain ways, altruistically or otherwise. One becomes a subject in acting out of the concern for the welfare of others, i.e. altruistically. Altruism is the condition of subjectivity, not the other way round. Levinas's phenomenology of subjectivity, elaborated in *Totality and Infinity*,[3] constitutes an argument for this claim. Levinas begins by showing that the subject, the "I," acquires its identity as subject by first separating or isolating itself from what is not itself. This is achieved in the process of satisfying desires, or the process of enjoyment, in which one becomes aware of one's own happiness and unhappiness, thus aware of one's own ipseity, or one's selfhood. Ipseity entails uniqueness, or "unicity" as Levinas puts it. Thus, to be aware of one's own ipseity, one's selfhood, is to be aware of one's uniqueness, one's unicity. For Levinas, enjoyment accomplishes this because "enjoyment ... is isolation" (TI, p.117) and isolation is the structure of the unicity of the I. To be aware of one's own ipseity, or unicity, is the first step toward the awareness of subjectivity. Given certain cognitive abilities, this first step leads to the awareness of objects of desires ("The separation accomplished as enjoyment ... becomes a consciousness of objects" - TI, p.139) and the conceptualization of them in language. It also leads to the awareness of other people who can contribute to or interfere with one's own enjoyment. The I has to deal with, or to be engaged in a commerce with, other people, with "the Other" (*l'autrui*). Given the linguistic ability, the use of language in the commerce with the Other is inevitable. Thus, we have a community of language users.

If this is all there is to the development of the I, of subjectivity, then the priority of subjectivity to moral choices is confirmed. If the subject is just a language user then there can be subjectivity before moral choices. However, Levinas insists that the entity that exists completely for itself in its dealings with others is not yet an I, or an entity with full subjectivity. As he puts it, the enjoyment in which "I am absolutely for myself" (TI, p.134) "assuredly does not render the concrete man" (TI, p.139). This is so because in being "absolutely for myself," there is no real separation between the I and the others. There is real separation only when the others are recognized by me as having a radical alterity, an otherness that cannot be absorbed by me into my being. Metaphysically, real separation manifests itself in a desire, or "Desire" as Levinas puts it, to transcend the totality of one's own being and to reach the infinity that lies on the hither side of one's being. In Levinas's own words and emphasis, this is the "metaphysical desire [that] tends toward *something else entirely*, toward the *absolutely other*" (TI, p.33). This "something else," this "absolutely other," is designated by the term "the other" (*l'autre*). The separation that constitutes subjectivity is completed only in the desire for the other. This desire, in turn, is fulfilled only in my commerce with the Other.

Fleshed out in logical terms, Levinas's argument is as follows. To be an I with full subjectivity is to be aware of one's own ipseity, to be aware of oneself as a unique identity, or as a "unicity." The I, then, must be completely separated from what is not itself, and furthermore, must have an awareness of this separation. To say the same thing differently, the I must be aware of the limits of its own being. As Hegel has shown us, the idea of the limit implies the idea of the beyond, of that which lies on the other side of the limit. Thus, the separation that constitutes the I requires awareness of what lies on the hither side of one's own being. To be totally absorbed in one's being without this awareness, to be "absolutely for myself," is not to be "the concrete man." It follows that subjectivity is confirmed only when there is an awareness of what is radically other than oneself, of radical alterity. As Levinas puts it in *Otherwise than Being*,[4] the subjectivity of the I is constituted as a "node and a denouement" of being and the otherwise than being, "of essence and the essence's other" (OB, p.10). The next step in the argument is to show that it is in my commerce with the Other, with my fellow human beings, that I can satisfy the metaphysical desire for subjectivity, which is logically the desire for what is absolutely other, for infinity, for transcendence.

In my commerce with my fellow human beings, I can either conceptualize and thematize them, and deal with them out of a concern for my own being, or I can see them as radically other than myself. To conceptualize and to thematize others is to reduce them to the categories of my own thought, to bring them within the limits of my being. To deal with them out of a concern for my own being is to see them as nothing but extensions of oneself. I can never successfully do this to my fellow human beings, or to the Other. To begin with, insofar as my commerce with them is conducted in language, I already realize that my fellow human beings possess an alterity that cannot be absorbed into the totality of my being. I realize that the meanings of my utterances depend not just on me but also on my interlocutors. As Levinas puts it, the "relationship of language implies transcendence, radical separation, the revelation of the other to me" (TI, p.73). Furthermore, my experiences with others will show me that they have their own intentions and purposes, that the Other is "*not under a category*" and has "only a reference to himself" (TI, 69). It follows that the Other possesses a radical alterity, an absolute otherness, that which can confirm my subjectivity. It follows further that it is in the commerce with the Other that the desire for subjectivity can be fulfilled. The next stage in Levinas's argument is to show that we can fulfill this desire, thus become an I with full subjectivity, only by maintaining the radical alterity in others, and we can do so only by acting altruistically.

To experience radical alterity, I have to behave in a way such that my enjoyment is not "absolutely for myself." In Levinas's own words, we have to behave in a way such that "the goods of this world break forth from the exclusive property of enjoyment," or from the "egoist and solitary enjoyment" (TI, p.76). Levinas characterizes this behaviour as "without utility, in pure loss, gratuitously, without referring to anything else, in pure expenditure" (TI, p.133). To do otherwise, i.e. referring only to oneself, or egoistically, is to fail to accomplish the separation that is constitutive of subjectivity. To see myself as a unique I, I have to draw the boundaries between what is myself and what is not, and I can only do so by recognizing what is radically other than myself, and this in turn only by "breaking forth from ... egoist and solitary enjoyment." Furthermore, I have to *maintain* the boundaries between myself and the other and I can only do this by maintaining the Other, my fellow human beings, in their heterogeneity, in their radical alterity. Maintaining the boundaries is my responsibility as an I in its full subjectivity. I can do this only by making myself sensible of the radical alterity of the Other, and this, in turn, by accepting that I am *responsible* for the Other as absolutely other, that is, out of a concern for the Other as other, not out of a concern for myself. It is this "responsibility [that] confirms the subjectivity" of the I (TI, p.245). Levinas goes on: "To utter 'I,' to affirm the irreducible singularity ..., means to possess a privileged place with regard to responsibilities for which no one can replace me and from which no one can release me. To be unable to shirk: this is the I." To utter "I," then, means to act altruistically toward others.

Clearly then, acting altruistically is not a choice available to the subject, nor is it something that moralists can cite in evaluating a subject. One is a subject by acting altruistically in the first place. This is why Levinas claims that responsibility for the Other is primordial and arises before freedom. My own subjectivity "comes from the impossibility of escaping responsibility" (OB, p.14). As a subject, I have to accept it in a passivity rather than assuming it in a positive act of freedom. As Levinas puts it, the responsibility that confirms my subjectivity, "in its antecedence to my freedom, its antecedence to the present and to representation, is a passivity more passive than all passivity, an exposure to the other without this exposure being assumed ..." (OB, p.15). Specifically, to be a subject and to maintain my subjectivity, I have to be exposed to the Other. Furthermore, I need to sharpen my sensibility of the absolutely other, hence the sensibility of my own subjectivity, by making myself vulnerable to the Other, by exposing myself "to outrage, to wounding" (OB, p.15). Better still, I have to substitute myself for the Other as a "hostage who substitutes himself for the others" (OB, p.15), to feel responsible for all their "faults and misfortune" (OB, p.10), to offer them "even the bread out of one's own mouth and the coat from one's shoulders" (OB, p.55). Ultimately, subjectivity is confirmed in the "ultimate offering (of) oneself, or suffering in the offering of oneself" (OB, p.54). The I in its full subjectivity cannot be egoistic. God did not create a subject and subsequently gave it the freedom to choose to act altruistically or egoistically. God created a subject that is already altruistic, already moral: "The miracle of creation lies in creating a moral being" (TI, p.89).

It may be objected at this point that if the responsibility for the Other is primordial and arose prior to freedom then it must be the case that under the right conditions the concern for the Other will *cause* me to act for their sake and if so, I cannot be acting altruistically. However, this objection misconstrues the responsibility for the Other as a causal condition of subjectivity whereas for Levinas, it is a metaphysical condition, not a physical one at all. Physically, I can still choose to act either for the sake of the Other or "absolutely for myself." As Levinas puts it, while "I can recognize the gaze of the stranger, the widow, and the orphan only in giving or in refusing; I am free to give or to refuse..." (TI, p.77). To refuse, to act absolutely for myself, means to deny my own subjectivity, to act inauthentically or in bad faith as existentialists would say. It means to act contrary to one's own metaphysical desire, contrary to the humanity that was the miracle of creation, bearing the mark of the original sin. Physically, when I *choose* to act for the sake of the Other, I do not choose to do so as an authoritative subject, or an I with full subjectivity, but rather as a fallen subject trying to rise up again, as a damaged subjectivity trying to repair itself. The I with full subjectivity does not choose to act altruistically; it is through acting altruistically that one becomes an I with full subjectivity. This I does not choose but is in a sense chosen, or commanded as Levinas says, by the Other to be "the first on the scene, [who] makes me approach him, makes me his neighbor" (OB, p.11). The I with full subjectivity acts altruistically not in an active choice but in a passivity "more passive than all patience" (OB, p.15). Nevertheless, to be chosen, to act in a passivity, is not to be caused. It is still to act for the sake of the Other "in the order of reasons," thus satisfying Rescher's condition for acting altruistically. Indeed, to sharpen the sensibility for the absolutely other, thus the sensibility for one's own subjectivity, responsibility for the Other, though primordial, must be brought to the cognitive level, or made to operate "in the order of reasons." This turns out to be easy enough because responsibility is already an "incessant murmur [that] strikes with absurdity" (OB, p.164).

The response above points to another possible objection. Thus, it may be said that insofar as the I acts for the sake of others only to confirm its subjectivity, to satisfy its metaphysical desire, it acts really for itself and not altruistically. Fortunately, Bishop Butler has taught us how to deflect this kind of objection. Following Butler, we can say that the critic has conflated the psychological with the ethical. Psychologically, all motivations must originate in me, but that does not mean that my actions cannot be genuinely ethical, genuinely altruistic. In any case, Levinas' metaphysical desire for transcendence is not a physical desire such as the desire to be loved or respected which may motivate someone to act for the sake of others. Genuine altruism is in no way incompatible with the satisfaction of the metaphysical desire for what is absolutely other. How such desire operates is not a matter of psychology or psychiatry but a matter of phenomenology. Likewise, subjectivity is not something sought by the subject as an end in performing something else as a means; it is revealed in my dealings with my fellow human beings.

3. PRACTICAL ALTRUISM AND PITY

What I have done so far is to construct an argument, based on the writings of Levinas, for the claim that altruism is the condition of subjectivity, not the other way round. If I am right then for people who think of themselves, or are aware of themselves, as beings with unique identities, as definite quiddities rather than amorphous beings with no definite boundaries, altruism is already embedded in their humanity. Such people do not ask whether they should act altruistically, and do not need the theoretical altruist to give them a justification for doing so. If they are also reflective people, they will not come up with an ethical theory as an account of altruistic behaviour but rather with an ethics as a metaphysics of being, or as Levinas would put it, ethics as first philosophy. Still, it may be asked if there is any empirical evidence for the claim above. While the notion of responsibility is not grounded in psychology, it may still be asked if there is anything in human psychology that helps or hinders our metaphysical yearning for the absolutely other. In what follows, I suggest that evidence can be found in the phenomenon of pity. Indeed, I shall argue that the phenomenology of pity maps neatly on to Levinas' phenomenology of responsibility.

It may be thought that pity is an inappropriate emotion to be grafted on to Levinas's ethics. The thought is that it is inappropriate because according to the Oxford English Dictionary, there is in the meaning of "pity" an implication of "slight contempt." Understandably, it is often the case that people find it offensive to be pitied. Indeed, many philosophers, ranging from the Stoics to Kant and Nietzsche, give pity a negative moral value. However, it is worth noting that the implication of "slight contempt" is a recent acquisition. The O.E.D. itself tells us that the term "pity" was not fully differentiated from the term "piety" until the late 1600s. According to Martha Nussbaum, it is only "from the Victorian era onward" that the term "pity" has acquired "nuances of condescension and superiority to the sufferer."[5] Worth noting also is the fact that the moral status of pity can be defended against critics such as Kant and Nietzsche, and Nussbaum is one of many philosophers who have done so.[6] I have elsewhere given my own defense of pity.[7] For the purpose of this paper, it suffices to point out that there are clearly cases of pity which are totally free from "nuances of condescension and superiority," cases in which pity is craved for rather than rejected as offensive. There is such a thing as "good pity," the kind for which Lear cries out in *King Lear* and Oedipus begs in *Oedipus at Colonus*,[8] the same kind of pity shown by the Virgin Mary toward the suffering Christ as depicted by Michelangelo's *Pietà*. It is this kind of pity that I want to graft on to Levinas's ethics.

According to Aristotle (*Rhetoric* 1385-6), we pity someone because he or she suffers from a serious and undeserved misfortune. Aristotle also stresses the fact that the circumstances of the pitied have to be such that the pitier can identify with, such that the pitier himself or herself could well fall into. To pity someone, the pitier must be circumstantially close to the pitied, close enough to realize that the misfortune of the pitied could well be one's own. Rousseau understands well this conceptual requirement. Thus, he claims that pity cannot be taught to the person who "considers ... alien to him" the sufferings of others, and that one learns to pity others only if one understands that "their ills are there in the ground beneath his feet."[9] It is not unreasonable to suggest that what both Aristotle and Rousseau stress is the circumstantial *proximity* between the pitier and the pitied. Finally, implicit in the meaning of pity are the feeling of compassion toward the sufferer and the desire to relieve the sufferer's distress. These are the main conceptual requirements of the notion of "pity." They are distilled from actual experiences of pity and thus can be cashed back out in phenomenological terms.

As I have pointed out elsewhere,[10] phenomenologically, the pitier feels as if he or she has the duty or the responsibility to relieve the distress experienced by the pitied, as if he or she is somehow responsible for the latter's suffering. This is consistent with the fact that "pity" is etymologically linked to "piety" as pointed out above, and that the Latin root of "piety" is *pietas*, meaning "dutifulness." The circumstantial proximity with the pitied typically makes the pitier feel that he or she has somehow escaped the misfortune that should have been his or hers, a feeling akin to what psychologists have identified in those caught up in a tragic event but somehow escaped the tragic consequences while others, the victims, were traumatized. This feeling can turn into the desire to take the sufferer's place, *to substitute* oneself for the sufferer. However, it is typical of pity that the condition for which we pity someone is such that both the pitier and the pitied are helpless in the face of it. Indeed, when the situation is not hopeless, when something can be done to stop the suffering, pity may well be inappropriate because it could well lead the pitier to adopting the attitude of passive acceptance. "Good pity" is felt when the pitier and the pitied believe that nothing can be done to remove the cause of suffering. The pitier realizes that the responsibility to stop the suffering cannot be discharged, that the desire to do so cannot be satisfied, that all that can be done is to suffer the suffering of the pitied.

Pity, as I have characterized it, is a human emotion to which we are all vulnerable, a feeling of which we are all susceptible. It is as if biologically hard wired into human beings, part of what Kant calls "the subjective conditions" of human nature. This is evidenced by the fact that the cry of distress is something that a human creature cannot ignore. When babies hear the cry of distress, they invariably feel the distress and invariably cry in response. In adult human beings, this empathetic response takes many forms. It has been observed, for instance, that the call of another human being is something that we find very difficult to ignore. The ringing telephone somehow demands to be answered. However, it is in the form of the feeling of pity that the empathetic response can operate cognitively, or "in the order of reasons." The feeling of pity invokes the desire to take on the responsibility to relieve the suffering. As in babies, it is felt before one has the chance to reflect, before one decides what to do, before freedom. The responsibility to relieve the distress that one feels in pitying comes from the primordial region of biology and is a responsibility that the biological I cannot shirk, any more than a baby can ignore the distressing cry of another baby. Coming from the primordial region, the feeling of pity signals a proximity without a distance, a closeness so close that the response is automatic, unmediated by reflection. Clearly then, if we are in search of a human subjective condition that helps us fulfill the metaphysics of morals as outlined by Levinas, the feeling of pity emerges as the prime candidate. Indeed, nothing else seems to fit the bill. Only through the feeling of pity that the Other appeals to me "with its destitution and nudity – its hunger – without my being able to be deaf to that appeal" (TI, p.200).

How does the feeling of pity help human beings fulfill Levinas's metaphysics of morals? Given the characterization of pity above, particularly its phenomenology, it is clear that the subjectivity of the I, already presupposed, emerges in the feeling of pity. In pity, it is the I that feels for the distressed Other. The pitier becomes aware of an-other who is suffering, of a separation between the I and the Other. Put in the terminology of *Totality and Infinity*, we may say that in pity the enjoyment of the I is interrupted, and the subjectivity of the I is confirmed through such interruption. In pity, the I is exposed "to outrage, to wounding." Yet, as we have seen, the feeling of pity arises from a primordial proximity, from the sensibility of a responsibility for an-other, a responsibility that the I cannot shirk, evidenced in the impossibility of ignoring a distressing cry. Furthermore, the feeling of pity not just reveals the subjectivity of the I, it also puts the I in question: Why this Other and not me? Why they rather than me? As Levinas has pointed out, morality consists just in this putting oneself in question. To be sure, in many people, the feeling of pity operates as a physical cause, in the same way as the crying of one baby affects other babies. However, the phenomenology of pity reveals that, typically, pity brings to our cognition the possibility of acting simply for the sake of others. It is in this way that the feeling of pity can fulfill Levinas's metaphysics of morals.

The question asked earlier, namely whether there is any empirical counterpart to the theoretical I who maintains its subjectivity in acting for the sake of others, can now be answered. It is the person who is susceptible to the feeling of pity and who responds to it in acts of altruism. However, it may still be asked why anyone should be motivated to respond to the feeling of pity by acting altruistically. I have compared the feeling of pity with the cry of a baby caused by another baby's cry of distress. The cry of a baby is meant to motivate its carer to remove the cause of the discomfort. Unfortunately, this biological motivation does not translate itself straightforwardly into the case of pity. It is true that no human being is able to ignore a cry of distress, or to ignore the upsurge inside one's own breast of the sensibility of responsibility toward the distressed Other. Nevertheless, in adult human beings, freedom often enough interferes. As we have seen, Levinas himself acknowledges that "I am free to give or to refuse" (TI, p.77). The question is: What motivates me to respond to the upsurge of responsibility by giving rather than refusing? As freedom takes over biology, the motivational question returns. Aware of Hecuba's suffering and of the sensibility arising within myself as a result, Levinas acknowledges that I can still ask "What is Hecuba to me?" (OB, p.117).

The answer is that in the feeling of pity, it is not just the pain of the distressed Other that I have to respond to: it is also, and primarily, my own pain that I have to respond to. As pointed out above, pity is such that the pitier and the pitied are impotent with respect to the cause of the misfortune. Thus, the desire to relieve the suffering will not be fulfilled: there is nothing the Virgin Mary can do to remove the cause of Christ's suffering, and this impotence is constitutive of her pity. The unfulfilled desire on the part of the pitier results in a suffering in the pitier himself or herself, in addition to the suffering of the pitied. It is like the pain of a baby caused by the cry of pain of another baby. However, while neither baby can do anything to ease its own pain other than crying to motivate others to do it, the pitier can and his or her own pain is the motivation. The feeling of pity has a motivational force because in pitying, the pitier has his or her own pain to deal with. Since the source of the pitier's pain is the pain of the pitied, the pitier is motivated to give "the bread out of one's own mouth and the coat from one's own shoulders." This is not to say that the concern for the Other, for Hecuba, for my brother, is a selfish one, having to do only with relieving my own pain. This is not the experiential characteristic of pity, which is the exact opposite. The concern is genuinely for the Other. As pointed out above, the fact that the motivational force originates from within oneself does not render the resulting actions egoistic.

In *Otherwise than Being*, Levinas speaks of "identity gnawing away at itself — in a remorse" (OB, p.114). We have seen that the feeling of pity accomplishes his metaphysics of identity insofar as it is a pain that both gnaws away inside the pitier and motivates the pitier to share bread with the famished and to welcome the wretched. Furthermore, there is no escape from the pain of pity because, as pointed out above, the desire to alleviate the pain cannot be satisfied, the responsibility sensed by the pitier cannot be discharged. Given the fact of pain and suffering and given our vulnerability and our susceptibility to the distress of others, the pitiful is always out there, traumatizing us and holding us hostage. It is out there as an "incessant murmur [that] strikes with absurdity" (OB, p.164), as that which puts us "under the traumatic effect of persecution" and as that by virtue of which the "subject is a hostage" (OB, p.112). In a passage that comes closest to what I have argued here, Levinas claims that it is "through the condition of being hostage that there can be in the world pity, compassion, pardon and proximity" (OB, p.117). In the empirical world, or what Levinas calls "the said," it is through the condition of being hostage to pity that there can be in the world morality as we know it. Those who still ask "Why should I be moral?" are those who have not felt the force of pity. No doubt, there have been and will continue to be people born with an immunity to it. The more fortunate among them can count on either the susceptibility to the force of practical reason as Kant had envisaged, or the Humean sentiment of sympathy, as an entry ticket into the moral community. Toward the less fortunate, we must show an appropriate moral stance developed from a good pity, a Levinasian readiness to embrace the Other with the words "Here I am." One can and should act altruistically even to an egoist.

If Levinas, as I interpret him here, is right, altruism as an ethical theory is otiose. For a human subject, to justify altruism makes no more sense than for, say, an existentialist to justify freedom, or a Christian to justify the existence of God. The subject is already moral, already altruistic. Does it mean, then, that we are all equally altruistic? It seems that, on Levinas' account, we are forced to say "yes" to this question, which is counter-intuitive. For, surely, mother Teresa is much more altruistic than I am. This is perhaps the final possible objection. The answer to it is a complex one and I can only gesture at it here. It has to do with Levinas' distinction between the metaphysical dimension, or what he calls *the saying*, and the empirical dimension, or what he calls *the said*. In the metaphysical realm, or on the level of *the saying*, we as human subjects are all equally moral, equally altruistic. However, in the empirical realm, or on the level of *the said*, there are other factors intruding into the attainment of subjectivity, making it into a struggle for it, the struggle to "accomplish metaphysics" as Levinas puts it. These factors include physical desires, the presence of what Levinas calls "the third party," or my neighbor's neighbor, and social and political institutions. The effect of these factors is such that in the empirical world, *the said*, we can only be more or less altruistic, more or less moral. However, it does not take a moral theory to determine the right degree of altruism. What it takes are psychology, politics and social science, and perhaps a theology that tells us how far the children of God, outside of Eden, have fallen and how they can atone for the Fall. Philosophers can afford the luxury of the utopian vision of a community of human subjects in which our subjectivity is confirmed and maintained by responsibility for the Other, a community in which we all are, already, equally altruistic, equally moral.

Notes

■ A slightly longer version of this paper was published in *American Catholic Philosophical Quarterly*, Vol.74(2000), pp.637-652. Permission from the editors of *ACPQ* to have the paper reprinted here is gratefully acknowledged.

1. I take it that passing the salt to someone at the dinner table, tipping the porter, giving the beggar one's loose change, etc. are not acts of altruism.
2. Nicholas Rescher, *Unselfishness: The Role of Vicarious Affects in Moral Philosophy and Social Theory* (Pittsburgh: University of Pittsburgh Press, 1975), p.6.
3. Emmanuel Levinas, *Totality and Infinity*, trans. Alphonso Lingis (Pittsburgh, Pa.: Duquesne University Press, 1969). Quotations from this work are indicated by TI followed by page numbers.
4. Emmanuel Levinas, *Otherwise than Being or Beyond Essence*, trans. Alphonso Lingis (The Hague: Martinus Nijhoff, 1981). Quotations from this work are indicated by OB followed by page numbers.
5. Martha Nussbaum, "Compassion: The Basic Social Emotion," *Social Philosophy and Policy*, Vol.13(1996), pp.27-58, at p.29.
6. See also Felicia Ackerman, "Pity as a Moral Concept/The Morality of Pity," *Midwest Studies in Philosophy*, Vol.20(1995), pp.59-66, and Eamonn Callan, "The Moral Status of Pity," *Canadian Journal of Philosophy*, Vol.18(1998), pp.1-12.
7. "Pity," *Southern Journal of Philosophy*, Vol.37(1999), pp.77-87.
8. A most poor man, made tame by fortune's blows;
   Who, by the art of known and feeling sorrows,
   Am pregnant to good pity.
   King Lear, Act IV, Scene VI.
9. Jean-Jacques Rousseau, *Emile*, trans. Allan Bloom (New York: Basic Books, 1976), p.224.
10. Nuyen, *op.cit.*

Chapter 5

Altruism, Risk And Sibling Rivalry

MICHAEL COLLINS

1. INTRODUCTION: WRIGHT, MAHATHIR AND THE NEED FOR ALTRUISM

In 1955 Richard Wright, an American writer who wanted to hear "the human race speaking," traveled to Bandung, Indonesia to cover the unprecedented gathering of Asian—and a few African—leaders that has become known as the Bandung Conference. *The Color Curtain,* Wright's book about the conference, is among other things an appeal for altruism, a call for the West to nurture the new-born countries represented at Bandung--even if that would mean grooming potential rivals.

With both Western and developing world audiences in his peripheral vision, Wright counsels the West to abandon fears of a shift in the balance of power even as he underscores his view that the result will be a kind of abdication: "When the day comes that Asian and African raw materials are processed in Asia and Africa," he asserts, "the supremacy of the Western world, economic, cultural, and political, will have been broken once and for all. . . ."[1] Wright clearly does not foresee the shift of the most prosperous states towards knowledge-based economies. But what remains relevant to present debates are his basic points—that power would be diffused and advantage undone by widespread development and that, for some, this prospect is cause for fear and for rejecting altruism.

The continuing topicality of Wright's concerns is clear when one compares them to those expressed by Malaysian Prime Minister Dr. Mahathir Mohamad in his 1999 work, *A New Deal for Asia*. In this volume, Mahathir replies to his critics in his usual brash style. In one Wright-like passage, he asserts that his region's rise to economic power was probably viewed in the West "with a mixture of awe and anxiety. Awe at the speed and relentlessness which brought the East Asian economies to prominence, and anxiety at the prospect of losing centuries of world domination." [2]

The similarities with Wright become even more striking when Mahathir, recalling the attacks on East Asian currencies in 1997-98, writes that "Within a period of days this diabolically simple, seemingly non-lethal weapon [currency speculation] had forced the emerging and obstreperous countries of East Asia to buckle under and surrender." Mahathir even calls for altruism, in the form of an end to "beggar-thy-neighbor" zero-sum economics and the establishment of a "World Century based on coexistence and greater prosperity for everyone." Of course the arguments of Wright the self-exiled writer and Mahathir the national leader also have striking differences.

Wright, writing in the chill of the cold war, speaks not so much of new deals and centuries as of tolerable and intolerable levels of fear and risk. Indeed, he couches his call for the West to voluntarily give up its supremacy in terms of the *risk* of not doing so—the risk of *not* helping Asia and Africa industrialize, and thus leaving the field open for the West's sworn enemies, the Communists, to step in with their aid.

To this end, Wright emphasizes the role of one of the participants in the conference, Chinese Premier Zhou En-lai. In a portrait that is something of a caricature, Wright paints Zhou as an arch manipulator rather than the rational and skillful diplomat most accounts limn. Playing on the chills he expected Zhou's role to send up the West's spines, Wright argues that "Unless the Western world can meet the challenge of the miraculous unity of Bandung openly and selflessly, it faces an Asian-African attempt at [modernizing] under the guidance of Mr. [Zhou] En-lai and his drastic theories and practices of endless secular sacrifices." The drastic theories Wright referred to were those of Stalinism, which perhaps for literary convenience, or perhaps because he was unaware of tensions between Beijing and Moscow, he conflates with Maoism.

Of course, Wright was himself under suspicion and surveillance as a former member of the American communist party, and he may have wished to distance himself from Zhou, whose five principles of peaceful coexistence heavily influenced the Bandung Conference's final "Declaration on the Promotion of World Peace and Cooperation."

Wright in any case drives his points home by closing *The Color Curtain* (whose title is a play on Winston Churchill's cold war phrase, "the iron curtain") with an exposition of what he believes leads to Stalinism—namely, an overwhelming consciousness of risk that manifests itself first as fear, then as totalitarianism. "Seen through the perspective of Bandung," he writes, "I think that it can be said that FEAR of the loss of their power, FEAR of re-enslavement, FEAR of attack was the key to the actions of the Russian Stalinists who felt that any efforts to modernize their nation would be preferable to a return to the status quo. . . ."

Scholarship on the Soviet dictator has confirmed that Stalin's bloody drive to industrialize was indeed fueled in large part by his fears of losing his power base and being unprepared for a war with foreign or domestic opponents. Indeed, in a 1931 speech, Stalin declared that if Russia did not catch up with the advanced industrialized countries, "they will crush us." Stalin's complete lack of altruism, however, not only built the Soviet Union but also made it too rigid, brittle and intolerant to survive. This suggests that a certain amount of altruism is necessary in human societies. At the very least, the counterexample of Stalin suggests that altruism must be a part not only of the rhetoric of the society—as it certainly was in the Stalinist utopia—but also of the structure of the society: that altruism must be built into laws and practices that put a limit on ruthlessness and the sort of top-down control that not only crushes response but also increases uncertainty and bewilderment—and inefficiency--even as it cows.

2. RISK AND ALTRUISM

But what exactly is altruism? This paper thus far has ducked that crucial question, since a proper answer would require another essay. But, briefly, for the purposes of this paper, *altruism* is a function of risk. More specifically, *Risk* is danger to a person's or a community's life or hopes, and *altruism* is action, undertaken at some risk to the actor, to save another person's—or a community's—life or hopes.

Biologist Richard Dawkins writes that an "entity, such as a baboon, is said to be altruistic if it behaves in such a way as to increase another such entity's welfare at the expense of its own. . . . 'Welfare' is defined as 'chances of survival', even if the effect on actual life and death prospects is so small as to seem negligible . . . . It is important to realize that the above definitions of altruism and selfishness are behavioural, not subjective. . . . I am not going to argue about whether people who behave altruistically are 'really' doing it for secret or subconscious selfish motives. . . . My definition is concerned only with whether the *effect* of an act is to lower or raise the survival prospects of the presumed altruist and the survival prospects of the presumed beneficiary."[3]

This paper agrees with every detail of Dawkins' definition. It simply tries to humanize the definition a bit by adding risky acts aimed at preserving a person's or community's *hopes*, and not only its life, to the honor roll of altruism. The role of hope is clear when one considers that, if Wright's African ancestors had been saved from a sinking slave ship but then sent on into slavery, their lives would have been preserved, but their hopes would have been dashed. Indeed, the investors in the voyage of the slave ship might in this case have been the beneficiaries of the altruistic act. As for the question of what so often stops altruism before it reaches slaves and other outsiders, the answer lies in what *starts* altruism.

Biologists have noted that the most natural—one might say the most Darwinian—form of altruism is kin-based altruism: a mother's altruism toward her child, a sister's altruism toward her brother. The reason? When we help our children or even our siblings, we in all likelihood help genes that match our own to survive.

Altruism begins to run into problems outside the family. But, under the right pressures, it can be stretched first across an extended family—aunts, cousins, second cousins—and then across metaphorical families—tribes, ethnic groups, nations even. In all its forms, altruism is a mechanism for defense against risk: The mother protects and trains her child; the tribe protects and honors its mothers; the nation establishes laws and rituals that encourage even mutually competitive groups to behave as if they were one people, one extended family. In an era of globalization, some scholars have noted, the nation can become for some of its citizens an indispensable anchor of identity and source of altruism (for instance, protective tariffs) even as it yields some of its sovereignty to supranational entities and cash flows. By the same token, global entities (like the UN High Commissioner for Refugees) can become the identity-savers and sources of altruism for those living in strife-torn nations that become the equivalent of dysfunctional families.

Conflicts persist because of competing altruisms and because, so far in human history, outsiders—nonrelatives, foreigners, speakers of foreign languages, "funny looking" people, the IMF and the forces of globalization--are encountered sooner or later: At this point, uncertainty and perhaps even fear set in. And once fear arises, the possibility of discrimination, deceit, aggression, and even warfare—where all risks are unleashed—becomes real.

3. A STEP BACK: SIBLING RIVALRY

Some zoological research suggests that the situation is even more grave than this. For even within the family there is sibling rivalry, immortalized in the story of Cain and Abel. The choice between rivalry and altruism turns on the fact that an altruist "purchases" a unit of another's survival in coins of risk. Person Y must decide how much person X's survival is worth to her.

The biological perspective suggests that the decision is made on the basis of the degree of genetic identity—the extent to which Y's genes mirror X's genes--and of behavioural identification. According to what is known as Hamilton's rule, after its originator W.D. Hamilton, the benefit to Y of an altruistic act by X is a function of the benefit to Y multiplied by the degree of relatedness (r) of X and Y and *less* the cost of the act to X. (In symbols this can be written as $r\mathbf{b}_y - \mathbf{c}_x$). If this amount is greater than zero (i.e., if $r\mathbf{b}_y - \mathbf{c}_x > 0$) then the rules of genetic fitness will permit the altruistic act to be performed, since the prospects of genes that probably match the altruist's own are improved more than the altruist's own genes are hurt.

But, as Douglas W. Mock and Geoffrey A. Parker have pointed out, if the benefit to the recipient of the deed, less the cost to the altruist, is less than zero (if $r\mathbf{b}_y - \mathbf{c}_x < 0$) then X will have a genetic incentive to act selfishly rather than altruistically. In a bird nest, where the nestlings increasingly compete for food as brood size increases, this can result in one sibling killing another, in what Mock and Parker call "sibicide". In short, altruism and sibling rivalry are opposite poles of a continuum that turns on degrees of perceived relatedness and perceived risk. Mock and Parker note that even full siblings, with half their genes in common, have the option of looking at each other as half identical (a glass half full, as Mock and Parker put it) or half alien (a glass half empty). Sibling X kills sibling Y because he looks at Y as a half-empty glass that wants to fill itself with food X needs for health and survival. [4]

The altruistic perspective is the one that sees the glass as half full; the selfish or egoistic perspective sees it as half empty. The altruist identifies. The egoist stresses his difference. The key to the emergence of one perspective or another is a perceived abundance or scarcity of resources. In the world Mock and Parker describe, altruism is favored by abundance; egoism by scarcity. As the two scientists put it, in the nest, a chick's well being is "a function of Self's fitness plus half the fitness of the remaining chicks".[5] So the survival of other individuals (even siblings) is worth half as much to Self as Self's own survival.

Taken out of its context and made into a kind of metaphor for interaction in general, this Self-and-other function can be viewed as a metaphor for interaction in general. It implies that the most we can expect from the altruistic perspective is that it values the survival of another at half the value of the altruist's survival. Even altruistic suicide is possible if a sufficient number of siblings and their genes (including those that match the suicide's) benefit from the elimination of a Self whose survival is threatened anyway, and whose elimination is a component of the survival of more sets of some of its own genes than it itself has.[6]

This suicide possibility shows that even if another's survival is worth ½ the Self's, there are cases when this other (or set of others) looms larger than the Self. In human society, this larger other is the Leader or the Cause or the Idea or the Love for which a person sacrifices himself or herself.

A key difference between human society and the average sibicidal bird nest is that in human societies sacrifices are made not only to preserve genes but also to preserve what Dawkins calls "memes". Memes as Dawkins portrays them are self-propagating ideas that spread "from brain to brain".[7] Dawkins writes that "when you plant a fertile meme in my mind you literally parasitize my brain, turning it into a vehicle for the meme's propagation in just the way that a virus may parasitize the genetic mechanism of a host cell. And this isn't just a way of talking—the meme, for, say, 'belief in life after death' is actually realized physically, millions of times over, as a structure in the nervous systems of individual men the world over."[8]

If shared genes make people genetic siblings, shared memes make them cultural siblings. But because memes spread more easily than genes (one need only think of the English language, which inhabits far more bodies than do English genes), the phenomenon of identical memetic twins is more common than identical genetic twins. Nationalism, for instance, is designed to create memetic twins. The resulting "extensivity" of memes should make altruism culturally more likely than sibling rivalry and sibicide. This is borne out in the fact that heroes, who risk themselves for their communities, are everywhere highly regarded: the hero meme is celebrated. Today, furthermore, most people live in cooperating, altruism-rewarding units that are larger than gene-based units like families, clans or tribes. Psychologist Susan Blackmore has suggested that "among the [more] successful memes are altruistic, cooperative, and generous ways of behaving" and that, indeed, the evolution of "genes for human altruism could have been meme-driven—making us genetically more altruistic than we would otherwise be."[9]

Still, if family harmony is limited by sibling rivalry and, sometimes, by parental sacrifice of offspring, how much can we expect from the memes from which societies arise? Consider the nation, which, since the era of the American and French revolutions, has increasingly become the metaphorical family of choice. Itself a meme universalized by imperialism, the nation has been accepted as the boundary of competing meme pools. But if the world is a single nest in which meme pools hatch, it is a nest full of sibling rivalry. Even within nations, divisions have been based on perceived gene-meme conflicts, and sometimes on gene-meme confusion. Gender conflicts and ethnic and racial conflicts are the most obvious examples.

At the root of it all, arguably, is the conflict between extensive altruism memes (including maxims like the golden rule) and gene-centered, self-centering memes like the one summed up in the phrase "look out for number one". This conflict suggests that the key to peace and tolerance is the propagation of the right memes—or rather, the *proper balancing* of other-directed and self-centered memes. But underlying tensions between risk and altruism make this easier said than done.

Wright, of course, played on these tensions like a master, hoping to create new altruistic, risk-controlling harmonies: new memes to live by. Wright emphasized the point that the West's own memes were thriving in Asia and that the leaders of the new countries hatching in the region were sibling countries worthy of a kind of kin-based altruism. In a sense, he sought to remind the West that the leaders of the emerging nations were, in a memetic sense, its sons. Though thinkers like Amartya Sen would dispute the view that the notions of equity and political freedom Wright champions flow exclusively from the West, there is no question about the West's economic and political power at the time Wright wrote—and of the fact that, as he emphasizes in *White Man, Listen!*, many of the leaders of the emerging nations had been educated in the West. Nevertheless, the Greek myth of Saturn devouring his children reminds us that even acceptance of humanity as one big family would not bring conflict to an end.

4. THE ELIAN GONZALEZ EXAMPLE

Thus, even if one sets aside as rarities the Saturn who devours his children or the Oedipus who slays his father, one must still contend with the surprising commonness of sibling rivalry. An excellent example of the way it works on the memetic level is provided by the ongoing ideological struggle between Cuba and Miami's "little Havana." This struggle was dramatized by the Elian Gonzalez case of 2000. As many will recall, the case centered on an international custody battle for six-year-old Elian, who was the sole survivor from a capsized boat in which his mother and other Cubans had sought to reach the United States and its opportunities. Backed by Fidel Castro, Elian's father demanded the boy's return to Cuba. Backed by Miami's fanatically anti-Castro Cuban community, Elian's paternal great uncle Lazaro refused. Lazaro, like most of the rest of Cuban Miami, dismissed Castro as the devil incarnate and as the puppet master moving Elian's father's mouth. With Castro's blessing, the father traveled to the United States. There followed protracted negotiations in which the Miami relatives refused to allow a reunion between the boy and his father. In the end, U.S. Attorney General Janet Reno broke the logjam by sending armed federal marshals in to seize the boy from Lazaro's home.

The Havana-little Havana dispute dramatizes the lengths to which genetic kin will go in a battle for the survival of their (in this case equal and opposite) memes and, as importantly, to secure the identities built on those memes. As in the bird nests already discussed, the battle here is for resources: the resource of legitimacy in the eyes of the world, the resources (in terms of physical and human capital) of the island of Cuba itself and, finally, the present value, so to speak, of shaping the personality and identity of a bright little boy.

The Elian case is a perfect illustration of a point made by the game theorist and moral philosopher John Harsanyi—that "Though some or all the players [in a "game" or decision situation like the Elian case] may very well assign high utilities to clearly altruistic objectives, this need not prevent a conflict of interest between them, since they may possibly assign high utilities to quite different, and perhaps strongly conflicting altruistic objectives."[10]

The root of the conflict, as the Elian case makes clear, lies in the need to choose and protect an identity—to provide answers to questions such as the following: *what kind of altruist (or egoist) am I, Lazaro, or I, Fidel Castro, or I, Janet Reno?* The irony is that all these people probably view themselves as altruists, and their opponents as grotesque egoists. From each identity, in short, flows certain preferences and styles of interpretation, and from each bundle of preferences and interpretative styles, flows certain approaches to decision-making, as well as certain approaches to altruism and negotiation.

5. IDENTITY AS RISK MANAGEMENT

If, as this paper assumes, all human actions are motivated by the need to manage risk, then an identity is a risk management tool. Among communal species like humans, identities survive as a result of combinations of personal and structural altruism. An example of personal altruism is that provided by a parent who works in a dangerous job to support her family. A somewhat controversial example of structural altruism, which for reasons to be shortly explained might also be called legislated extensivity, is the welfare state. "The welfare state reforms of Scandinavia are a collective reaction to the inequalities and injustices of early capitalism," Ronald Cohen argues in his essay "Altruism and the Evolution of Civil Society".[11] He adds that "over a number of years, each new reform carried these societies a step further to a political culture that has turned the state into the manager of altruistic relations. Each individual recognizes the obligation to give up income for utilitarian goals."

If one asked Samuel and Pearl Oliner, they would likely say that this recognition of the need for financial sacrifice (and the small risk of future financial embarrassment it entails) flows from "extensivity." They define this as "the tendency to assume commitments and responsibilities toward diverse groups of people. Extensivity includes two elements: the propensity to attach oneself to others in committed interpersonal relationships; and the propensity toward inclusiveness with respect to the diversity of individuals and groups to whom one will assume obligations."[12]

The Oliners go on to contrast extensivity with its opposite, which they call "constrictedness". They note that while "extensivity implies attachment and inclusiveness, constrictedness implies detachment and exclusiveness . . . detachment reflects a sense of boundedness in which the self is not only distinct from others but is also not bound to others in relationships of obligation."[13] But, of course, detachment at its alienated extreme is but the zero point of extensiveness, which at the other extreme becomes a feeling of connectedness to the universe and the other. The Oliners, drawing on data from their monumental study of rescuers of Jews in Nazi Germany, report that the deep altruists who rescued Jews were "more likely [than non-rescuers] to be extensive people."

But extensivity, the Oliners add, tends to be socially constructed: "If peer groups, schools, religious or ethnic groups, and the workplace fail to provide experiences conducive to an extensive altruistic orientation, then even already predisposed individuals may be threatened with losing it. When family beginnings are less than benevolent, the need for other institutions to provide such encouraging experiences increases. We thus assume that people are most likely to develop an extensive orientation towards others if the institutions in which they live most of their lives support it."[14]

In other words, even if there is a programmed predisposition, such as a gene for altruism in humans, it still requires the right meme to trigger it. We might expect, for instance, that the Swedish welfare state will trigger extensive relations, at least among Swedes. But this raises another question—namely, *of exactly what does extensivity consist*? What are its emotional or intellectual components?

Again the Oliners suggest the answers. "For some rescuers," they write in *The Altruistic Personality: Rescuers of Jews in Nazi Europe*, "helping Jews was a matter of heightened empathy for people in pain. For others, it was due to internalized norms of social groups to whom they were strongly attached. And for a small minority, it was a question of loyalty to overriding autonomous principles rooted in justice or caring."[15] Empathy, internalized norms of social groups such as church groups, principles of caring, principles of justice and duty (like Kant's categorical imperative)--what all these have in common, as the term extensivity indicates, is a perspective that goes beyond the personal. But now that we know its elements, we still need to discover how to make extensivity more, so to speak, extensive.

6. HARSANYI EXTENSIVITY

Here John Harsanyi, who himself benefited from altruism when he was sheltered from the Nazis by a Jesuit priest during World War II, provides some answers. In the course of his long and brilliant career, Harsanyi articulated a formula that makes extensivity mathematically clear at the same time that it shows how difficult it is to attain. When there is a dispute between two parties, Harsanyi once wrote, "the natural inclination of each party will be to judge the situation from his own one-sided point of view." A "moral" point of view, on the other hand, requires a special intellectual exercise, almost a special state of mind, which I call *Harsanyi extensivity*. Harsanyi explains that

> if individual *i* wants to make a moral value judgment about the merits of alternative social situations A, B, . . . , he must make a serious attempt not to assess these social situations simply in terms of his own personal preferences and personal interests but rather in terms of some impersonal criteria. For example, if individual *i* expresses certain views about how rich men and poor men, or motorists and pedestrians, or teachers and students, and so on, should behave toward each other, these views will qualify as true moral value judgments only if they are not significantly influenced by the fact that he himself happens to be a rich man or a poor man, a motorist or a pedestrian, a teacher or a student. . . . Individual *i*'s choice among alternative social situations would certainly satisfy this requirement of impartiality and impersonality, if he simply *did not know in advance* what his own social position would be in each social situation—so that he would not know whether he himself would be a rich man or a poor man, a motorist or a pedestrian, a teacher or a student, a member of one social group or a member of another social group, and so forth. More specifically this requirement would be satisfied if he thought he would have equal probability of being put in the place of any one among the n individual members of society, from the first individual (say the one in the best social position) to the nth individual (say, the one in the worst social position). But then, technically, his choice among alternative social situations would be a choice among alternative

> *risky prospects*. . . . his choice would be rational only if it maximized his *expected utility* [i.e. his expected degree of satisfaction with his position].[16]

Harsanyi goes on to distinguish between a social welfare function that would capture an individual's moral or social preferences (thereby suggesting the sorts of moral choices he would be likely to make) and an individual utility [degree of satisfaction] function that would capture his individual preferences and likely choices.

The difficulty here is that human rationality and imagination are constrained by the limits of the brain and of the lifespan--game theorist Reinhard Selten has compared economic investigations based on the assumption of perfect rationality to theology! Bounded rationality and imagination limit our ability to place ourselves in other shoes--to say nothing of situations where shoes are a luxury. This inevitably places a limit on the perfectibility of the social welfare function, and a limit on altruism. The altruism of humans is always bounded. But Harsanyi's ignorance assumption goes a long way toward coping with the boundedness. By forcing an individual to contemplate the risk of being anyone in any social situation, Harsanyi tips the scales in favor of extensivity and altruism. Some human-brained bird who could not know where it would end up in the nest would be likely to agree in advance that sibicide be banned, and that the altruistic perspective in which siblings view each other as glasses half full be cultivated.

7. CHEATING

But this brings us to the phenomenon of cheating. For moral rules, conventions and laws are broken most often by people who know them perfectly well. Sibicide in the nest and out of it, recall, is driven by the risk of being crowded out of crucial resources. In the human world, when risk and the fear of it heats up, morality is likely to melt quickly away. Thucydides, describing the effects of the plague at Athens, writes of "the rapidity with which men caught the infection; dying like sheep if they attended on one another". He adds that "When they were afraid to visit one another, the sufferers died in their solitude, so that many houses were empty because there had been no one left to take care of the sick. . . ." So much for the pressure risk places on altruism.

The opposite pressure that norm-based altruism places on risk is more surprising. Those who ventured to care for the sick, Thucydides writes, "perished, especially those who aspired to heroism. For they went to see their friends without thought of themselves and were ashamed to leave them, at a time when the very relations of the dying were at last growing weary and ceased even to make lamentations, overwhelmed by the vastness of the calamity." Here, the intensity of the risk destroys ordinary familial altruism, so that only those almost superhumanly driven by the norms of friendship, in this case without hope of reciprocation, are able to act.

Again, despite these exceptions, custom and morality in general broke down under the pressure of the apparently limitless and unmanageable risk. Thucydides writes that "the violence of the calamity was such that men, not knowing where to turn, grew reckless of all law, human and divine. . . . Who would be willing to sacrifice himself to the law of honor when he knew not whether he would ever live to be held in honor? . . . No fear of Gods or law of man deterred a criminal. Those who saw all perishing alike, thought that the worship or neglect of the Gods made no difference. For offences against human law no punishment was to be feared; no one would live long enough to be called to account. Already a far heavier sentence had been passed and was hanging over a man's head. . . ."[17]

The disorder Thucydides describes throws into relief the extent to which society is a system of carefully distributed risks, whose calibration in laws or censures of varying intensity is essential to the maintenance of social intercourse. The horrors of the plague also show that altruism fares badly when the focus on risk becomes too great. They show, too, the extent to which cheating is encouraged when a) rationality is seen to be futile and b) extensivity is widely perceived as being punishable by death.[18] Altruism, in short, is above all else a decision problem, a part of the larger question of rational behaviour, and the crux of the tension between the "coldly rational" and the "humane." Oddly, some of the deepest insights into altruism have come from the super-rational shop of the man who created Harsanyi's discipline, John von Neumann, the great Hungarian mathematician.

8. JOHN VON NEUMANN AND RISK

What one must know about von Neumann is that he lived in dangerous times and appeared to have been deeply influenced by them. When asked what accounted for the extraordinarily high percentage of geniuses in his generation of Hungarians, he "would say that it was a coincidence of some cultural factors which he could not make precise: an external pressure on the whole society of this part of Central Europe, a subconscious feeling of extreme insecurity in individuals, and the necessity of producing the unusual or facing extinction," according to his friend Stanislaw Ulam. Nowhere is the tie between risk and the structure of society more eloquently expressed than in this analysis of a generation.

Perhaps in line with the dangers he felt himself immersed in, von Neumann had a low opinion of human nature, and he found confirmation of his views in Thucydides. A biographer of von Neumann's, Steve J. Heims, notes that one of von Neumann's favorite passages, "which he knew by heart and often quoted to his friends, is the dialogue between the Athenians [at the height of their power] and the Melians in Thucydides' *History of the Peloponnesian War.* During the period when he was advocating a policy of preventive war against the USSR, von Neumann came back often to the Athenians arguments; For example, he liked the rationality of their advice to the weaker Melians:

> We recommend that you should try to get what it is possible for you to get, taking into consideration what we both really do think; since you know as well as we do that, when these matters are discussed by practical people, the standard of justice depends on the equality of power to compel and that in fact the strong do what they have the power to do and the weak accept what they have to accept.[19]

The advice of the Athenians is an almost perfect verbal anticipation of a crucial breakthrough in von Neumann's development of game theory, the minimax theorem. Here von Neumann proved that in a zero sum game (a chess or boxing match or war, for instance, in which one side wins what the other loses), there is a rational way for each player to proceed—a strategy. If the one in the stronger position plays rationally, he can maximize the winnings he can extract from the weaker ("the strong do what they have the power to do"). If the weaker plays rationally, he can minimize his losses ("the weak accept what they have to accept"—but no more). [20]

The importance here of rationality—rather than, say, courage or battle frenzy--cannot be overstated. "It is possible to argue that in a zero-sum two-person game the rationality of the opponent can be assumed," von Neumann and Morgenstern write in *Theory of Games and Economic Behaviour*, "because the irrationality of his opponent can never harm a player." This might as well be a translation of the Athenians' remark that "you should try to get what it is possible for you to get, taking into consideration what we both really do think; since you know as well as we do that, when these matters are discussed by practical [i.e. rational] people" there can be no outcome that is not rational.

Steve J. Heims sharply criticizes von Neumann, for he believes the minimax theorem was not only a von Neumann mathematical theorem, but a von Neumann worldview. Von Neumann was admittedly an architect of the atomic bomb whose Cold War hawkishness made him a model for Dr. Strangelove in the Stanley Kubrick film. According to Heims, he "found himself emotionally in tune with men of power" and fit the profile of power-loving men who, in a theory attributed to Hans J. Morgenthau, are embittered by failure to achieve "the totality of commitment that characterizes. . . love". Such men therefore resort to a "daemonic and frantic striving for ever more power"—a striving that in von Neumann's case, Heims suggests, culminated in the tireless quest for atomic dominance. But in the Cold War era this was nothing more than an extreme form of the old human lust for dominance over risk. It is not surprising that, for the committed cold warrior, the pure pursuit of power came to "risk dominate," to borrow a term from Harsanyi, the pursuit of extensivity.

9. RISK DOMINANCE AS THE PATH TO ALTRUISM

Harsanyi developed the idea of risk dominance by reformulating an approach originated by Danish economist Fredrik Zeuthen. Zeuthen observed that at any given stage in rounds of bargaining between two players, the player most likely to make the next concession is the one "less willing to face the risk of a conflict."[21] Zeuthen then reasoned that each player has a risk limit that is determined by the ratio of the cost to him of accepting the opponent's terms (conceding), to the cost to him of insisting on his own terms and risking a conflict (i.e. a breakdown of negotiations and no agreement at all). The higher the cost of conceding relative to the cost of conflict, the higher the risk limit. But the more averse (or, perhaps, ill-equipped) the player is to conflict, the lower the risk limit.[22] If one player has a lower risk limit than his opponent, he is less willing to risk conflict and more liable to concede than is his opponent. His risk limit is the "highest risk (the highest subjective probability of a conflict) that player *i* would be willing to face in order to obtain an agreement on his own terms. . . rather than on his opponent's terms. . . .."[23]

Harsanyi concludes that "If the two players have to choose between two alternative offers A*1* and A*2*, they will always choose that A*i* which corresponds to a higher risk limit. . . . We can express this by saying that Zeuthen's Principle establishes a dominance-like relation between any offer A*i* corresponding to a higher risk limit . . . and any offer A*j* corresponding to a lower risk limit. . . . We call this dominance-like relation *risk dominance* . . . ."[24] In other words, the player with the higher risk limit will get his way.

In a development of his argument in another part of his book, Harsanyi notes that if players 1 and 2 must choose between payments in which either player 1 gets more than 2 or player 2 gets more than 1, risk dominance will decide the issue. In a particular strategic situation Harsanyi describes, if player 1 aims at the higher payoff, he runs the risk of "a much heavier loss. . . . Hence it is natural to argue that player 1 will be more afraid to use [a strategy will either secure him the bigger payment or the bigger loss] .. . than player 2 will be to use [a strategy that might get him the bigger payment or a loss much smaller than the one player 1 risks]." Harsanyi goes on to show that player 1's risk limit is much lower than player 2's, and therefore the outcome that secures the higher payment for player 2 will enjoy "*risk-dominance*."[25]

For Morgenthau's leaders (and von Neumann if he was indeed like them), the costs of cold conflict were much lower than the costs of conceding. The cold conflict was designed to avert the need to concede. Therefore cold conflict (warmed by hot proxy wars), and conflictual situations (such as the arms race) were "safer." Those advocating them had higher risk limits than those advocating serious attempts to extend extensivity in such a way as to include current adversaries under its umbrella. Conflict and conflictual stances risk dominated concession and extensive stances. Thus in the cold war, and in cold war-like situations, the sides choose between two "offers": 1) perpetual arms race, spying and deceit and 2) disarmament, maximum openness, maximum trust. For both sides, 1 risk dominated 2, and, until the era of détente, each side chose conflict (including the already mentioned proxy wars) over the concessions that began with détente. It should be noted that Norman MacRae, whose sympathetic portrait of von Neumann is arguably fairer than Heims', believes von Neumann's tough stance helped save the world from Stalinism.

Altruism comes back into the equation when one realizes that it is itself a kind of necessary skin that protects humans. Von Neumann, for all his genius, and, in the Stalinist moment, for all his prescience, was probably blocked from realizing this by the fact that he saw humans as irredeemably selfish: "It is just as foolish to complain that people are selfish and treacherous as it is to complain that the magnetic field does not increase unless the electric field has a curl. Both are laws of nature," von Neumann once said.[26] On this view, Harsanyi extensivity is either a miracle or an impossibility. But Immanuel Kant and Thucydides himself have shown that, actually, extensivity and selfishness are intimately linked.

In the very minimax perspective itself, one must consider one's enemy, if only so as to find the best way of countering him. And then there is the phenomenon of loyalty, the already-mentioned willingness to go so far as to sacrifice the self to preserve the memes out of which the self is made. The Corinthians in Thucydides' history at one point describe the Athenians thus: "Their bodies they devote to their country as though they belonged to other men; their true self is their mind [their meme hoard], which is most truly their own when employed in her service".[27]

But on the eve of the Peloponnesian war, it is a delegation of these brave Athenians that prophetically warns the Peloponnesians (the other side in their cold war) against rashly entering into a hot war. Their words show that, at least in imperfect form, something like Harsanyi extensivity always emerges, even if it takes abandonment of the perspective to drive home the lesson of its value: "Realize, while there is time, the inscrutable nature of war; and how when protracted it generally ends in becoming a mere matter of chance, over which neither of us can have any control, the event being equally unknown and equally hazardous to both. The misfortune is that in their hurry to go to war, men begin with blows, and when a reverse comes upon them, then have no recourse to words. . . . Let our differences be determined by arbitration, according to the treaty."

War and the plague are not dissimilar, since they make risk unmanageable (with victory becoming "a mere matter of chance . . . the event being equally unknown and hazardous to both"). Arbitration, which requires seeing both sides (if only in their relative power positions), is a key step towards confirming and perhaps extending the frozen extensivity that a treaty is. But the fact that Thucydides grew old writing down the events of the 27-year-long war and died, manuscript unfinished, in the Athens that the war had humbled, shows that something more than treaties is needed.

Kant recommended the categorical imperative, and showed how his version of rationality made it imperative even for the selfish to accept it. In a famous passage he describes how someone who is thriving, but who "sees others who have to struggle with great hardships (and who he could easily help); and he thinks: What does it matter to me? . . . .Now admittedly if such an attitude were a universal law of nature, mankind could get on perfectly well—better no doubt than if everybody prates about sympathy and good will, and even takes pain, on occasions to practice them, but on the other hand cheats when he can. . . . [But] a will which decided in this way would be in conflict with itself, since many a situation might arise in which the man needed love and sympathy from others, and in which, by such a law of nature sprung from his own will, he would rob himself of all hope of the help he wants for himself."[28]

In her essay on this passage, philosopher Barbara Herman rightly points out that "this argument will yield a strong duty of beneficence for some (low-risk tolerators) and a decreasingly stringent duty of beneficence for those who have greater tolerance for risks. . . . The form of the argument urges our thinking about the duty of beneficence as a kind of (hypothetical) insurance policy." But, she adds, "To center moral deliberation on a strategy for even hypothetical self [protection] provides a lesson one would not have expected Kant to endorse" [since his moral law is to be followed with indifference to personal preferences].[29] For the purposes of this paper, however, it is fine for the duty of beneficence to be an insurance policy. The important thing is that what she calls the "CI [categorical imperative] procedure" forces one away from the strictly personal perspective in which another's suffering does not matter. Herman prefers to emphasize the fact that it is not rational to reject nonbeneficence rather than the fact that it is frightening to do so.

"It is a fact of our nature as rational beings that we cannot guarantee that we shall always be capable of realizing our ends unaided. . . . The willing of a world of nonbeneficence thus conflicts with the practical consequences of the conditions of human rationality: the natural limitations of our powers as agents. This does not involve questions of risk and thus of prudence. The natural limits of our powers as agents set the conditions of rational willing within which prudential calculations are made. It is because these limits are not transcended by good fortune that considerations of risk and likelihood are not relevant." [30]

These observations, made as a way of making the moral law absolute, and not dependent on levels of risk tolerance, nevertheless overlook the fact that the critical human limit is mortality—the inevitability of death and the constant risk of death gives meaning to terms like "good fortune" and "reason". The latter, an evolved tool for steering through risk, can be used to create effective medicines as surely as it can be used to track the path to Kant's Kingdom of Ends. The human body and the brain, the seat of reason, are themselves products of risks overcome in the course of evolution. So considerations of risk are never irrelevant: they are the essence of the human condition. While people have different levels of risk tolerance, everybody has his "price" in terms of risk—a price for which some minimal commitment to extensivity can be bought. For considerations of risk are the only constant links between the world of the self and the world of the other.

If, as Harsanyi (a rule utilitarian) has noted, "There is no reason whatsoever to assume that we have direct intuitive access to moral truths,"[31] then risk is the only spur we have to the discovery of the need for extensivity, altruism and moral codes. Even zero sum game theory presupposes the existence of consistent rules within which rationality can operate. Even amoral "rules" are, if consistent, a substrate of morality and cannot succeed without at least hypocritical acknowledgement of the need for structural promise keeping—for a reliability and dutifulness that can be taken advantage of, betrayed.

Considerations of risk are also the route to resolving conflicts among self-proclaimed altruists (as in the Elian case or the Cold War), as well as the route to deciding how altruism should be built into society—whether that society is the global one Wright had his sights on, or the national one of the Scandinavian welfare state or Mahathir's Malaysia. As in the Asian values debate Mahathir raises, a focus on risk can also indicate what form altruism should take. *For it is by keeping an eye on the distribution—the extensivity—of risk that we can insure that each person is given the freedom and the capacity to choose the risks he or she can tolerate and, on the upside, take advantage of.* Ideally, a chooser of his or her own risks could decide to live in a welfare state, or the sort of Marshall plan developing world Richard Wright called for, and acquire capabilities from the educational systems available in these places[32]. The capabilities would then raise that person's risk limit, put him or her in a stronger position in bargaining situations where risk dominance comes into play, and make him or her less needful of direct (or even structural) altruism. Such a person might then choose to become an agent of extensivity—might take, say, his or her medical or diplomatic skills to a civil war zone, where risks and the consequent chances to be altruistic--to heal the wounded or to reconcile warring siblings--are high.

Notes

1. Richard Wright: *The Color Curtain* (Jackson: University of Mississippi Press, 1956), pp.85 – 86.
2. Mahathir Mohamad: *A New Deal for Asia* (Kelana Jaya: Pelanduk Publications, 1999), p.27.
3. Richard Dawkins: *The Selfish Gene* (Oxford; New York; Tokyo: Oxford University Press,1998), p. 4.
4. Douglas W. Mock and Geoffrey A. Parker: *The Evolution of Sibling Rivalry* (Oxford; New York; Tokyo: Oxford University Press, 1997), p.2.
5. ibid, p77.
6. ibid, p78.
7. Dawkins explains his selection of the term "meme" in the following passage: "We need a name for the new replicator, a noun that conveys the idea of a unit of cultural transmission, or a unit of *imitation*. 'Mimeme' comes from a suitable Greek root, but I want a monosyllable that sounds a bit like 'gene.' I hope my classicist friends will forgive me if I abbreviate mimeme to *meme*. . . . Examples of memes are tunes, ideas, catch-phrases, clothes fashions, ways of making pots or of building arches. Just as genes propagate themselves in the gene pool by leaping from body to body via sperms or eggs, so memes propagate themselves in the meme pool by leaping from brain to brain via a process which, in the broad sense, can be called imitation."-- Dawkins: *The Selfish Gene*, p.192.
8. ibid.
9. Susan Blackmore: *The Meme Machine* (Oxford; New York; Tokyo: Oxford University Press, 1999), pp 154, 160.
10. John Harsanyi: *Essays on ethics, social* behaviour, *and scientific explanation* (Dordrecht, Holland: Boston: D. Reidel Publishing Company, 1976), p.97.
11. Ronald Cohen: "Altruism and the Evolution of Civil Society," in Pearl M. Oliner, Samuel P. Oliner, Lawrence Baron, Lawrence A. Blum, Dennis L. Krebs and M. Zuuzanna Smolenska, editors: *Embracing the Other: Philosophical, Psychological and Historical Perspectives on Altruism* (New York: New York University Press, 1992), p.111.

12. ibid, p.370.
13. ibid, p.373.
14. ibid, p.377.
15. Samuel P. Oliner and Pearl M. Oliner: *The Altruistic Personality: Rescuers of Jews in Nazi Europe* (New York: The Free Press, 1992), p249.
16. John Harsanyi: *Rational Behaviour and Bargaining Equilibrium in Games and Social Situations* (Cambridge; London; New York; Melbourne: Cambridge University Press, 1977), pp.49 – 50.
17. Thucydides: *History of the Peloponnesian War*, translated by Benjamin Jowett (Amherst: Prometheus Books), Book II, pp139-140.
18. The rescuers of Jews and those who cared for their stricken friends during the plague in Athens went against this rule, but they were literally heroic exceptions.
19. Steve J. Heims: *John von Neumann and Norbert Wiener: From Mathematics to the Technologies of Life and Death* (Cambridge, Massachusetts and London, England: The MIT Press, 1981), p.329.
20. In their classic *Theory of Games and Economic Behaviour*, von Neumann and Morgenstern formulate it thus at one point: "Player 2[in this case the weaker] can, by playing appropriately, make it sure that the gain of player 2 is ≤ v i.e. prevent him from gaining > v irrespective of what player 1 does. "Player 1[in this case the stronger] can, by playing appropriately, make it sure that the gain of player 2 is ≤ - v i.e. prevent him from gaining > - v irrespective of what player 2 does."—John von Neumann and Oskar Morgenstern: *Theory of Games and Economic Behaviour* (Princeton: Princeton University Press, 1953), p.108.
21. John Harsanyi: *Rational Behaviour and Bargaining Equilibrium in Games and Social Situations* (Cambridge University Press, 1977), p.150.
22. As Harsanyi puts it, "The quantity **r***i* [the risk limit] can . . . be interpreted as a ratio of two utility differences. The numerator, the difference U*i*(A*i*) – U*i*(A*j*), is the cost to player *i* of reaching an agreement on the opponent's terms instead of an agreement on player *i*'s own terms. The denominator, the difference U*i*(A*i*) – U*i*(C), is the cost to player *i* of reaching no agreement at all. In other words, the first difference is the *cost of a total concession*, while the second is the *cost of a conflict*. Therefore the ratio of these two differences, the quantity **r***i* itself, is a measure of the strength of player *i*'s incentives for insisting on his own last offer rather than accepting his opponent's last offer. . . . To sum up, the quantity **r***i* is the highest risk that player *i* is willing to take rather than to accept his opponent's terms; and it also measures player *i*'s incentives to take a high risk rather than to accept his opponent's terms."—*Rational Behaviour and Bargaining Equilibrium in Games and Social Situations,* p.151.
23. ibid.
24. ibid, p164.
25. ibid, p275, p276.
26. Heims, p327.
27. Thucydides, Book I, p48.
28. Barbara Herman: "Mutual Aid and Respect for Persons," in Ruth F. Chadwick, editor: *Immanuel Kant: Critical Assessments, vol III: Kant's Moral and Political Philosophy* (London and New York: Routledge, 1992), p. 116.
29. ibid, pp120 – 121.
30. ibid, p125.

31. Werner Leinfellner and Eckehart Köhler, editors: *Game Theory, Experience, Rationality: Foundations of Social Sciences, Economics and Ethics: In Honor of John Harsanyi* (Dordrecht/Boston/London: Kluwer Academic Publishers, 1998), p.296.
32. The term "capabilities" is used here in the sense developed by Amartya Sen, who writes of the "'capabilities' of persons to lead the kind of lives they value. . . . These capabilities can be enhanced by public policy, but also, on the other side, the direction of public policy can be influenced by the effective use of participatory capabilities by the public." With regard to poverty and inequality, he writes, "Deprivation of elementary capabilities can be reflected in premature mortality, significant undernourishment (especially of children), persistent morbidity, widespread illiteracy and other failures."—Amartya Sen: *Development as Freedom* (New York: Alfred A. Knopf, 1999), p. 18, p.20.

Chapter 6

Empathy And Helping

ANTHONY CHANG

1. INTRODUCTION

Empathy is considered to be "one of the basic human attributes supportive of social life" (Hoffman, 1977a, p. 169). This makes it an attractive construct to study. Empathy has been considered to be a critical element in social understanding and in the regulation or reduction of antisocial behaviours such as aggression (Eisenberg & Miller, 1987; Feshbach, 1975; Krebs, 1970; Miller & Eisenberg, 1988). It has also been considered a useful explanatory concept for the development of altruism (Eisenberg, 1986, 1989; Batson & Coke, 1981; Krebs, 1970; Hoffman, 1975). Rushton (1995) suggested that we ought to characterize human beings as "helpful, cooperative, empathic, loving, kind, and considerate" (p. 382). Thus, it is not surprising that attempts have been made to find a biological basis for empathic tendency.

According to MacLean (1973), the human brain structures have made it possible for earlier primitive affect to be experienced in conjunction with cognitively more advanced social awareness or insight into others. By extrapolation, social animals too, have this innate facility for responsiveness to facial expressions and affective stimuli (Darwin, 1965; Moore, 1990). Buck & Ginsburg (1997) suggested that "the biological capacity for communication is primordial and inheres in the genes" (p. 19) in their communicative gene hypothesis' of empathy. Hemispheric lateralization of emotions gives credence to this hypothesis.[1]

Sullivan (1953) viewed empathy as a "peculiar emotional linkage" between mother and neonate. Through both the kinesthetic and olfactory senses the link between mother and infant provides a "psychological umbilical cord" by which the infant has direct access to the mother's inner self. He suggested that "long before there are signs of any understanding of emotional expression, there is evidence of this emotional contagion or communion" (p. 17).

Similarly, during the first week of life, female infants demonstrate an affective orientation to other infants (Hoffman & Levine, 1976; Sagi & Hoffman, 1976) which may represent a constitutionally based, "early precursor of empathy" (Hoffman, 1978, p. 233). One- and two-day-old infants have been found to show distress and cry to the sound of another infant's cry (Hoffman, 1977b). Quite interestingly, infants responded in a more subdued manner to a computer-simulated cry of equal intensity (Hoffman, 1975). While the infant's "primitive empathic response" to another infant's apparent distress appears quite spontaneous and intense, it cannot be considered to even approach a mature empathic response because the infant lacks a cognitive awareness of the self or other. Such emotional contagion, at least early in development, occurs in the absence of the ability to delineate emotion through other sensory channels.

MacLean (1973) said that the word 'affect' refers to the subjective state and can only be experienced by us as individuals. The existence of affects in another individual must be inferred through some kind of verbal or nonverbal behaviour (MacLean, 1973). Stotland (1969) referred to empathy as "an observer's reacting emotionally because he perceives that another is experiencing or is about to experience an emotion" (p. 272). Similarly, Hoffman (1977a, 1977b, 1982b) defined empathy as the arousal of affect in the observer that is a vicarious response to another person rather than a reaction to one's own situation. This sharing of another person's experience, particularly, shared emotions, is often involuntary, although may be mediated by a number of cognitive processes, which may change with cognitive growth and social experience (Hoffman, 1983; Eisenberg, Murphy, & Shepard, 1997; Strayer, 1986). In addition, one can empathize with a broad range of affects so long as the shared emotional response is congruent with the other's emotional state or situation (Eisenberg & Strayer, 1987; Zahn-Waxler, Radke-Yarrow, & King, 1979).

Much research work in empathy has operationally defined empathy as affect matching. Affect matching refers to matching of congruent (Feshbach & Roe, 1968; Feshbach, 1975, 1978, 1980; Borke, 1971, 1973) and incongruent (Burns & Cavey, 1957; Deutsch, 1974; Deutsch & Madle, 1975; Chandler & Greenspan, 1972; Iannotti, 1975, 1978, 1985; Gnepp, 1983; Gnepp & Hess, 1986; Reichenbach & Masters, 1983) person- and situation-based cues. Affect match measures employing only incongruent items have also been used to explore the relative contributions of expressive and situational information to the understanding of the emotions of others (Eisenberg, Murphy, & Shepard, 1997; Hoffner & Badzinski, 1989; Reichenbach & Masters, 1983; Wallbott, 1988).

Affective responsiveness to the experience of other persons in need has also been cited as a possible contributor to the motivation of helping (Feshbach, 1975; Hoffman, 1975, 1981; Iannotti, 1975; Krebs, 1975; Eisenberg-Berg & Mussen, 1978; Radke-Yarrow, Zahn-Waxler & Chapman, 1983; Shantz, 1983). Researchers have examined the relationship between empathy and prosocial behaviour (Coke, Batson & McDavis, 1978; Eisenberg & Miller, 1987; Hoffman, 1976) and found empathy to be an important variable in helping.

2. HISTORICAL BACKGROUND

The empathy concept was called *Einfuhlung* ("feeling oneself into") in the 19th century. Lipps (1903) conceptualized *Einfuhlung* as "feeling oneself into" the object so that "the object is myself and by the very same token this self of mine the object" (p. 372). Therefore, in *Einfuhlung* one knows that one is relating oneself to the other. Titchener (1909) translated *Einfuhlung* to empathy (Boring, 1929) which literally translates as "in suffering", whereas *Einfuhlung* means to "feel oneself into". Titchener (1909) thought that knowledge of another's consciousness could only be obtained through kinaesthetic sensations or imagery: "Not only do I see...but I feel or act them in my mind's muscles" (p. 21). Empathy then referred to the subject's awareness in imagination of the emotions of another person.

McDougall (1908) referred to the empathic processes in terms of sympathy. He defined primitive sympathy as... "a suffering with, the experiencing of any feeling or emotion when and because we observe in other persons or creatures the expression of that feeling or emotion" (p. 78), an idea which he attributed to Spencer (1897). McDougall (1908) observed that primitive sympathy or emotional contagion was existent in children. He noted that children cry in response to others' cries and laugh in response to laughter.

The historical references to, and conceptualizations of, empathy have consistently alluded to four phases within the empathic process. These four phases are basically an elaboration of Reik's (1948) conceptualization of the empathic process which involves the interaction of both cognitive and affective components (Katz, 1963). The first two phases in Reik's (1948) model concern the identification with, and the incorporation of, the object of empathy. Phases three and four are symbiotically dependent on each other so that the (perhaps, forceful) affect experienced in phase three (the "reverberation phase") becomes more appropriate to someone else's situation than to one's own situation (Hoffman, 1975). Thus, the critical element in the empathic process is the ultimate distinction between self and other in contrast to Lipps' (1903) conceptualization.

3. COGNITIVE AND AFFECTIVE COMPONENTS OF EMPATHY

Empathy has a history of problems particularly, because it is a difficult phenomenon to demonstrate experimentally (Moore, 1990; Sawin, 1979; Smither, 1977; Wispe, 1986). The major problem with this elusive construct (Chang, 1987) is the disagreement over whether empathy is a cognitive, affective or cognitive-affective phenomenon (Deutsch and Madle, 1975). This disagreement is reflected in the diverse definitions of empathy such as emotional contagion, identification, projection, affective and cognitive role-taking and especially, sympathy - all of which may or may not refer to identical psychological processes (Eisenberg and Lennon, 1983). Davis (1994) suggested that the problems identifying empathy was not unlike that of the fabled blind men with the elephant: "each one was convinced that the part of the creature he was holding defined its nature" (p. 11). Stotland (1969) felt that the lack of consistency in demonstrating empathy was "quite troublesome" and delineated the need for more accurate measurements of empathy.

Typically, empathy is conceptualized either as an affective or cognitive phenomenon. An affective definition of empathy specifies that the person not only understands the affective situation of the other person, but also feels as the other does. Stotland (1969) defined empathy as "an observer's reacting emotionally because he perceives that another is experiencing or is about to experience an emotion" (p.2). This definition is similar to McDougall (1908)'s definition (see page 3). Thus, empathy is defined as the vicarious experiencing or "sharing" of the observed affective state of another person (Aronfreed, 1970; Feshbach, 1975; Hoffman, 1977a; Staub, 1970, 71, 74, 78). But, this empathic response must be "more appropriate to another's situation than to one's own" (Hoffman, 1982b, p. 289).

This affective definition contrasts with the cognitive conceptualization of empathy as the accuracy of social insight, emotion detection, or social/affective role-taking (Borke, 1971, 1973; Chandler & Greenspan, 1972; Dymond, 1950). Such a cognitive conceptualization assesses whether the observer understands how another person feels (Flavell, Botkin, Fry, Wright, & Jarvis, 1968; Strayer, 1987). For example, Dymond (1950) defined empathy as "... the imaginative transposing of oneself into the thinking, feeling, and the acting of another" (p. 343). Rogers (1975), suggested that "in empathy, I act as if I were the other person" (p. 4), "but always maintaining separateness" (Flavell et al., 1968). Hoffman (1982c), quoting Adam Smith, said "by the imagination we place ourselves in the other's situation" (p. 87). He suggested that "the use of imagination actually generates the empathic affect" (Hoffman, 1977a, p. 210).

Kagan (1978) cautioned that the use of separate affective and cognitive categories of empathy merely represents the particular aspects of the empathic response that one wishes to emphasize. These categories are not normally explanatory. Hoffman (1975) said that if cognitive processes helped to determine how even the simplest emotion is experienced, then distinguishing the empathic response as cognitive or affective may be artificial.

4. MULTIDIMENSIONAL MODELS OF EMPATHY

A third conceptualization of empathy combines both cognitive and affective approaches. Thus, the person not only understands the affective situation of the other, but also feels as the other does (Feshbach, 1975, 1978; Hoffman, 1975; Staub 1971, 1974). This conceptualization of empathy has its roots in Reik's (1948) model.

Hoffman (1975) said that cognitive factors are "indispensable to any formulation of emotion" (p. 610). Causal attributions clarify the vague empathic affect: "until we know what caused the other's feeling, our empathy remains imperfect" (Hoffman, 1982a, p. 287). Piaget and Inhelder (1969) claimed that although cognitive and affective aspects are not considered to be reducible to one single aspect they are inseparable and complementary, both occurring as a result of a single integrative process.

A developmental and motivational model of empathy is generally preferred (Hoffman, 1975, 1976, 1977a, 1984). Such a model postulates that the affective component of empathy is experienced differently as the child matures cognitively. This model suggests a "developmental synthesis" of affect and cognition. *Synthesis* refers to "a reciprocal process in which the empathic and the cognitive enhance each other" (Hoffman, 1984, p. 136) and does not mean "an instantaneous occurrence" (p. 136). Thus, the development of empathy corresponds with cognitive development, for example, the development of a cognitive sense of the other. The development of the capacity for role-taking occurs as a result of the "integrative process" of self-other differentiation (Piaget and Inhelder, 1969) and mediates the gradual shift from a self-oriented emotional reaction (e.g., emotion contagion) to others' distress to a more other-oriented reaction of sympathy and concern. Thus, empathically aroused affect combines with an image of the other person's plight. At its highest level, empathy becomes transformed into sympathy so that the motivation to reduce another's distress or prosocial helping may occur (Hoffman, 1977a).

5. EMPATHY AS A MOTIVATIONAL PHENOMENON

The question then, of how empathy, once it is aroused becomes translated into prosocial action is an intriguing one.

Studies suggest that it is the emotional and not the cognitive aspect of empathy that most strongly predicts behaviours on behalf of others (Rushton, 1980; Batson & Coke, 1981; Hoffman, 1975, 1981; Krebs, 1970, 1982; Piliavin, Dovidio, Gaertner & Clark, 1981, 1982). Typically, sadness is viewed as an important variable that mediates the relation between sympathy/empathy and helping. Hoffman (1975) argued that empathy is motivated by vicarious distress, a term conceptually similar to sadness. Strayer (1989) indicated that "feeling into" others' sadness is the emotion typically felt by parents and adult students when empathy is referenced. According to Hoffman (1977a), pure empathic distress as part of a person's response to another's misfortune may result in prosocial action because it is an aversive state that can often be alleviated by giving help to the victim. Furthermore, the direction of attention whether to self or other, is an important factor in determining whether helping will occur. For example, empathic sadness, being other-oriented has been found to promote helping, whereas egocentric sadness retarded helping (Barnett, Howard, Melton, & Dino, 1982).

However, the motive to help is under cognitive control (Hoffman, 1975; 1977a). Cognitive processes serve the motivational component of empathy since they are "obviously involved in assessing what, if anything, should be done to help the other person" (Hoffman, 1977a, p. 210). But, the relationship between empathy and helping is less consistent and weaker in research conducted with children than those conducted with adults (Eisenberg & Miller, 1987). Children may have limited helping skills and may not have the competence to enact altruistic behaviours even if they would like to (Peterson, 1983). However, their affective responses and behavioural reactions become more integrated with age (Eisenberg & Miller, 1987). In general, "people of all ages do respond empathically and with some attempt to help the victim" (Hoffman, 1982b, p. 296).

Nevertheless, empathy and prosocial behaviour, although compatible and synchronous, need not inevitably be associated (Feshbach, 1982; Feshbach & Feshbach, 1986). Empathy merely is a necessary, although not sufficient precondition, for prosocial behaviour (Eisenberg-Berg & Mussen, 1978).

6. LOCAL STUDIES ON EMPATHY

In order to study more thoroughly the relationship between empathy and helping, I conducted several studies on empathy using a mood-induction procedure with two instructional sets, observe-other and imagine-other (Stotland, 1969). The resultant empathic mood was measured with the Toi & Batson (1982) questionnaire (e.g., sympathy, compassion, warmth, tenderness). This method assessed empathy as a cognitive-affective construct. It has been shown that instructions to take the role of the other person have been used successfully to induce empathic emotion in both children and adults (Barnett et al., 1982; Barnett, King, & Howard, 1979; Batson, 1987; Batson, Early, & Salvarani, 1997; Coke, Batson, & McDavis, 1978; Davis, Hull, Young & Warren, 1987; Howard & Barnett, 1981; Toi & Batson, 1982). For example, in studies with adults, Davis (1983) and Toi and Batson (1982) found that "imagine-other" instructions heightened feelings of sympathy. Likewise, Stotland (1969) manipulated two perceptual sets, "imagine-other" and "observe-other". Adults instructed to imagine themselves or to imagine a target person's reactions in a painful situation (undergoing painful heat treatment) had greater empathic arousal (indicated both physiologically and verbally) than did adults instructed to merely observe closely the target person's movements and posture. Furthermore, Davis et al. (1987) found that individuals high in perspective-taking showed stimulus-congruent emotional reactions when instructed to imagine the feelings of the target, whereas objective-set instructions did not result in differences in emotional experiences for high or low perspective-takers.

I also varied the number of participants in a group from one participant per group to as many as four participants per group. In all my studies, I found that empathic mood was successfully induced using this procedure. Empathic mood was greater in the imagine-set condition compared to the objective-set condition. Empathic mood also varied according to the size of the group. Higher empathic mood was induced in the smaller compared to the larger groups, indicating that the process of diffusion due to increased numbers also affected empathic mood. More importantly, although helping did occur in some of my studies, subsequent helping need not consistently follow from the empathic mood generated. However, in one study, where I made salient the cues for helping, helping was consequent to the empathic mood induction. Thus, the relationship between empathy and helping is probably, moderated by other factors such as group size or salience of cues.

7. CONCLUSION

This paper has given a historical background to empathy, its evolution from diverse definitions to its current conceptualization as a cognitive-affective phenomenon. It is now accepted that empathy conjointly entails concordant emotions and their cognitive mediation in response to another's emotional context (Eisenberg & Strayer, 1987) with elements of concern (Batson & Coke, 1981).

The local studies I conducted demonstrated unequivocally that empathy can be induced under laboratory conditions. This fact indicates that, under particular conditions, everyone can be empathic and gives credence to Rushton's (1995) notion that we ought to be perceived as empathic and caring. That feelings of empathy need not always, or necessarily, be accompanied by helpful responses should not cause one to devalue empathy in itself. Its relationship with helping is probably, moderated by other factors (such as costs to self, presence of others, salience of cues) which we need to identify and understand better. In itself, empathy might be merely a cognitive-affective response, but viewed in the broad, social context of a likely linkage with prosocial helping (Eisenberg, N., & Fabes, R. A., 1990, 1993, 1997) and reduction of aggression (Miller & Eisenberg, 1988), social and emotional understanding (EQ?) and the capacity to love others, it becomes an important socio-psychological phenomenon (Davis, 1994).

Notes

1. Emotional expressions and recognition are processed in the right hemisphere of the brain.

References

1. Aronfreed, J. (1970). The socialization of altruistic and sympathetic behaviour: Some theoretical and experimental analyses. In J. Macaulay & L. Berkowitz (Eds.), *Altruism and helping behaviour* (pp. 103-106). New York: Academic Press.
2. Barnett, M. A., Howard, J. A., Melton, E. M., & Dino, G. A. (1982). Effect of inducing sadness about self or other on helping behaviour in high- and low- empathic children. *Child Development, 53,* 920-923.
3. Barnett, M. A., King, L. M., & Howard, J. A. (1979). Inducing affect about self or other: Effects on generosity in children. *Developmental Psychology, 15,* 164-167.
4. Batson, C. D. (1987). Prosocial motivation: Is it ever altruistic? In L. Berkowitz (Ed.), *Advances in experimental social psychology* (Vol. 20, pp. 65-122). New York: Academic Press.
5. Batson, C. D., & Coke, J. S. (1981). Empathy: A source of altruistic motivation for helping? In J. P. Rushton & R. M. Sorrentino (Eds.), *Altruism and helping behaviour: Social, personality, and developmental perspectives* (pp. 167-211). Hillsdale, NJ: Erlbaum.
6. Batson, C. D., Early, S., & Salvarani, G. (1997). Perspective taking: Imagining how another feels versus imagining how you would feel. *Personality & Social Psychology Bulletin, 23 (7),* 751-758.
7. Boring, E. G. (1929). *History of experimental psychology.* New York: Appleton-Century-Crofts.
8. Borke, H. (1971). Interpersonal perception of young children. *Developmental Psychology, 5 (2),* 263-269.
9. Borke, H. (1973). The development of empathy in Chinese and American children between three and six years of age. *Developmental Psychology, 9,* 102-108.
10. Buck, R., & Ginsburg, B. (1997). Communicative genes and the evolution of empathy. In W. Ickes (Ed.), *Empathic Accuracy.* New York: Guilford Press.
11. Burns, N., & Cavey, L. (1957). Age differences in empathic ability among children. *Canadian Journal of Psychology, 11,* 227-230.
12. Chandler, M. J., & Greenspan, S. (1972). Ersatz egocentrism: A reply to Borke. *Developmental Psychology, 7,* 104-106.
13. Chang, A. (1987). Empathy: An elusive construct or an illusion? *Singapore Psychologist,* 3 (2), 41-52.
14. Coke, J. S., Batson, C. D., & McDavis, K. (1978). Empathic mediation of helping: A two-stage model. *Journal of Personality and Social Psychology, 36,* 752-766.
15. Darwin, C. (1965). *The expression of emotions in man and animals.* Chicago: University of Chicago Press. (Original work published 1872).
16. Davis, M. H. (1983). Measuring individual differences in empathy: Evidence for a multidimensional approach. *Journal of Personality and Social Psychology, 44,* 113-126.
17. Davis, M. H. (1994). *Empathy: A social psychological approach.* Brown & Benchmark: Madison, Wisconsin.
18. Davis, M. H., Hull, J. G., Young, R. D., & Warren, G. G. (1987). Emotional reactions to dramatic film stimuli: The influence of cognitive and emotional empathy. *Journal of Personality and Social Psychology, 52 (1),* 126-133.

19. Deutsch, F. (1974). Female preschoolers' perceptions of affective responses and interpersonal behaviour in videotaped episodes. *Developmental Psychology, 10,* 733-740.
20. Deutsch, F., & Madle, R. (1975). Empathy: Historic and current conceptualization, measurement, and a cognitive theoretical perspective. *Human Development, 18,* 267-287.
21. Dymond, R. (1950). Personality and empathy. *Journal of Consulting Psychology, 4,* 343-350.
22. Eisenberg, N. (1986). *Altruistic emotion, cognition, and behaviour.* Hillsdale, NJ: Erlbaum.
23. Eisenberg, N. (1989). *New directions in child development: Empathy and related emotional responses* (Vol. 44). San Francisco: Jossey-Bass.
24. Eisenberg, N., & Fabes, R. A. (1990). Empathy: Conceptualization, measurement and relation to prosocial behaviour. *Motivation and Emotion, 14 (2),* 131-149.
25. Eisenberg, N., & Fabes, R. A. (1993). Prosocial behaviour and empathy: A multimethod developmental perspective. In Clark, M. S. (Ed.), *Prosocial Behaviour* (pp. 34-61). London: Sage Publications.
26. Eisenberg, N. & Fabes, R.A. (1997). Prosocial development (Ch. 11). In N. Eisenberg (volume Ed.), Social ,emotional, and personality development. In W. Damon (series Ed.), *The handbook of child psychology,* Vol. 3. New York: Wiley.
27. Eisenberg, N., & Lennon, R. (1983). Emotional displays associated with preschoolers' prosocial behaviour. *Child Development, 58,* 992-1000.
28. Eisenberg, N., & Miller, P. A. (1987). The relation of empathy to prosocial and related behaviours. *Psychological Bulletin, 101 (1),* 91-119.
29. Eisenberg, N., & Strayer, J. (1987). Critical issues in the study of empathy. In N. Eisenberg & J. Strayer (Eds.), *Empathy and its development* (pp.271-291). New York: Cambridge University Press.
30. Eisenberg, N., Murphy, B. C., & Shepard, S. (1997). The development of empathic accuracy. In W. Ickes (Ed.), *Empathic accuracy* (pp.73-116). New York: Guildford Press.
31. Eisenberg-Berg, N., & Mussen, P (1978). *Empathy and moral development in adolescence.* Developmental Psychology, 14, 185-186.
32. Feshbach, N. D. (1975). Empathy in children: Some theoretical and empirical considerations. *The Counseling Psychologist, 5,* 25-30.
33. Feshbach, N.D. (1978). Studies in empathic behaviour in children. In B.A. Maher (Ed.), *Progress in experimental personality research* (Vol. 8). New York: Academic Press.
34. Feshbach, N. D. (1980). *The psychology of empathy and the empathy of psychology.* Presidential address, 60th Annual Meeting of the Western Psychological Association, Honolulu, Hawaii.
35. Feshbach, N. D. (1982). Sex differences in empathy and social behaviour in children. In N. Eisenberg (Ed.), *The development of prosocial behaviour* (pp. 315-338). New York: Academic Press.
36. Feshbach, S., & Feshbach, N. D. (1986). Aggression and altruism: A personality perspective. In C. Zahn-Waxler, E. M. Cummings, & R. Iannotti (Eds.), *Altruism and aggression: Biological and social origins* (pp. 189-217). New York: Cambridge University Press.
37. Feshbach, N., & Roe, K. (1968). Empathy in six- and seven-year-olds. *Child Development, 39,* 133-145.
38. Flavell, J. H., Botkin, P. T., Fry, C. L., Wright, J., & Jarvis, P. (1968). *The development of role-taking and communication skills in children.* New York: Wiley.

39. Gnepp, J. (1983). Children's social sensitivity: inferring emotions from conflicting cues. *Developmental Psychology, 19 (6),* 805-814.
40. Gnepp, J., & Hess, D. L. R. (1986). Children's understanding of verbal and facial display rules. *Developmental Psychology, 22 (1),* 103-108.
41. Hoffman, M. L. (1975). Developmental synthesis of affect and cognition and its implications for altruistic motivation. *Developmental Psychology, 11,* 607-622.
42. Hoffman, M. L. (1976). Empathy, role-taking, guilt, and development of altruistic motives. In T. Lickona (Ed.), *Moral development and behaviour: Theory, research, and social issues* (pp. 124-143). New York: Holt, Rhinehart & Winston.
43. Hoffman, M. L. (1977a). Empathy, its development and prosocial implications. In C. B. Keasey (Ed.), *Nebraska Symposium on Motivation* (Vol. 25, pp.169-218). Lincoln: University of Nebraska Press.
44. Hoffman, M. L. (1977b). Sex differences in empathy and related behaviours. *Psychological Bulletin, 84 (4),* 712-722.
45. Hoffman, M. (1978). Toward a theory of empathic arousal and development. In M. Lewis & L. Rosenblum (Eds.), *The development of affect* (pp. 227-256). New York: Plenum.
46. Hoffman, M. L. (1981). Is altruism part of human nature? *Journal of Personality and Social Psychology, 11,* 607-622.
47. Hoffman, M. L. (1982a). The measurement of empathy. In C. E. Izard (Ed.), *Measuring emotions in infants and children* (pp. 279-296). Cambridge: Cambridge University Press.
48. Hoffman, M. L. (1982b). Development of prosocial motivation: Empathy and guilt. In N. Eisenberg (Ed.), *The development of prosocial behaviour* (pp. 281-313). New York: Academic Press.
49. Hoffman, M. L. (1982c). Affect and moral development. In D. Cicchetti & P. Hesse (Ed.), *New directions in child development* (pp. 83-103). New York: Academic Press.
50. Hoffman, M. L. (1983). Affective and cognitive processes in moral internalization. In E. T. Higgins, D. N. Ruble, & W. W. Hartup (Eds.), *Social cognition and social development: A sociocultural perspective* (pp. 236-274). Cambridge: Cambridge University Press.
51. Hoffman, M. L. (1984). Interaction of affect and cognition in empathy. In C. Izard, J. Kagan, & R. Zajonc (Eds.), *Emotions, cognition, and behaviour* (pp. 103-131). New York: Cambridge University Press.
52. Hoffman, M. L., & Levine, L. E. (1976). Early sex differences in empathy. *Developmental Psychology, 12 (6),* 557-558.
53. Hoffner, C., & Badzinski, D. M. (1989). Children's integration of facial and situational cues to emotion. *Child Development, 60,* 411-422.
54. Howard, J. A., & Barnett, M. A. (1981). Arousal of empathy and subsequent generosity in young children. *Journal of Genetic Psychology, 138,* 307-308.
55. Iannotti, R. J. (1975). The nature and measurement of empathy in children. *The Counseling Psychologist, 5,* 21-25.
56. Iannotti, R. J. (1978). Effect of role-taking experiences on role taking, empathy, altruism, and aggression. *Developmental Psychology, 14,* 119- 124.
57. Iannotti, R. J. (1985). Naturalistic and structured assessments of prosocial behaviour in preschool children: The influence of empathy and perspective taking. *Developmental Psychology, 21 (1),* 46-55.
58. Kagan, J. (1978). On emotion and its development: A working paper. In M. Lewis and L. A. Rosenblum (Eds.). *The development of affect* (pp.11-42). New York: Plenum Press.

59. Katz, R. L. (1963). *Empathy: Its nature and uses.* New York: Free Press.
60. Krebs, D. (1970). Altruism - an examination of the concept and a review of the literature. *Psychological Bulletin, 73,* 258-302.
61. Krebs, D. (1975). Empathy and altruism. *Journal of Personality and Social Psychology, 32 (6),* 1134-1146.
62. Krebs, D. (1982). Altruism - a rational approach. In N. Eisenberg (Ed.), *The development of prosocial behaviour* (pp. 53-76). New York: Academic Press.
63. Lipps, T. (1903/1979). Empathy, inner imitation and sense feelings. In M. Rader (Ed.), *A modern book of esthetics* (pp. 371-378). New York: Holt, Rhinehart & Winston.
64. MacLean, P.D. (1973). *A triune concept of brain and behaviour.* Toronto: University of Toronto Press.
65. McDougall, W. (1908/1936). *An introduction to social psychology.* London: Methuen.
66. Miller, P. A., & Eisenberg, N. (1988). The relation of empathy to aggressive and externalizing/antisocial behaviour. *Psychological Bulletin, 103 (3),* 324-344.
67. Moore, B.S (1990). The origins and development of empathy. *Motivation and Emotion, 14 (2),* 75-80.
68. Peterson, L. (1983). Influence of age, task competence, and responsibility focus on children's altruism. *Developmental Psychology, 19,* 141-148.
69. Piaget, J., & Inhelder, B. (1969). *The psychology of the child.* New York: Basic Books.
70. Piliavin, J. A., Dovidio, J. F., Gaertner, S. L., & Clark, R. D., III. (1981). *Emergency intervention.* New York: Academic Press.
71. Piliavin, J. A., Dovidio, J. F., Gaertner, S. L., & Clark, R. D., III. (1982). Responsive bystanders: The process of intervention. In V. J. Derlega & J. Grzelak (Eds.), *Cooperation and helping behaviour: Theories and research* (pp. 279-304). New York: Academic Press.
72. Radke-Yarrow, M., Zahn-Waxler, C., & Chapman, M. (1983). Children's prosocial dispositions and behaviour. In P. H. Mussen (Ed.), *Handbook of child psychology.* (Vol. 4, pp. 469-545). New York: Wiley.
73. Reichenbach, L., & Masters, J. C. (1983). Children's use of expressive and contextual cues in judgments of emotion. *Child Development, 54,* 993-1004.
74. Reik, T. (1948). *Listening with the third ear: The inner experience of the psychoanalyst.* New York: Grove.
75. Rogers, C. (1975). Empathic: An unappreciated way of being. *The Counseling Psychologist, 2,* 2-10.
76. Rushton, J. P. (1980). *Altruism, socialization, and society.* Englewood Cliffs, NJ: Prentice-Hall.
77. Rushton, J. P. (1995). Altruism and society: A social learning perspective. In S. Zamagni (Ed.), *The economics of altruism* (382-403). Elgar: Great Britain.
78. Sagi, A., & Hoffman, M. L. (1976). Empathic distress in the newborn. *Developmental Psychology, 12,* 175-176.
79. Sawin, D. B. (1979, April). *Assessing empathy in children: A search for an elusive construct.* Paper presented at the meeting of the Society for Research in Child Development, San Francisco.
80. Shantz, C. U. (1983). Social-cognition. In P. H. Mussen (Ed.), *Handbook of child psychology* (Vol. 3, pp. 495-555) New York: Wiley.
81. Smither, S. (1977). A reconsideration of the developmental study of empathy. *Human Development, 20,* 253-276.
82. Spencer, H. (1897). *The principles of psychology (Vol. II).* New York: D. Appleton & Company.

83. Staub, E. (1970). A child in distress: The influence of age and number of witnesses on children's attempts to help. *Journal of Personality and Social Psychology, 14 (2),* 130-140.
84. Staub, E. (1971). A child in distress: The influence of nurturance and modeling on children's attempts to help. *Developmental Psychology, 5 (1),* 124-132.
85. Staub, E. (1974). Helping a distressed person: Social, personality, and stimulus determinants. In L. Berkowitz (Ed.), *Advances in experimental social psychology* (Vol. 7, pp. 293-241). New York: Academic Press.
86. Staub, E. (1978). *Positive social behaviour and morality: Social and personal influences (Vol. 1).* New York: Academic Press.
87. Stotland, E. (1969). Exploratory investigations of empathy. In L. Berkowitz (Ed.), *Advances in experimental social psychology* (Vol. 4, pp. 271-312). New York: Academic Press.
88. Strayer, J. (1986). Children's attributions regarding the situational determinants of emotion in self and others. *Developmental Psychology, 22,* 649-654.
89. Strayer, J. (1987). Affective and cognitive perspectives on empathy. In N. Eisenberg & J. Strayer (Eds.), *Empathy and its development* (pp. 218-244). New York: Cambridge University Press.
90. Strayer, J. (1989). What children know and feel in response to witnessing affective events. In C. Saarni & P. L. Harris (Eds.), *Children's understanding of emotions (pp.259-289).* New York: Cambridge University Press.
91. Sullivan, H. (1953). *The interpersonal theory of psychiatry.* New York: W. Norton.
92. Titchener, E. (1909). *Experimental psychology of the thought processes.* New York: MacMillan.
93. Toi, M., & Batson, C. D. (1982). More evidence that empathy is a source of altruistic motivation. *Journal of Personality and Social Psychology, 42,* 281-292.
94. Wallbott, H. G. (1988). Faces in context: The relative importance of facial expression and context information in determining emotion attributions. In K. R. Scherer (Ed.), *Facets of Emotion* (pp. 139-159). Hillsdale, NJ: Erlbaum.
95. Wispe, L. G. (1986). The distinction between empathy and sympathy: To call forth a concept, a word is needed. *Journal of Personality and Social Psychology, 50,* 314-321.
96. Zahn-Waxler, C., Radke-Yarrow, M., & King, R. A. (1979). Child rearing and children's prosocial initiations toward victims of distress. *Child Development, 50,* 319-330.

Chapter 7

Altruism Or Social Exchange?

ELIZABETH NAIR

1. INTRODUCTION

1.1 Altruism, prosocial acts and social exchange

Altruism refers to an act performed voluntarily to help someone else when there is no expectation of receiving a reward in any form (Schroeder, Penner, Dovidio & Piliavin, 1995). This is qualitatively different from prosocial behaviour, which is a much broader category and includes any act that helps or is designed to help others, regardless of the helper's motives.

Many prosocial acts are not altruistic. One example is when one volunteers to work for a charity to impress friends or to build up one's resume for future job opportunities (Taylor, Peplau & Sears, 1997). Prosocial behaviour ranges over a continuum from the most selfless acts of altruism to helpful acts motivated entirely by self-interest.

According to social exchange theory, any time individuals interact, certain *costs* must be paid and certain *rewards* result. An increased sense of power is one of the rewards a helper receives from the interaction. This sense flows from the fact that the helper demonstrated useful abilities and resources and was able to influence other people. The increased sense of power is independent of anything the recipient does to repay the helper. Often the increased sense of power offsets the cost of helping, which, from the helper's point of view, makes the interaction worthwhile. In contrast, an increased sense of powerlessness is a cost that the recipient experiences from the interaction, for the recipient has been forced to acknowledge dependence (Worchel, Cooper, Goethals & Olson, 2000).

Social psychologist Rubin (1973) wrote:

"Exchange theory postulates that human relationships are based first and foremost on self-interest. As such, it often seems to portray friendship as motivated only from what one person can get from another and to redefine love as a devious power game.....But although we might prefer to believe otherwise, we must face up to the fact that our attitudes toward other people are determined to a large extent by our assessments of the rewards they hold for us".(p.82).

Thus, in the discipline of social psychology, Worchel et al (2000) and Rubin (1973) describe a social exchange motivated act as one that involves calculation of costs and benefits, inclusive of psychological rewards and costs such as pleasure, happiness, feeling of empowerment, embarrassment, owing a debt of gratitude and lowering of self-esteem.

1.2 Empathy, egoism and other-regarding altruism

Empathy is the capacity to envision the sentiments, thoughts and feelings of another person. Social psychology research has demonstrated that an empathetic perspective may more likely lead to prosocial behaviour. The motivation guiding the action may be either to relieve one's own sense of discomfort, referred to as egoism (Batson, Fultz & Schoenrade, 1987) or mainly to alleviate the situation of the person in distress. Depending on which is the dominant motivation, the act of helping may be classified accordingly as either other-regarding altruism or self-regarding in nature.

When the main motivation to help is empathic joy, described as personal pleasure derived from feedback that the victim had been helped by the intervention, this feeling is egoistic in that we all like to feel good. It is also empathic in the sense that there is sharing of the good feeling imparted to the person who was helped. Following a series of experiments, Batson and his colleagues concluded that empathic joy may constitute another form of egoistic motivation that can lead to helping when people are not focused on the altruistic goal of reducing another person's distress (Batson, Batson, Singlsby, Harrell, Peekna, & Todd, 1991).

1.3 Present research : social exchange hypothesis

Singapore society is predominantly pragmatic, achievement-oriented and disciplined, and the measure of success apparently decided by accumulated material assets (Nair, 1997). Social exchange principles of reciprocity, balancing costs and benefits and re-paying one's debts, are more likely to prevail rather than altruistic actions which would be uncalculating, selfless and self-effacing in outlook. Arguably, it is these very principles guiding social and business transactions, which have contributed to the prosperity and stability in the country. In the present research, it is proposed that in the Singapore context, empirical data would support the hypothesis that social exchange motives would be reflected in the reported choices made in a series of five ipsative or "forced choice" statements. The standard item format for ipsative tests is to present the participant with a choice between two or more alternatives for each test item. The participant's task is to choose which of the alternatives is preferred. The ipsative format in testing strategy therefore enables an examination of how strong the preferences are for specific attributes within individuals (Murphy & Davidshofer, 1994).

1.4 Developmental and cultural differences in orientation

It is expected that while the gender of the Singapore respondent may not make a difference in the choices they make, there may be a difference in outlook between younger and older respondents and across the three main ethnic groups. With increasing age, the process of socialization in the values and norms of the community would be better entrenched. Conversely, it is also likely that the socially acceptable response may be better learned with increasing age, and for this reason, altruistic responses may be reported in preference to social exchange motivated responses. In view of differences in the cultural and philosophical orientations of the three ethnic groups, it is expected that differences would be found. Specifically, Chinese are deemed to be more pragmatic than Malays and Indians, and it is therefore anticipated that they would be more likely to report a social exchange motivated response.

2. METHOD

2.1 Subjects

A total of 464 subjects participated in this study, ranging from upper primary school students to secondary school and Junior College students, as well as a cohort of undergraduates. They readily agreed to participate as the questionnaire was short and appeared interesting to them. Most of the questionnaires were completed within a classroom context.

2.2 Instrument

FORM EN/ALTQUEST started with a brief note of introduction to respondents instructing them to make a "forced choice" for each of the following statements. They were reassured that there was no right or wrong answer, and to choose the answer which "fits best". They were not required to write down their names.

The questionnaire consisted of five statements requiring ipsative choice, each pertaining to an aspect of prosocial behaviour that could be interpreted as either altruistic or social exchange motivated. The test items in the questionnaire are detailed in the following section.

A section requesting personal particulars of gender, ethnic group and age followed this. Finally, the researcher had a brief personal note thanking respondents for their participation and informing them of the conference where the paper was to be presented.

2.3 Test items

2.3.1 Repaying a social exchange debt of gratitude

A recipient of help would be in a situation of obligation to the helper, and would acknowledge this. Thus for the first statement "I would take care of my parents in their old age", it is postulated that the predominant response would be .... *because they gave me life*, instead of ...*if they need my help*. This is the same rationale that would govern the choice made to the third statement that reads " I would be pleased to help ...", and it is postulated that in line with social exchange theory the choice would be for *...someone who has helped me before*, rather than *...anyone who needs help.* [1]

2.3.2 Determining more "deserving" helpee

Research on helping behaviour has shown that we are more likely to help someone if we believe the cause of the problem is outside the person's control (Meyer & Mulherin, 1980). If altruism was the basis for helping behaviour, then this value judgement of merit or otherwise should not feature in the choice of who to help, and we would be blind to whether the person had "earned the right" to be helped. For the second statement that reads " I would rather give a donation for the training of ..." it is hypothesized that value judgments would prevail and there would be an inclination to choose *...a handicapped person*, in preference to *...a drug addict*. The underlying rationale for this would be the viewpoint that the drug addict brought his predicament on himself voluntarily through his own actions and therefore bankrupted his balance sheet of merit, while the handicapped person had no personal choice with regard to his situation and therefore did not earn any demerit points.[2]

2.3.3 Sociobiological rationale for choice of helpee

The sociobiological perspective would predict a tendency to help others who may have a high survival value for the individual's genes. This is the explanation proffered by this theory for defensive and protective behaviour by the individual to ensure that one's tribe, clan or countrymen can survive as a group, though the individual may perish in heroic action. In line with this, it is predicted that the response to the fourth statement would be "It is better to*...help one's own community group"*, in preference to *...help any community that needs help.*

2.3.4 Interpersonal interaction guided by utility or altruism ?

Social exchange theory would predict that we would seek to maximize our benefits, and this would govern our interpersonal interaction. In response to the fifth statement, it is hypothesized that the reported perception would be that "In order to be a success in life *...you must make useful friends"*, rather than *...one must be kind to everyone*. Implicit in this choice would be the assumption that "success in life" would be deemed to be based on assets that could be enhanced by "useful friends" rather than any estimation of spiritual, artistic or cultural measures of success, which would be blind to the "usefulness" of another person.

2.4 Analysis

The data was analyzed using the Statistical Package for the Social Sciences (SPsS). Frequencies and means were calculated across groups for each item, and independent t-tests conducted to check for significant differences.

3. RESULTS

The demographic analysis of the sample is presented followed by the significant results for the five ipsative statements.

3.1 Demographics

The sample consisted of 153 males (33%) and 304 females (66%). 7 had not indicated their gender. 172 (37%) were aged from 12 to 16 years, 196 (42%) were 17 to 19 years old and 92 (20%) were mostly from 20 years to 23 years of age. 4 had not indicated their age. 352 (76%) were ethnic Chinese, 42 (9%) were Malay, while 55 (12%) were Indian. The remaining 3% comprised of Eurasians and others. No attempt was made to parallel the demographic profile of the population in Singapore in terms of older age groups and different occupations. The inferences would be strictly comparative in nature, across sampled categories. The sample size and the fairly large cell sizes would permit such inferential analyses across categories.

3.2 Taking care of parents in old age

The predominant response to this was the social exchange rationale ...*because they gave me life* (n=416) as compared to ...*if they need my help* (n=48). There was no difference between males and females or between the ethnic groups on this item. Analysis by age groups reflected a tendency for the younger age groups to be more committed to the social exchange position than the older age groups.

Thus the youngest age category of 12 to 16 years (mean=1.06) differed significantly from the next higher age category of 17-19 year olds (mean=1.10), $F\ (1,\ 366)=7.05$, $p=0.008$. The youngest age group differed significantly from the oldest category of 20 to 23 years (mean=1.17), F (1, 262)=32.79, *p*=0.00. The two older age categories also differed significantly from each other, F (1, 286)=11.41, *p*=0.001. The trend would appear to support identification of a developmental difference.

3.3 Giving a donation for training

The predominant response to this was to the arguably social exchange choice of ....*a handicapped person* (*n*=377) rather than to ... *a drug addict* (*n*=85). Women (mean=1.17) were found to be more committed to this position compared to men (mean=1.21), F (1, 455) = 4.30, *p*=0.04.

Analysis by ethnic group showed significant differences across the three main ethnic groups. The Malay response (mean=1.12) differed significantly from the Chinese (mean=1.18), F (1, 391)=4.84, *p*=0.03. The Malay response also differed significantly from the Indian (mean=1.25), F (1, 95)=12.85, *p*=0.001. The Chinese and Indian responses were also significantly different from each other, F(1, 404)=5.38, *p*=0.02.The Malays were more committed to helping in the training of a handicapped person, while the Indians were more committed to the apparently less judgmental position of making a donation to the training of a drug addict.

3.4 Reciprocity in helping behaviour

The sample endorsed helping ...*anyone who needs help*, (*n*=386) in preference to employing the reciprocity principle of ...*someone who has helped me before* (*n*=78). No gender difference was found on this item. Analysis by ethnic group showed no significant difference between Chinese and Malays on this item. There was a significant difference between Indians (mean=1.93) and both Chinese (mean=1.84), F (1, 405)=15.50, *p*=0.00, and Malays (mean=1.79) F (1,95)=18.37, *p*=0.00. Indians endorsed helping anyone who needs help more than the other two ethnic groups.

The youngest age group of 12 to 16 years old (mean=1.94) also reflected this altruistic sentiment more strongly than the two older age groups of 16 to 19 years (mean=1.79), F (1, 366)=84.86, *p*=0.00, and 20 to 23 years (mean=1.75), F (1, 262)=84.27, *p*=0.00.

3.5 Sociobiological perspective on helping

The sample reported that it was better to ...*help any community that needs help* (n=405) rather than ...*help one's own community group* (n=59). This would assume an altruistic stance rather than a sociobiologically driven position. A significant gender difference was found on this item, with females (mean=1.89) endorsing this position more strongly than males (mean=1.84), $F(1, 455)=10.74$, $p=0.001$.

The Chinese (mean=1.85) endorsed this less strongly compared to both Malays (mean=1.93), $F(1, 392)=9.28$, $p=0.002$ and Indians (mean=1.95), $F(1, 405)=18.52$, $p=0.00$. Malays and Indians did not differ significantly on this response.

There were significant differences across all three age categories, with the younger groups endorsing the altruistic stance more than the sociobiological position. The youngest category of 12 to 16 year olds (mean=1.93) differed from the next higher age category of 17 to 19 year olds (mean=1.87), $F(1, 366)=14.17$, $p=0.00$. The former also differed significantly from the oldest age category of 20 to 23 year olds (mean=1.77) $F(1, 262)=59.58$, $p=0.00$. The older age groups also differed significantly from each other, $F(1, 286)=17.85$, $p=0.00$.

3.6 Criteria for success

The sample endorsed the altruistic perspective of ...*one must be kind to everyone* (n=355) in preference to the social exchange calculation that ... *you must make useful friends*. No gender or ethnic differences were found for this item.

Analysis by age categories showed a difference between the oldest age group, 20 to 23 years (mean=1.68) and the two younger age groups of 12 to 16 years (mean=1.80), $F(1, 262)=14.51$, $p=0.00$, as well as with the 17 to 19 years group (mean=1.78) $F(1, 286)=10.72$, $p=0.001$. The oldest age category endorsed the social exchange utilitarian position of making *useful friends* compared to the younger respondents.

4. DISCUSSION

The sample endorsed the social exchange driven choice only for the first two statements. On the last three statements, they endorsed the apparently altruistic position. There is a likelihood that this may have been an artifact of responding in a perceived socially more acceptable fashion. However this bears closer analysis of the responses by the demographic variables such as age to check for any variations.

4.1 Social exchange debt to parents

In terms of the rationale of caring for elderly parents, there appears to be a clear message to the younger age categories that they owe a debt to their parents. With increasing age, the rationale changes to one of the parents' need rather than a social exchange debt owed by the children. It may be that early socialization by the parents emphasizes the sacrifices they make on behalf of the children, and thus the social exchange perspective of the younger age categories. It is interesting to note that a perceived "obligation" or "debt" is more calculative and may be less generous of spirit and may be less affectionate. [3]

A participant at the Altruism seminar pointed out that a reverse interpretation was possible, insofar as helping one's parents *....because they gave me life* may be a way of expressing sentiments of love towards them, while the alternative of *.... if they need my help* may reflect a more calculative social exchange stance, i.e. I am not prepared to help my parents irrespective of whether they need my help or not.[2] An argument in favour of this reverse interpretation arises out of the empirical findings in which the younger subjects favoured *... they gave me life* more than the older subjects. As the younger subjects generally appeared to be more altruistic in their answers to other questions, Kapur has suggested in informal comments that it would appear to be logically consistent to expect the younger subjects to be more altruistic in answering this question as well. Such a reverse interpretation would indeed facilitate a more parsimonious explanation of the findings.

4.2 The meaning of not opting to help a drug addict

Opting to help a handicapped person in preference to a drug addict was interpreted to be a judgmental stance, and it was predicted that there would be a clear preference to help the handicapped person. The findings did indeed support this prediction. Women were found to differ significantly from men in this endorsement. An alternative interpretation could be the calculation that a handicapped person may be more likely to maximize the investment in his training, while a drug addict may revert back to his habits, and not utilize his training to best effect. In the context of other-regarding psychological rewards falling under the umbrella of altruism, a preference to help a handicapped person rather than a drug addict could reflect an 'altruistic' assessment that the former may be less likely to squander the help extended to him and thereby not become any better off. This may even be interpreted as a deeper altruism in the sense that the giver took the time to assess the likely effects of his help on the receiver, and thus showed greater interest in and concern for the latter.

In view of the over-representation of drug addicts in the Singapore Malay community, it may well be the knowledge of the high recidivism (Nair, 1992) amongst drug addicts that led to the Malay sample opting significantly more than the other ethnic groups to invest in preferential training for the handicapped. This choice would again lend support to other-regarding altruistic calculation governing the decision-making.

4.3 Whither the principle of reciprocity or you scratch my back ?

This sample did not endorse the principle of reciprocity, which is often vaunted as the back-bone of the business community and the work world in general. Part of the explanation may lie in the age range of this sample. The oldest category is still young adults. An entirely different picture may emerge if the question was put to older adults. There is some support for this explanation in the youngest age category of 12 to 16 year olds reflecting a significantly more altruistic perspective than the older age groups.

It is interesting to note the Indian sentiment of wanting to help ...*anyone who needs help* significantly more so than the other ethnic groups. It is possible that this stems from their unique cultural, historical and philosophical orientation. It is arguable that this apparently admirable sentiment could be translated into less focused efforts to materially uplift the Indian community (Nair, 1998), in not clearly subscribing to transactional practices.

4.4 Ethnic based self-help groups and the Community Chest

The preponderant endorsement that the sample would rather *...help any community that needs help* begs the question of what values have been transmitted to the young Singaporeans as far as the ethnic-based self-help organizations such as CDAC, MENDAKI and SINDA are concerned. The responses seem to reflect a denial of any inclination to favour one's own community. It may well be an indication of the classic psychological phenomena of reactance (Brehm, 1966). This theory espouses that when an individual's freedom of action is perceived to be compromised, the individual is likely to react in a defiant manner, contrary to imposed expectations. This is particularly well demonstrated in the behaviour of children and teenagers.

It is also pertinent to note that there has been a concerted ongoing public education program, both in the mass media and in the schools, regarding the "nationhood" of Singapore. The message emphasizes that across all groupings "...We are Singapore". This message may be the most salient to the sample. It would seem that one of the objectives of the Community Chest to "...unite the diverse ethnic communities of our country to contribute towards building a more compassionate, concerned and united society" (Ee-Chooi, 1997, p. 438) has been accomplished at least to a measurable extent.

It is interesting that the analysis by ethnic groups showed that the Chinese, generally acknowledged as traditionally clan oriented and pragmatic, were more inclined than the others to favour the sociobiological choice of helping *...one's own community group.*

There was also a significant age difference across all three categories. The direction of choice showed the younger categories of schoolchildren reflecting the more altruistic and uncalculating position of helping *....any community that needs help.*

4.5 Who is a successful man?

The answer to the fifth statement requires that the respondent has an opinion on the criteria by which to evaluate whether or not a man is a success. An altruist's definition of a successful man would differ from a predominantly social exchange motivated perspective on the definition of a successful man. While the former would prioritize giving without counting how much is given, the latter would prioritize balance in giving and taking. Respondents who interpret being "a success in life" narrowly in terms of material success only would endorse that strategically it is better ....*to make useful friends*. The altruistic position would be to disregard utility in making friends since altruists are deemed to be non-calculating for their self-enhancement and not committed to materialistic goals as a priority over being other-oriented. Here the strength of the ipsative format of the questionnaire is clear in forcing a preferential choice by the individual.

It is likely that the youthfulness of this sample also accounts for their rejection of this option in favour of being ...*kind to everyone*, since the young are generally thought to be more idealistic and uncalculating. (The New Testament teaching specifically states that to enter the kingdom of heaven, one must be like a child and that it is easier for a camel to go through the eye of a needle than for a rich man to enter heaven). Indeed the analysis by age categories supports this interpretation, as the youngest group was significantly different from the older age groups, who inclined more towards utilitarianism in choice of friends.

5. CONCLUSION

The postulation that social exchange and not altruism would be the guiding principle in reported behaviour was only partially supported. The analysis of the data by demographic variables adds to the robustness of the findings for the sample. Alternative interpretations of the findings offered by participants at the Altruism seminar contributed to a more parsimonious explanation of the findings in favour of a clearly altruistic stand. A resolution of these issues can most fruitfully be determined with further follow-up research that asks participants to state their reasons for the choices made.

The encouraging indication that Singaporeans are prepared to help any community that needs help suggests that there should be more 'mobility' across the ethnic self-help groups. There is scope for encouragement to participate in the activities of ethnic-based self-help groups other than their own. To the extent that they would be engaging in cooperative activities on an equal footing, this would help to strengthen social cohesion in line with the contact hypothesis (Pettigrew, 1969).

The detailed analysis by demographic variables concurrently lends strong support to the premise that the youthfulness of this sample may well explain the prevalence of the altruistic stance. An older adult population may reflect a different picture, and this interpretation is borne out by the significant age-based differences observed in the responses. One possibility is that the adult response reflects the ingrained process of social conditioning. Should there be a wish to change this trend, such a broad-reaching societal attitude change can only be achieved with coordinated efforts by the leaders in business, the professions, religious and secular, as well as the political leadership in the country. Such efforts could include public statements on altruistic acts as desirable and endorsement of such behaviours as the acceptable norm for the country.

Notes

1. Kapur's informal comments are acknowledged that "pleased" was not an optimum choice for this item, in view of the connotations with regard to psychological rewards.
2. Other interpretations to 2.3.1 and 2.3.2. will be discussed later.
3. A parent in *need* may also be judged harshly to be "careless" in providing for their own old age, and incur a social exchange debt by imposing themselves on their children in their old age.

References

1. Batson, C.D., Batson, J.G., Singlsby, J.K., Harrell, K.L., Peekna, H.M., & Todd, R.M. (1991). Empathy joy and the empathy-altruism hypothesis. *Journal of Personality and Social Psychology, 61*, 413-426.
2. Batson, C.D., Fultz, J., & Schoenrade, P.A. (1987). Distress and empathy: Two qualitatively distinct vicarious emotions with different motivational consequences. *Journal of Personality, 55*, 19-39.
3. Brehm, J.W. (1966). *A theory of psychological reactance*. New York : Academic Press.
4. Ee-Chooi, T. (1997). *Father of charity and ...my father : Ee Peng Liang*. Singapore : SNP Printing Pte Ltd.
5. Meyer, J.P. and Mulherin, A. (1980). From attribution to helping : An analysis of the mediating effects of affect and expectancy. *Journal of Personality and Social Psychology, 39*, 201-210.
6. Murphy, K.R. & Davidshofer, C.O. (1994). *Psychological Testing : Principles and Applications*. New Jersey : Prentice-Hall International, Inc.
7. Nair, E. (1992). *Recidivism amongst prisoners and probationers in Singapore : A demographic analysis and a study of selected psychological variables*. Singapore : National University of Singapore.
8. Nair, E. (1997). *Work Ethic : A Cross-Cultural Study of India and Singapore*. Calcutta: Indian Institute of Management Calcutta.
9. Nair, E. (1998). *Underachievement by Indian Singaporeans : A qualitative study*. Singapore : SINDA Research Monograph Series.
10. Pettigrew, T.F. (1969). Racially separate or together ? *Journal of Social Issues; 25*, 43-69.
11. Rubin, Z. (1973). *Liking and loving : An invitation to social psychology*. New York : Holt, Rinehart and Winston.
12. Schroeder, D.A., Penner, L.A., Dovidio, J.E. and Pilaivin, J.A. (1995). *The psychology of helping and altruism : Problems and puzzles*. New York : McGraw Hill.
13. Taylor, S.E., Peplau, L.A. and Sears, D.O. (1997). *Social Psychology*. Singapore : Simon & Schuster Asia Pte Ltd.

14. Worchel, S., Cooper, J., Goethals, G.R. and Olson. J.M. (2000). *Social Psychology*. Singapore : Wadsworth.2.

Chapter 8

Economic Consequences of Altruism

A Two-Group Growth Model of the Welfare Economy

WEI-BIN ZHANG

1. INTRODUCTION

Over years many efforts have been made to enlarge the scope of economic analysis. Social and economic issues such as family, morality, law, discrimination, altruism, communitarianism, and sexual relationships have been integrated into economic analyses (e.g., Becker, 1957, 1981a, Casson, 1997a, 1997b, Kapur, 1999, Zhang, 1999a). It has become clear that introduction of 'non-economic variables' into economic analysis often provides new insights about relations between individuals and society. 'Invisible relationships' between different social and economic phenomena are often 'discovered' by new analytical connections.

The purpose of this study is to examine some economic consequences of altruism. In our approach, we say that one acts altruistically when one feels and acts as if the welfare of others is an end in itself. Irrespective of the fact that the literature on the economics of altruism is increasing (Becker, 1981, Sugden, 1984, Stark, 1995), it may be argued that most of the economic studies have been concerned with rational and self-interested individuals. One of reasons that economists put little attention to altruism may be that it is believed that egoism is productive while altruism is not. It is argued that economic efficiency is attained in a perfectly competitive market between egoistic individuals. Smith argued that a capitalist, in making an investment which raised the country's output, is led by an invisible hand to promote an end which is not a part of his intention. Smith's point is that by pursuing his own interest the capitalist frequently promotes that of the society more effectively than when he really intends to promote for the public good. It is worthwhile to mention that from the economic literature we may conclude that the impact of altruism on economic growth is situation-dependent. It is known that Malthus (who was concerned with growth of supply-driven economy) held that altruist might neither benefit the poor nor enrich the rich. He argued that by redistributing income from the rich to the poor, the saving rate of the economy tends to decrease, thus reducing capital accumulation. In contrast to Malthus, Keynes (who was concerned with growth of demand-driven economy) held that redistribution policy (which may be considered as altruist behaviour) would benefit the poor and would not harm the rich. He argued that by redistributing income, the saving rate of the economy tends to decrease, thus raising the level of aggregate demand in the economy. The economic performance of the system as a whole will be improved. There are many other studies on the relationships between altruism and efficiency in economic literature (Phelps, 1975, Collard, 1978, Zamagni, 1995). For instance, Kolm (1983) addressed issues related to altruism and economic efficiency, trying to take account of preferences, sentiments, and action within a compact framework. Kolm discussed the logical impossibilities of obtaining altruistic behaviour, together with the corresponding attitudes and sentiments, through agreements and exchanges. He tried to provide insights into why the major religious and secular moralities such as in Christianity and socialism failed to realize altruism, though they advocate altruism while condemning egoism.

This paper tries to make a contribution to the literature by proposing a two-group growth model with altruism. In our approach, altruism is reflected in income transfers from one group to the other. In particular, the model is constructed to provide some insights into economic mechanisms of welfare economies. Many viewpoints have been proposed to justify for the existence of welfare states. According to Sugden's (1984) 'conditional co-operation' thesis, that people are prepared to contribute their 'fair share' to help the needy only if they perceive others to be doing likewise, and as such some level of compulsory contributions to welfare through the tax system may have advantages over a purely voluntary system. Miller (1988) examined the question of whether it is possible to explain the existence of welfare states in terms of the altruistic concern that people generally feel for the welfare of their compatriots. The existence of altruism means that people have the willingness to be taxed to provide welfare for others. It is argued that the welfare of the society is improved by redistribution through the government tax policy because everyone would be happier when some resources are transferred from the well-endowed to the needy. But it is pointed out that if people are altruistic, it is possible for them to make private arrangements to express their altruism through charitable giving. It is argued that the liberal institution is superior to the welfare state in two ways. People can express genuine altruism without being forced to do. People donate the amount of their own choice without being asked to do so. Miller (1988) also provides other explanations for the existence of welfare states. For instance, the welfare state may be seen as an insurance scheme taken out by the rich to buy off the discontented poor. The welfare state is also considered as a device used by the poor, through majority voting, to benefit from the income transfers. It is argued that the welfare institution is the creation of a professional class that lives off its proceeds. The welfare state is seen also as a scheme of mutual insurance against remote and often unpredictable events. This study is not concerned with people's motives and beliefs that they would contract voluntarily into a welfare state. It is obvious that altruism cannot fully explain the existence and scale of tax policy in the welfare states. Our purpose is to see what will happen to the economic system if the altruist rich transfers his income to the poor.

The understanding of dynamics of national growth and differences of living conditions and wealth between different groups of people is one of the essential aspects for understanding modern socioeconomic evolution. The issues related to economic growth and distribution are the main concerns of classical economists such as Ricardo and Marx. But there are only a few dynamic (mathematical) models with endogenous savings and income and wealth distribution. Our approach is influenced by the post-Keynesian theory of growth and distribution (Panico and Salvadori, 1993). Kaldor first formulated this theory in his seminal article (Kaldor, 1955). In 1962, Pasinetti reformulated the Kaldor model and introduced explicitly the assumption of steady growth. He also suggested a change in the saving function of workers and set the interest rate equal to the profit rate. After the publication of these seminal works, many papers about the issue have been published (e.g., Sato, 1966, Samuelson and Modigliani, 1966, Pasinetti, 1974, Marglin, 1984, Salvadori, 1991, Zhang, 1999a). The key feature of this theory is that it groups the population into different groups, whose consumption and saving behaviour are homogenous within each group and are different among the groups. Our paper examines a dynamic interdependence of two groups with different productivity and preferences. We follow this modeling framework in this study; but we introduce income transfers between groups. Assuming that altruism affects income transfers between the two groups, we try to show how altruism and differences in preference structures and productivity between the two groups may affect national wealth accumulation, income and wealth distribution, and consumption levels over time.

The remainder of this paper is organized as follows. Section 2 defines the model. Section 3 guarantees the existence of a unique equilibrium. The stability conditions are provided in the appendix. Section 4 studies the impact of changes in altruism on income and wealth distribution. Section 5 examines the impact of changes in altruism on the system when productivity of the altruism-receiving group is dependent on altruism. Section 6 concludes the study.

2. THE TWO-GROUP MODEL WITH INCOME TRANSFERS

The production aspects of the economic system under consideration are similar to the one-sector neoclassical growth model (Burmeister and Dobell, 1970, Zhang, 1989). The output and the rate of interest are denoted respectively by $F(t)$ and $r(t)$. Similar to multi-group models by Zhang (1999a), the population is classified into two groups, indexed respectively by group 1 and group 2. We introduce the following indexes

N_j —the fixed population of group j, $j = 1, 2$;

$K_j(t)$ —capital owned by group j at time t;

$C_j(t)$ and $S_j(t)$ —consumption level of and savings made by group j; and

$w_j(t)$ —wage rate of group j.

We assume that the labor and capital are always fully employed. The total capital stock $K(t)$ and the total qualified labor force N^* are given by

$$K_1 + K_2 = K, \; N^* = N_1 + zN_2 \tag{1}$$

where the parameter z is the human capital difference index. The parameter z distinguishes the difference in productivity of the two groups. Here, we omit issues related to endogenous human capital. We neglect possible impact of education, training and other learning efforts on human capital. It can be shown that it is not difficult to introduce human capital dynamics within the modeling framework of this study (Zhang, 1999a). With group 1's human capital as the basis of measurement, the terms, N_1 and zN_2, are respectively the qualified labor force of groups 1 and 2. The production function of the economy is given by

$$F(t) = K^{\alpha} N^{*\beta}, \ \alpha + \beta = 1. \tag{2}$$

The marginal conditions are given by

$$r = \frac{\alpha F}{K}, \ w_1 = \frac{\beta F}{N^*}, \ w_2 = \frac{\beta z F}{N^*}. \tag{3}$$

From (3), we have $w_2 / w_1 = z$. The ratio of wage rates is equal to the difference in human capital between the two groups. This relation implies that there is no discrimination in the labor market.

If there is no income transfer between the two groups, group j's income is given by: $rK_j + w_j N_j$, $j = 1, 2$. We assume that group 1 is altruist. It is assumed that some part of group 1's income is distributed to group 2, for instance, through government tax policy. Let parameter φ stand for the income transfer rate from group 1 to group 2. It should be noted that if group 2 is more highly educated and holds more wealth than group 1, a positive φ may be interpreted as 'exploitation' rather than altruism. We will specify differences in productivity, preferences, income and wealth between the two groups in order to propose reasonable values of φ. The net income Y_j of each group consists of its wage income $w_j N_j$, payment rK_j of interest for its capital, and the income due to income transfers. The net incomes, Y_j, $j = 1, 2$, are given by

$$Y_1 = (1-\varphi)(rK_1 + w_1N_1),$$
$$Y_2 = rK_2 + w_2N_2 + \varphi(rK_1 + w_1N_1), \quad 0 \le \varphi < 1. \tag{4}$$

We may write (4) in terms of per capita as follows

$$y_1 = (1-\varphi)(rk_1 + w_1), \quad y_2 = rk_2 + w_2 + n\varphi(rk_1 + w_1)$$

where $y_j \equiv Y_j / N_j$, $k_j \equiv K_j / N_j$, and $n \equiv N_1 / N_2$. If the ratio n between the population of the altruist and the altruism-receiving groups is low and the altruists are not rich, the altruist group can hardly change living conditions of group 2. Moreover, if group 2 is lowly educated (which implies a low wage rate) and does not accumulate, then the difference in incomes between the two groups is large if group 1's altruism is weak.

This study is only concerned with the above-simplified way of income transfers. There are many possible ways in which a person may take account of welfare of others. For simplicity, we assume that changes in φ are motivated by altruism. Our interpretation of income transfer due to altruism is obviously a limited yet essential case of income transfers in reality. Gifts may be given due to egoistic purposes. One may give gifts to others with a view, for instance, to forcing a counter-gift, to buying recognition or benevolence, or to showing one's superiority or to confirming a high social state. Transfers of income, wealth and in-kind services may be actually motivated by many considerations. They may be motivated by economic punishments or rewards, 'forced' by social duty or legal requirements, or by altruism. It is difficult to differentiate altruistic and self-interested behaviour, for instance, when one's concern for the welfare of others is merely an instrument for promoting one's own longer-term ends. Moreover, we simply assume that the transfer rate is exogenously given. People may care about the well-being of others in a way that is directly related to the actual living conditions of others. This consideration can be treated in our framework by assuming that the altruist group has a utility function which includes the altruism-receiving group's utility level. Since the utility level of others is dependent on φ, we can thus make φ as an endogenous variable.

We now examine the conditions that the altruist group has higher income than group 2, i.e., $y_1 > y_2$. By the above equations, we have

$$(1 - \varphi - n\varphi)(rk_1 + w_1) > rk_2 + w_2 .$$

We see that if $\varphi > 1/(1 + n)$, then the altruist group's income per capita will be lower than the altruism-receiving group, irrespective of the two groups' income levels. This may happen, for instance, if n is sufficiently large. The condition means that if the altruism-receiving group's population is much smaller than the altruist group, income inequality among the people can be largely reduced even with small increases in φ. From the above discussion, we see that it is reasonable to assume the inequality $(1 - \varphi - n\varphi)(rk_1 + w_1) > rk_2 + w_2$.

The financial budget constraint for group j is given by

$$C_j + S_j = Y_j . \quad (5)$$

It is assumed that group j's savings is given as follows

$$S_j = \lambda_j Y_j - \upsilon_j K_j , \quad 0 \le \lambda_j < 1, \quad 0 \le \upsilon_j < 1 \quad (6)$$

where λ_j and υ_j are non-negative parameters. Similar to the savings rate in the Solow-Swan model, the parameter λ_j is group j's savings rate out of the income. The term $-\upsilon_j K_j$ in group j's savings equation means that when group j's wealth is higher, the group's saving is lower (wealthier people have less need to save for the future, for instance).

According to the definitions of S_j, group j's capital accumulation is given by

$$\frac{dK_j}{dt} = S_j - \delta_k K_j$$

where δ_k is the fixed rate of capital depreciation. Substituting (6) into the above equations yields

$$\frac{dK_j}{dt} = \lambda_j Y_j - (\upsilon_j + \delta_k)K_j. \tag{7}$$

As the product is either consumed or invested, we have

$$C_1 + S_1 + C_2 + S_2 = F. \tag{8}$$

It should be noted that if (4), $C_j + S_j = Y_j$, (1), and (3) are satisfied, then (8) is satisfied. This implies that the above equation is dependent on the other equations in the system. It should be remarked that we can easily relax the assumption of fixed population by allowing the two groups' population to grow at the same fixed positive rate. If the two groups' population grows at the same rate, our analytical results with regards to variables per capita would not be affected. Since our main interest is to examine the relative living conditions between the households of the two groups, the assumption of the fixed population is acceptable.

We have thus built the dynamic model. The dynamics consist of two-dimensional differential equations for K_1 and K_2. In order to analyze properties of the dynamic system, it is necessary to express the dynamics in terms of the two variables at any point of time. From $K_1 + K_2 = K$, (3), (4), and the definitions of $Y_j(t)$ we see that the dynamics of the system are given by the two-dimensional dynamic system (7) with two variables $K_1(t)$ and $K_2(t)$. It is straightforward to show that all the other variables are uniquely determined as functions of $K_1(t)$ and $K_2(t)$ at any point of time.

3. PROPERTIES OF THE DYNAMIC SYSTEM

As all the other variables are uniquely determined as functions of $K_1(t)$ and $K_2(t)$, it is sufficient to examine dynamic properties of (7). Equilibrium is given as a solution of the following equations

$$\lambda_j Y_j = (\upsilon_j + \delta_k)K_j. \tag{9}$$

By (4) and (3), we get

$$Y_1 = \left(\frac{\alpha K_1}{K} + \frac{\beta N_1}{N^*} \right) \varphi_0 F ,$$

$$Y_2 = \left(\frac{\alpha K_2}{K} + \frac{\beta z N_2}{N^*} + \frac{\varphi \alpha K_1}{K} + \frac{\varphi \beta N_1}{N^*} \right) F \tag{10}$$

where $\varphi_0 \equiv 1 - \varphi$. Substituting (10) into (9) yields

$$\left(\frac{\alpha K_1}{K} + \frac{\beta N_1}{N^*} \right) \varphi_0 F = \delta_1 K_1 ,$$

$$\left(\frac{\alpha K_2}{K} + \frac{\beta z N_2}{N^*} + \frac{\varphi \alpha K_1}{K} + \frac{\varphi \beta N_1}{N^*} \right) F = \delta_2 K_2 \tag{11}$$

in which $\delta_j \equiv (\upsilon_j + \delta_k) / \lambda_j$, $j = 1, 2$. Dividing the first equation in (11) by the second one, we get

$$\left(\frac{\alpha \Lambda}{1 + \Lambda} + \frac{\beta N_1}{N^*} \right) \varphi_0 = \delta \Lambda \left(\frac{\alpha}{1 + \Lambda} + \frac{\beta z N_2}{N^*} + \frac{\varphi \alpha \Lambda}{1 + \Lambda} + \frac{\varphi \beta N_1}{N^*} \right) \tag{12}$$

in which $\delta \equiv \delta_1 / \delta_2$ and $\Lambda \equiv K_1 / K_2$. The above equation has only one positive solution as follows

$$\Lambda = \left(b^2 + c \right)^{1/2} - b \tag{13}$$

in which

$$a \equiv \left(\frac{\beta z N_2}{N^*} + \frac{\varphi \beta N_1}{N^*} + \alpha \varphi \right) \frac{\delta}{\varphi_0}, \quad b \equiv \frac{1}{2a} \left\{ a - \left(\alpha + \frac{\beta N_1}{N^*} \right) \right\},$$

$$c \equiv \frac{\beta N_1}{a N^*}.$$

From the first equation in (11), (2), $\Lambda \equiv K_1 / K_2$ and $K_1 + K_2 = K$, we solve K_1 and K_2 as follows

$$K_1 = \left\{ \left(\frac{\Lambda}{1 + \Lambda} + \frac{\beta N_1}{N^*} \right) \left(\frac{\Lambda}{1 + \Lambda} \right)^{\alpha} \frac{\varphi_0}{\delta_1} \right\}^{1/\beta} N^*, \quad K_2 = \frac{K_1}{\Lambda}. \tag{14}$$

We determine the steady state values of all the variables by the following process: K_1 and K_2 by (14) $\rightarrow$ K by (1) $\rightarrow$ F by (2) $\rightarrow$ r and w_j, $j = 1, 2$ by (3) $\rightarrow$ Y_1 and Y_2 by (4) $\rightarrow$ S_j by (6) $\rightarrow$ C_j (5).

Since it is difficult to explicitly interpret the stability condition, the eigenvalues are given in the appendix. When $\varphi = 0$, the model proposed in this study is identical to the two-group growth model proposed in Zhang (1999a). It should be remarked that the unique equilibrium might be either stable or unstable. For instance, if we assume the two groups are identical and neglect the income transfer, then the model is mathematically identical to the Solow-Swan growth model that has a unique stable equilibrium. In the case that any income transfer is omitted, and

$$\alpha = 0.5, \ \upsilon_1 = 10\upsilon_2, \ \delta_k = 0, \ z = 2, \ N_1 = 10N_2,$$

the dynamic system is unstable. If group 1's savings behaviour is more strongly affected by its wealth than group 2 (i.e., $\upsilon_1 = 10\upsilon_2$), group 2's human capital is higher than group 1's, and group 1's population is ten time of group 2's population, then the system is unstable.

PROPOSITION 1.

The dynamic system has a unique equilibrium. The equilibrium may be either stable or unstable, determined by the conditions provided in the appendix.

Before examining impact of changes in the parameter φ upon the equilibrium, we examine the conditions that the altruist group has higher income than the altruism-receiving group, i.e., $y_1 > y_2$ in the steady state. By (9), we get $Y_j = \delta_j K_j$. The condition $y_1 > y_2$ is guaranteed if $\delta\Lambda > n$ is held. Substituting (13) into $\delta\Lambda > n$ yields

$$c > \frac{2bn}{\delta} + \frac{n^2}{\delta^2}.$$

Using the definitions of c and b, the above inequality is rewritten as follows

$$\frac{n - \beta zn + \alpha - \alpha\delta n + \beta\delta - \delta z}{\delta\beta n + n^2 + \alpha nz + n + \alpha + \beta\delta} > \varphi. \quad (15)$$

It is straightforward to see that the denominator is larger than the numerator. Since φ is positive, it is necessary to require the numerator to be positive. It is straightforward to show that if we specify: $\varphi \le 1/2$, $\alpha = 0.3$, $z = 0.5$, $\delta = 0.4$ and $n < 0.26$, $y_1 > y_2$ is held at the steady state. In the case of $\delta = 1$ which holds if the two groups have the same preference, (15) is rewritten as

$$\frac{1 - z}{\varphi} > 1 + n + \frac{n + z}{1 + \beta n}\alpha n.$$

Since the two groups have the identical preference, we see that $y_1 > y_2$ can hold only if $1 > z$. That is, group 1's wage rate is higher than group 2's. For a fixed z (< 1), the above inequality (which guarantees $y_1 > y_2$) is held if φ and/or n are small.

4. THE IMPACT OF CHANGES IN φ

This section is concerned with impact of changes in φ on the equilibrium of the dynamic system. First, taking derivative of (13) with respect to φ yields

$$2(\Lambda + b)\frac{d\Lambda}{d\varphi} = \Lambda^* \equiv \frac{dc}{d\varphi} - 2\Lambda\frac{db}{d\varphi} = \frac{2b\Lambda - c}{a}\frac{da}{d\varphi} - \frac{b\delta\Lambda}{a\varphi_0^2} < 0 \tag{16}$$

where we use $2b\Lambda - c = -\Lambda^2 < 0$ and

$$\frac{da}{d\varphi} \equiv \left(\frac{\beta N_1}{N^*} + \alpha\right)\frac{\delta}{\varphi_0} + \frac{a}{\varphi_0} > 0.$$

The increase in φ reduces the ratio of the capital stock owned by the altruist and the altruism-receiving group.

We examine the ratios of consumption, wealth, and income per capita between the two groups. From $Y_j = \delta_j K_j$, we get $y_1 / y_2 = \delta\Lambda / n$. From (9), (5), and (6), we get

$$\frac{c_1}{c_2} = \frac{\delta_1 - \delta_k}{(\delta_2 - \delta_k)n}\Lambda, \quad c_j \equiv \frac{C_j}{N_j}, \quad j = 1, 2.$$

Taking derivatives of these equations with respect to φ yields

$$\frac{y_2}{y_1}\frac{d(y_1/y_2)}{d\varphi} = \frac{c_2}{c_1}\frac{d(c_1/c_2)}{d\varphi} = \frac{k_2}{k_1}\frac{d(k_1/k_2)}{d\varphi} = \frac{1}{\Lambda}\frac{d\Lambda}{d\varphi} < 0. \tag{17}$$

The ratios of consumption, wealth, and income per capita between the altruist group and the altruism-receiving group are reduced as the altruist group strengthens altruism.

From (14) and $K = (1+\Lambda)K_1/\Lambda$, we obtain

$$\frac{1}{K_1}\frac{dK_1}{d\varphi} = \left\{\frac{\alpha}{\Lambda} + \frac{N^*}{\Lambda N^* + \beta N_1(1+\Lambda)}\right\}\frac{1}{(1+\Lambda)\beta\Lambda}\frac{d\Lambda}{d\varphi} - \frac{1}{\varphi_0\beta} < 0,$$

$$\frac{1}{K_2}\frac{dK_2}{d\varphi} = \frac{1}{K_1}\frac{dK_1}{d\varphi} - \frac{1}{\Lambda}\frac{d\Lambda}{d\varphi},$$

$$\frac{1}{K}\frac{dK}{d\varphi} = \frac{1}{K_1}\frac{dK_1}{d\varphi} - \frac{1}{(1+\Lambda)\Lambda}\frac{d\Lambda}{d\varphi}. \tag{18}$$

The capital owned by the altruist group is reduced. Since the comparative static analysis is conducted without specifying any parameter value, we see that the altruist group's wealth is reduced when its altruism is strengthened. We will see in the next section that this may not be true when the altruism-group's working efficiency is related to the altruism. The total capital and group 2 's capital may be either increased or decreased. We see that even when group 2 's capital is increased, the total capital may be still reduced. It is straightforward to calculate the impact upon the consumption, income and capital per capita of the two groups as follows

$$\frac{1}{y_j}\frac{dy_j}{d\varphi}=\frac{1}{c_j}\frac{dc_j}{d\varphi}=\frac{1}{k_j}\frac{dk_j}{d\varphi}=\frac{1}{K_j}\frac{dK_j}{d\varphi}. \tag{19}$$

The altruist group's income, consumption, and capital per capita will be reduced as its altruism is strengthened. The impact upon the altruism-receiving group's living conditions is ambiguous. By (2) and (3), we get

$$\frac{1}{F}\frac{dF}{d\varphi}=\frac{1}{w_1}\frac{dw_1}{d\varphi}=\frac{1}{w_2}\frac{dw_2}{d\varphi}=\frac{\alpha}{K}\frac{dK}{d\varphi},\quad \frac{1}{r}\frac{dr}{d\varphi}=-\frac{\beta}{K}\frac{dK}{d\varphi}. \tag{20}$$

Since the impact on K is ambiguous, we see that it is necessary to further specify the parameter values in order to get explicit conclusions about the wages and the total output. In the case that K is reduced, the wage rate of each group and the total output are reduced and the interest rate is increased. In sum, we see that as the altruism is strengthened, the national output may be either increased or decreased, the altruism-receiving group's living conditions (in terms of consumption and wealth per capita) may be either improved or deteriorated, the altruist group's living conditions are reduced, and the gaps in living conditions between the two groups are reduced.

PROPOSITION 2

An increase in φ has the following impact on the steady state values: (i) the altruists' per capita capital, per capita consumption, and per capita income are reduced; (ii) the altruism-receiving group's per capita consumption, and per capita income may be either reduced or increased; and (iii) the national wealth and income may be either increased or decreased.

It is well known that steady state values of per capita variables in the neoclassical growth theory are dependent on the propensity to save. When one group transfers incomes to another group, the 'aggregated savings' behaviour would be changed when the two groups have different propensities to save. This change in savings behaviour (due to altruism) may result in increases or decreases of the national output and wealth. To illustrate this point, let us consider the case that the two groups have the identical preference, i.e., $\lambda \equiv \lambda_1 = \lambda_2$ and $\upsilon = \upsilon_1 = \upsilon_2$. In this case, adding the two equations in (10) yields $Y_1 + Y_2 = F$. Using this relation and adding the two equations in (9), we get $\lambda F = (\upsilon + \delta_k)K$. Solving the above equation yields

$$K = \left(\frac{\lambda}{\upsilon + \delta_k}\right)^{1/\beta} N^* \tag{21}$$

where we use (2). Using (21) and $K_2 = K/(1 + \Lambda)$, we get

$$\frac{dK}{d\varphi} = 0, \quad \frac{1}{K_2}\frac{dK_2}{d\varphi} = -\frac{1}{1+\Lambda}\frac{d\Lambda}{d\varphi} > 0. \tag{22}$$

We thus have the following corollary.

COROLLARY 2.1

Let the two groups have the identical preference. When the altruist groupstrengthens altruism (i.e., φ being increased), we have the following results: (i) the altruists' per capita capital, per capita consumption, and per capita income are reduced; (ii) the altruism-receiving group's per capita consumption, and per capita income are increased; and (iii) the national wealth and income are not affected.

Since the two groups have the same propensity to save, income transfers between the groups would not affect the 'aggregated savings behaviour'. It is reasonable to expect that the total capital will not be affected. The above corollary implies, for instance, that it is possible for a society to equalize its distribution of wealth and income without reducing its total capital and income if there is no taxation.

5. THE IMPACT OF CHANGES IN φ AND z

The previous section examined the impact of changes in the parameter φ on the economic system. We showed that if the altruism-receiving group does not change its preference and the group's human capital is not affected by changes in φ, then the altruist group would not economically benefit from giving money to the other group. We assumed that altruism has no impact on other aspects of the society except upon the endogenous variables. But it may be argued that altruism may affect some aspects of the society which are not taken into account so far. Possible influences of altruism are also dependent on the way in which wealth and income are spent. For instance, when the poor receives money from the rich, economic conditions would be different, depending on whether the poor spends the received money on education or eating. As mentioned by Keynes, if some labor force is unemployed, then monetary transfers from the rich to the poor would economically benefit the rich as well. Since we assume the full employment of labor force, to provide insights into the economic mechanism by Keynes, we may consider a case that the monetary transfer from the rich to the poor would increase the poor group's working efficiency. We now what will happen to the two groups' living conditions when the altruism-receiving group changes its work efficiency after receiving altruist contributions from the other group.

In this section, we consider a possible case that the altruism-receiving group's human capital is related to the income transfer rate from the altruist group. We assume

$$z = z_0 \varphi^m, \quad z_0 > 0, \quad 1 > \varphi > 0. \tag{23}$$

We are concerned with the impact of changes in φ on the system when m is taken on different values. It should be remarked that the previous section is a special case of this section with $m = 0$. If $m > 0$, it means that the altruism-receiving group will improve its human capital when the altruist group strengthens its altruism. The condition $m < 0$ means that the altruism-receiving group works less effectively when the altruist group strengthens its altruism. It is important to examine what will happen to the system when the altruism-receiving group reacts to altruism in different ways.

Taking derivatives of (13) with respect to φ yields

$$2(\Lambda + b)\frac{d\Lambda}{d\varphi} = \frac{dc}{d\varphi} - 2\Lambda\frac{db}{d\varphi} = \Lambda^* - \frac{\alpha\varphi c z^* N_2}{\beta z N_2 + \varphi\beta N_1 + \alpha\varphi N^*}$$

$$- \frac{\beta z^* \varphi N_1 N_2 \Lambda\varphi_0}{\left(\beta z N_2 + \varphi\beta N_1 + \alpha\varphi N^*\right)^2 \delta\varphi} \tag{24}$$

where $\Lambda^* < 0$ is defined as in (16) and $z^* \equiv dz / d\varphi = mz / \varphi$. We see that if $m > 0$, then Λ is decreased as φ increases. Since $m > 0$ implies that as group 2 receives more money from group 1, group 2 increases its working efficiency, it is reasonable to see that the capital ratio between the two groups is reduced when φ is increased. If $m < 0$, the sign of $d\Lambda / d\varphi$ is ambiguous. This means that if the income and wealth redistribution makes the altruism-receiving group to invest less in human capital and work less effectively, it is possible that the gap between the two groups' wealth is enlarged when altruism becomes stronger in society.

Similar to (17), we have

$$\frac{y_2}{y_1}\frac{d(y_1 / y_2)}{d\varphi} = \frac{c_2}{c_1}\frac{d(c_1 / c_2)}{d\varphi} = \frac{k_2}{k_1}\frac{d(k_1 / k_2)}{d\varphi} = \frac{1}{\Lambda}\frac{d\Lambda}{d\varphi}. \tag{25}$$

In the case of $m \geq 0$, the ratios of consumption, wealth, and income per capita between the altruist and altruism-receiving group are reduced as the first group strengthens altruism. In the case of $m < 0$, the impact is ambiguous.

From (14) and $K = (1 + \Lambda)K_1 / \Lambda$, we obtain

$$\frac{1}{K_1}\frac{dK_1}{d\varphi} = \left\{\frac{\alpha}{\Lambda} + \frac{N^*}{\Lambda N^* + \beta N_1(1 + \Lambda)}\right\}\frac{1}{(1 + \Lambda)\beta\Lambda}\frac{d\Lambda}{d\varphi} - \frac{1}{\varphi_0 \beta}$$
$$+ \left(\frac{\Lambda N^* - \alpha N_1(1 + \Lambda)}{\Lambda N^* + \beta N_1(1 + \Lambda)}\right)\frac{z^* N_2}{N^*},$$

$$\frac{1}{K_2}\frac{dK_2}{d\varphi} = \frac{1}{K_1}\frac{dK_1}{d\varphi} - \frac{1}{\Lambda}\frac{d\Lambda}{d\varphi},$$
$$\frac{1}{K}\frac{dK}{d\varphi} = \frac{1}{K_1}\frac{dK_1}{d\varphi} - \frac{1}{(1 + \Lambda)\Lambda}\frac{d\Lambda}{d\varphi} + \left(\frac{\Lambda N^* - \alpha N_1(1 + \Lambda)}{\Lambda N^* + \beta N_1(1 + \Lambda)}\right)\frac{z^* N_2}{N^*}$$

(26)

where K_1^*, K_2^* and K^* are defined in (18). In the remainder of this section, we require

$$\Lambda N^* - \alpha N_1(1 + \Lambda) = \left(\beta\Lambda + \frac{z\Lambda}{n} - \alpha\right)N_1 > 0.$$

Since we required $\Lambda / n > 1/\delta > 1$ (which we discussed in examining the condition for $y_1 > y_2$ in Section 3), we see that the above requirement is not strict.

In the case of $m < 0$, the capital owned by the altruist group is reduced. The total capital and group 2's capital may be either increased or decreased. In the case of $m > 0$, it is possible that K_1, K_2, and K are increased as φ is increased. This means that if the altruism increases the altruism-receiving group's incentive to accumulate human capital, even the altruist group's capital may be increased. Everyone can economically benefit from the altruism.

It is straightforward to calculate the impact upon the consumption, income and capital per capita of the two groups as follows

$$\frac{1}{y_j}\frac{dy_j}{d\varphi} = \frac{1}{c_j}\frac{dc_j}{d\varphi} = \frac{1}{k_j}\frac{dk_j}{d\varphi} = \frac{1}{K_j}\frac{dK_j}{d\varphi}. \qquad (27)$$

By (2) and (3), we get

$$\frac{1}{F}\frac{dF}{d\varphi} = \frac{\alpha}{K}\frac{dK}{d\varphi} + \frac{\beta z^* N_2}{N^*}, \quad \frac{1}{w_1}\frac{dw_1}{d\varphi} = \frac{\alpha}{K}\frac{dK}{d\varphi} - \frac{\beta z^* N_2}{N^*},$$

$$\frac{1}{w_2}\frac{dw_2}{d\varphi} = \frac{\alpha}{K}\frac{dK}{d\varphi} + \frac{z^*(N_1 + \alpha z N_2)}{zN^*}, \quad \frac{1}{r}\frac{dr}{d\varphi} = -\frac{\beta}{K}\frac{dK}{d\varphi} + \frac{\beta z^* N_2}{N^*}$$

$$(28)$$

It can be seen that that if the altruism-accepting group increases its human capital when altruism is strengthened, then everyone in the society may economically benefit. We now try to identify such a case (with $m > 0$).

Let us consider the case that the two groups have the identical preference, i.e., $\lambda \equiv \lambda_1 = \lambda_2$ and $\upsilon = \upsilon_1 = \upsilon_2$. In this case, we have $\delta = 1$, $Y_1 + Y_2 = F$, and K is given by (21). Using (21), $K_1 = \Lambda K/(1 + \Lambda)$, and $K_2 = K/(1 + \Lambda)$, we get

$$\frac{1}{K}\frac{dK}{d\varphi} = \frac{z^* N_2}{N^*} > 0, \quad \frac{1}{K_1}\frac{dK_1}{d\varphi} = \frac{z^* N_2}{N^*} + \frac{1}{(1+\Lambda)\Lambda}\frac{d\Lambda}{d\varphi},$$

$$\frac{1}{K_2}\frac{dK_2}{d\varphi} = \frac{1}{K}\frac{dK}{d\varphi} - \frac{1}{1+\Lambda}\frac{d\Lambda}{d\varphi} > 0. \tag{29}$$

We thus have the following corollary.

COROLLARY 5.1.

Let the two groups have the identical preference and $m > 0$. When the altruist group strengthens altruism (i.e., φ being increased), we have the following results: (i) the altruists' per capita capital, per capita consumption, and per capita income may be either increased or reduced; (ii) the altruism-receiving group's per capita consumption, and per capita income are increased; and (iii) the national wealth and income are increased.

It should be noted that if $m < 0$ (which may be interpreted as Malthus' assumption), the national wealth and the altruist group's wealth are definitely reduced. If the reduction in the altruism-receiving group's productivity is so high that Λ is increased, then we conclude that the altruism-receiving group's per capita consumption and wealth are reduced. In other words, Malthus' view that no one would benefit from strengthening altruism is justified.

6. CONCLUSIONS

This study proposed a growth model of two groups with different productivity and preferences. The altruism is reflected in income transfers between the two groups. We showed how altruism and differences in preference structures and productivity between the two groups affect national wealth accumulation, income and wealth distribution, and consumption levels over time.

There are different viewpoints about man's nature and interrelations between beliefs and action (Casson, 1997, Fonseca, 1991, Zhang, 1999, 2000). It is argued that altruism may not be a preexisting 'stock' as we assumed. For instance, Aristotle held that virtues are neither innate nor contrary to nature. But from the sustainable point of view, altruism may be conducted in large scales in the long term only when altruism has positive consequences not only for the altruism-receiving groups but also for the altruist groups. As far as society as a whole is concerned, it seems important to find out what kinds of altruist behaviour would promote welfare of different individuals and increase productivity of the society. It is well known that Adam Smith advocated that the government should intervene education in market economy so that all the social groups of the people would benefit from economic development. In our modeling framework Smith's idea may be interpreted as that 'altruism' would benefit all the groups if it were targeting at improving human capital through spreading education. Our analysis may also provide insights into Malthus' viewpoint that altruist may neither benefit the poor nor enrich the rich. Keynes' viewpoint about government's redistribution policy and economic growth is a proper example that 'social altruism' is in harmony with economic development and economic benefits of the different groups. It may be held that our analytical results provide insights into the viewpoints held by Smith, Malthus, and Keynes. Alfred Marshall (1890:9) held that "The supreme aim of the economist is to discover how this latent asset [being capable of more unselfish service than they generally render] can be developed more quickly and turned to account more wisely." Our simple model shows that there is no unique correspondence between altruism and economic consequences. In other words, altruism may either cause economic benefits or loss to the altruist group as well as to the altruism-receiving group.

APPENDIX: STABILITY CONDITIONS

Using (10) and (7), we calculate the Jacobian as follows

$$J = \begin{bmatrix} \lambda_1 Y_{11} - (\upsilon_1 + \delta_k) & \lambda_1 Y_{12} \\ \lambda_2 Y_{21} & \lambda_2 Y_{22} - (\upsilon_2 + \delta_k) \end{bmatrix}$$

where

$$Y_{11} \equiv \frac{\partial Y_1}{\partial K_1} = \frac{(1-\varphi)\alpha K_2 F}{K^2} + \left(\frac{\alpha K_1}{K} + \frac{\beta N_1}{N^*}\right)\frac{(1-\varphi)\alpha}{K},$$

$$Y_{12} \equiv \frac{\partial Y_1}{\partial K_2} = \left(\frac{N_1}{N^*} - \frac{K_1}{K}\right)\frac{(1-\varphi)\alpha\beta F}{K},$$

$$Y_{21} \equiv \frac{\partial Y_2}{\partial K_1} = -\frac{(1-\varphi)\alpha K_2 F}{K^2} + \left(\frac{\alpha K_2}{K} + \frac{\beta z N_2}{N^*} + \frac{\varphi\alpha K_1}{K} + \frac{\varphi\beta N_1}{N^*}\right)\frac{\alpha F}{K},$$

$$Y_{22} \equiv \frac{\partial Y_2}{\partial K_2} = \frac{(1-\varphi)\alpha K_1 F}{K^2} + \left(\frac{\alpha K_2}{K} + \frac{\beta z N_2}{N^*} + \frac{\varphi\alpha K_1}{K} + \frac{\varphi\beta N_1}{N^*}\right)\frac{\alpha F}{K}.$$

The two eigenvalues, ϕ_j, 1, 2, are given by

$$\phi_{1,2} = \theta_1 \pm \sqrt{\theta_1^2 + \theta_2}$$

where

$$\theta_1 \equiv \frac{\lambda_1 Y_{11} + \lambda_2 Y_{22} - \upsilon_1 - \upsilon_2}{2} - \delta_k,$$

$$\theta_2 \equiv \lambda_1\lambda_2 Y_{21} Y_{12} - (\lambda_1 Y_{11} - \upsilon_1 - \delta_k)(\lambda_2 Y_{22} - \upsilon_2 - \delta_k).$$

Since it is difficult to explicitly determine the sign of ϕ_j, we don't further examine the stability conditions.

References

1. Becker, G. (1957) *The Economics of Discrimination*. Chicago: The University of Chicago Press.
2. Becker, G.S. (1981) Altruism in the Family and Selfishness in the Market Place. *Economica* 48, 1-15.
3. Becker, G. (1981a) *A Treatise on the Family*. Mass., Cambridge: Harvard University Press.
4. Burmeister, E. and Dobell, A.R. (1970) *Mathematical Theories of Economic Growth*. London: Collier Macmillan Publishers.
5. Casson, M. (1997a) *Culture, Social Norms and Economics – Economic Behaviour*, Vol. I. Cheltenham: Edward Elgar Publishing Limited.
6. Casson, M. (1997b) *Culture, Social Norms and Economics - Economic Performance*, Vol. II. Cheltenham: Edward Elgar Publishing Limited.
7. Collard, D. (1978) *Altruism and Economy – A Study in Non-Selfish Economics*. Oxford: Martin Robertson & Company.
8. Fonseca, E.G. Da. (1991) *Beliefs in Action – Economic Philosophy and Social Change*. Cambridge: Cambridge University Press.
9. Kolm, S.C. (1983) Altruism and Efficiency. *Ethics* 94, 18-65.
10. Kaldor, N. (1955) Alternative Theories of Distribution. *Review of Economic Studies* 23, 83-100.
11. Kapur, B.K. (1999) A Communitarian Utility Function and Its Social and Economic Implications. *Economics and Philosophy* 15, 43-62.
12. Marglin, S.A. (1984) *Growth, Distribution, and Prices*. Cambridge: Harvard University Press.
13. Marshall, A. (1890) *Principles of Economics*. London: Macmillan.
14. Miller, D. (1988) Altruism and the Welfare State, in *Responsibility, Rights, and Welfare: The Theory of the Welfare State*, 163-88, edited by J.D.Moon. London: Westview Press.
15. Panico, C. and Salvadori, N. (1993, edited) *Post Keynesian Theory of Growth and Distribution*. Vermont: Elward Elgar Publishing Limited.
16. Pasinetti, L.L. (1974) *Growth and Income Distribution - Essays in Economic Theory*. Cambridge: Cambridge University Press.
17. Phelps, E.S. (1975, edited) *Altruism, Morality and Economic Theory*. New York: Russell Sage Foundation.
18. Salvadori, N. (1991) Post-Keynesian Theory of Distribution in the Long Run. In *Nicholas Kaldor and Mainstream Economics - Confrontation or Convergence*? edited by E.J Nell and W. Semmler, London: Macmillan.
19. Samuelson, P.A. and Modigliani, F. (1966) The Pasinetti Paradox in Neo-Classical and More General Models. *The eview of Economic Studies* XXXIII, 269-301.
20. Sato, K. (1966) The Neoclassical Theorem and Distribution of Income and Wealth. The *Review of Economic Studies* XXXIII, 331-336.
21. Stark, O. (1995) *Altruism and Beyond – An Economic Analysis of Transfers and Exchanges within Families and Groups*. Cambridge: Cambridge University Press.
22. Sugden, R. (1984) Reciprocity: The Supply of Public Goods Through Voluntary Contributions. *The Economic Journal* 94, 772-787.
23. Zamagni, S. (1995, Ed.) *The Economics of Altruism*. Vermont: Edward Elgar Publishing Co.
24. Zhang, W.B. (1989) *Economic Dynamic- Growth and Development*. Heidelberg: Springer.
25. Zhang, W.B. (1999) *Confucianism and Modernization*. London: Macmillan.

26. Zhang, W.B. (1999a) *Capital and Knowledge - Dynamics of Economic Structures with Non-Constant Returns*. Heidelberg: Springer.
27. Zhang, W.B. (2000) *Adam Smith and Confucius – The Theory of Moral Sentiments and The Analects*. New York: Nova Science.

Chapter 9

Charitable Giving By Individuals: An Empirical Perspective

VINCENT C.H. CHUA and C.M. WONG

1. INTRODUCTION

In his study of gift-giving in several pre-industrial societies, Marcel Mauss (1925, 1967) discovered that much of this activity is of a certain *quid pro quo* nature. However, unlike a market transaction that establishes a *quid pro quo* relation between objects exchanged, a gift establishes a *quid pro quo* relationship between the giver and the recipient. A gift involves giving away something of the self, which means the giver has given up something of value. The recipient has an obligation to receive the gift and is thus placed in a state of dependence upon the giver. Because the giver is not immediately compensated in the exchange, the receiver has an obligation to repay the gift. Mauss's work continues to be relevant in modern societies.

Alms giving, and more generally, charitable giving is a set of activities that closely resembles gift-giving but there are three distinct differences: (a) the objects transferred directly or indirectly satisfy some basic needs of the recipient; (b) reciprocation by the recipient is non-obligatory and the form of reciprocation is more restricted and less predictable due to a lack of means; and (c) giving could be to a total stranger that one may not likely encounter again. Moreover, because the ability or opportunity to reciprocate may be absent, some of these activities may fall into a category that Culyer (1973) termed "quids without quos". In the absence of compulsion, these activities are often associated with the term *altruism*.

In the next section of this paper, we discuss a variety of contrasting motives that may help explain why individuals engage in charitable giving and show that many such motives may stem from pure self-interest. That some of these activities may also be driven by "a love for one's neighbor" or by "a sense of duty" is also highlighted. We then proceed to an exposition of the interdependent utility framework that underpins much of the theoretical and empirical literature on altruism in economics. The remainder of the paper focuses on the empirical work on charitable giving by individuals. Issues such as (a) the effect of tax policy on the price of giving and consequently the level of contributions to the less fortunate, (b) the implications of the cost of fund raising on the organization of fund-raising activities, (c) the effect of economic growth and how this may affect the plight of the needy, and (d) the role of the government in helping the less fortunate are discussed with a view to providing policy makers with some broad directions for action. The emphasis here is on how economic factors can be altered to raise the level of giving. For a more enduring solution to the problem of the less fortunate, it may also be necessary for us to consider a change of the social mindset and to encourage individuals in our society to consciously cultivate an awareness of our duties towards others, for as Immanuel Kant noted, "... if none of us did any act of love and charity, but only kept inviolate the rights of every man, there would be no misery in the world except sickness and misfortune as do not spring from the violation of rights."

2. MOTIVES UNDERLYING CHARITABLE GIVING AND ALTRUISM

Undoubtedly, human history has been graced by the likes of Mother Teresa, Mahatma Gandhi and Joan of Arc, who had given much of themselves selflessly to the service of others, because they love their neighbors, because they cherish the brotherhood of man or because they possess an intensely strong sense of duty towards their countrymen or nation. But as with Mauss's discovery of the motives for gift-giving in a number of archaic societies, much of the charitable giving activities that we observe in modern societies may be primarily a result of self-interested behaviour. In his *Lectures on Ethics*, Kant suggests that much of the human involvement in charitable activities may be a result of the natural inclination in individuals to selectively express their love for their less fortunate neighbors. Such individuals, as Kant noted, stand in need of people to whom they can show their kindness and are not content until they find human beings towards whom they can be charitable. George Eliot's character Dorothea Brooke in *Middlemarch* typifies individuals of this behavioural type. That this disposition towards others is but a manifestation of self-interested behaviour may be deduced from the disappointment experienced by Dorothea when she realized the redundancy of the help that she could offer. Coincidentally or otherwise, the taxonomies of motives provided in Ireland (1973), Johnson (1973) and Clary and Snyder (1990) also point in this direction, that charitable actions by individuals could be largely motivated by self-interest. For instance, an individual may derive direct benefits from seeing the less fortunate better off because helping others serves to justify one's current well-being. This type of helping actions serves what Clary and Snyder (1990) term the *ego defensive* function. That is, helping others help givers reduce guilt feelings or make them feel deserving of desirable outcomes. In this context, some may regard the capacity to feel guilt as an indication that the individual is not totally self-interested. Regardless, if the motive for the action is primarily to alleviate one's guilt feeling, then it appears indisputable that the act is primarily a self-interested one.

Others may give because they anticipate responses of gratitude from the recipients or they may give because they derive satisfaction directly from the knowledge that they have carried out a good deed. Andreoni (1990) refers to these as the "warm-glow" effect. Here, it is useful to differentiate this "warm-glow" effect from the unintended warm glow that one experiences as a result of discharging one's moral obligation towards others. In the case of the latter, as discussed further below, there is a moralistic basis for the pleasure experienced.

Sometimes the relevant consideration may be to do with how other members of the social group to which one belongs regard our actions. As Becker (1974) noted, gaining the esteem of one's peers and/or avoiding their scorn may be important motives here. Likewise, one may give so as to avoid possible adverse repercussions from employers who strongly support, say, United Way contributions.

Giving actions motivated by one or more of the above self-interested considerations surely do not qualify as altruistic actions and to Kant, it is not such behaviour, the pursuit of individual gratification in one form or other, which ought to be cultivated. Such a pursuit based on the principle of individual gratification or happiness (eudemonism) if adopted will result in, as Abbott in his preface to Kant's *Metaphysical Elements of Ethics* (1780, 2000) noted, "the euthanasia (quiet death) of all morality". Rather it is behaviour originating from a clear understanding of an individual's obligation towards others, an obligation that stems from moral ethics, be it driven by pure reason or by Christian love, which requires cultivation. It is a duty for individuals to help their less fortunate counterparts and this duty ought to be carried out even when the impulse to help is absent.

When individuals are motivated to action by this clear understanding of duty and obligation, they also experience moral, as opposed to pathological, pleasure. Pleasure that must precede the obedience to a law in order that one may act according to the law is pathological, and the process follows from the physical order of nature; that which must be preceded by the law in order that it may be felt is in the moral order. To Abbott, "when the thinking man has conquered the temptations to vice, and is conscious of having done his (often hard) duty, he finds himself in a state of peace and satisfaction which may well be called happiness, in which virtue is her own reward". This is what appears to distinguish the unintended warm glow mentioned earlier from the "warm-glow" effect discussed in Andreoni's work.

But are all giving acts driven by one's moral obligation towards others necessarily altruistic acts? Surely there are many actions that we take on a daily basis that are driven by our moral sense of duty and at the same time consistent with our natural impulses, for example, caring for our young. Does helping a stranger we have a natural attraction to and in whom we derive great pleasure in helping qualify as an altruistic act? If not, what then is the type of activity that Culyer referred to as "quids without quos"? While it is enticing at this point to advance a definition of the term *altruism*, it suffices to mention that whatever this definition may be, we feel that it will involve at least two elements. First, the action taken must be driven not by impulse but by what is morally correct and second, it must involve some sort of a sacrifice on the part of the giver. The definition of altruism as "giving without regard to self" would be consistent with these requirements.

3. THE ECONOMIST'S FRAMEWORK

Most economists have studied altruism as an issue involving interdependent utilities [see, for instance, Warr (1982) and Clotfelter (1985)]. Let X_D be the consumption of individual D. If D were to exhibit purely self-interested behaviour, then his ordinal preference function U^D depends only on his own consumption X_D i.e. $U^D = U^D(X_D)$. Let X_R denote the consumption of the less fortunate (collectively defined) and, for simplicity, suppose the preference function of the less fortunate is linear in X_R i.e. $U^R = U^R(X_R) = X_R$. If individual D were to be altruistic, then his preference function will depend on both his consumption X_D and the consumption of the less fortunate X_R. We write D's preference function as $U^D = U^D(X_D, U^R(X_R)) = U^D(X_D, X_R)$. That is, individual D cares not only about his own consumption but also the consumption of the less fortunate and, being rational, D selects a most preferred division of his endowment which may be determined algebraically by solving the following problem:

$$\text{Maximize } U^D = U^D(X_D, X_R)$$
$$\text{subject to } X_D + X_R = E$$

where E is D's endowment of say, corn, and X_D is the amount of corn that he consumes and X_R is the amount that he has given to the less fortunate. In this instance, individual D is a donor and R denotes the recipient(s). Put simply, individual D, given the amount of resources that he has (E), will divide this between himself and the less fortunate in a way that is most preferred from his perspective.

In an environment involving more than one donor, however, individual D will quickly realize that the consumption of the less fortunate does not depend only on what he gives but on what every other donor is giving as well. Accordingly, although individual D cares about the consumption of the less fortunate X_R, the part of X_R that is directly within his control may constitute only a small fraction of it. Lest the less fortunate ends up with a level of consumption that would be generally regarded as excessive, individual D will want to take the amount other donors will be giving into consideration when deciding the amount he will give. Because of the inability of donors to coordinate their actions, an equilibrium outcome is likely to be characterized by a situation that is inefficient. This problem, also known as the *public good* or *free-rider* problem, will result in the less fortunate not receiving enough aid. In a large society, in the absence of other considerations, each individual donor will give very little to the less fortunate.

However, as discussed in Andreoni (1990), if individual donors have the capacity to experience and do desire the warm-glow effect, then this extreme situation can be averted to some extent. It should also be noted that a number of writers, seeking to explain how the free rider problem may be mitigated, have demonstrated that efficient or near efficient outcomes may be possible if individuals in society more fully embrace the Kantian motive [see, for instance, Collard (1978) and Sugden (1984)] or have communitarian sentiments [see, for instance, Margolis (1982) and Kapur (1999)]. These theoretical studies serve to remind us that more efficient and socially desirable outcomes may be possible through a systematic cultivation of the social mindset via public education, moral suasion, campaigns and the like. While there must already be a fair number of individuals in our society who already possess Kantian or communitarian sentiments, a systematic cultivation of the social mindset via public education, moral suasion and campaigns will still be necessary. But such a strategy for raising the welfare of the less fortunate, by its very nature, would require a considerable length of time to take effect. Thus the shortfall that may result from the free-rider problem remains a major concern.

There are also interpretative difficulties associated with the interdependent utility framework as a framework for the study of altruism. It is surely reasonable to state that if one is altruistic towards another individual, then the other individual's consumption will feature in some way in one's preference function. But setting up the problem as such makes the inclusion of the consumption of others in the preference function devoid of the motive for giving, information that is essential for determining whether an act is altruistic or otherwise. Another individual's consumption could feature in one's preference function because one is particularly concerned with the guilt feeling that it would otherwise induce in us. The same variable may enter in an identical fashion because one does care for the other person from a moral perspective and likewise if one is naturally inclined to do so. For this reason, Culyer (1973) emphasized that much of what has been put forward has to do not with the concept of altruism *per se* but with a related notion *generosity* and as long as one recognizes this, the work of economists in this area should become accessible to many non-economists.

The foregoing discussion points to the diversity of motives underlying charitable giving. It is with this as a premise that we proceed to discuss the large volume of empirical work on the determinants of charitable giving. In particular, if private voluntary contributions are insufficient to fund the needs of the less fortunate, what then are the possible measures that one could consider to help remedy this situation? Can the private sector contribution mechanism be improved or redesigned to help alleviate this problem? Is there room for a more active role by the public sector?

Reasonable answers to the queries posed in the preceding paragraph can come only from a better understanding of the giving behaviour of individuals and how public policy influences this behaviour. For this purpose, the vast majority of empirical work on the determinants of charitable giving by individuals have consistently directed attention at how the price of giving and the level of disposable income influence the level of individual charitable contributions and how private voluntary giving respond to public sector provisions. We proceed now to briefly review this literature.

4. THE PRICE OF GIVING

Private donors are essentially concerned about the consumption of the less fortunate. In this context, the price of giving for a donor refers to the amount the donor has to spend in order for the donor to raise the consumption of the less fortunate by a dollar. Following the direction suggested in Weisbrod and Dominguez (1986) and in Posnett and Sandler (1989), we write the price of giving as $(1+c_d)/[1-(c_f+c_a)]$, where c_d refers to the transaction cost the donor has to incur to get a dollar to the charity. As an example, in the context of a telethon, c_d may refer to the cost of making the telephone call divided by the dollar amount contributed. This cost may also refer to the resources that an individual will have to expend to determine the worthiness of a particular cause. The c_f and c_a variables, on the other hand, refer to the per dollar cost incurred by the charities in connection with fund raising and administration respectively. When a dollar is received by a charity, $1-(c_f+c_a)$ is the amount that ultimately gets to the beneficiaries. Obviously, the more efficient the charity is in fund raising and administration, the more of the dollar contributed will get to the less fortunate.

If donations to the charity are tax-deductible, this price is modified as follows. The price of giving is $(1+c_d-t)/[1-(c_f+c_a)]$, where t refers to the donor's marginal tax rate. Tax-deductibility reduces the price of giving for those subject to a positive rate of income taxation. Suppose the donor's marginal tax rate (t) is 25 percent, the per dollar transaction cost (c_d) of giving is 10 cents and the per dollar cost of fundraising and administration (c_f+c_a) is also 10 cents, if donations to the charity is not tax-deductible, then the price of raising the consumption of the less fortunate by a dollar is \$1.22. That is, \$1.22 is the amount the donor has to spend so as to get a dollar to the less fortunate. Exemption of charitable contributions from income taxation for the donor will bring the donor's price of giving down to 94 cents, which is less than a dollar. For an individual who possesses Kantian sentiments, and suppose he believes that it is his moral obligation to share a certain fraction of his income with the less fortunate, then the relevant price for him is also 94 cents since his ultimate concern is with how he consumes and how much the less fortunate consumes. The same applies when the warm-glow effect is present as long as the warm glow is generated by the extent to which the individual has enhanced the consumption of the recipient.

The price incentive effect will be larger for large donors whose motives for giving are those other than the public good motive, for instance, the publicity or social prestige motive. In this instance, the price for a "dollar" of publicity is \$0.75 since the administrative and fund raising cost of \$0.10 per dollar raised will lead only to reduction in benefits to the recipients without having any effect on the publicity impact. But if a large donor is motivated by the public good motive, then the reduction in public sector provision resulting from a reduction in government income tax revenue will be factored into his giving decision and accordingly, the price reduction effect of tax deductibility will be somewhat dampened.

The price of giving can thus vary considerably across individual donors and across motives. The nature of the available data however typically restricts our consideration to variation in prices brought about by the donors' differing tax circumstances, the tax-deductibility status of their benefits and the efficiency of their respective benefits in fund raising and administration. Nonetheless, this price variation across donors has been an indispensable source of information for studying the responsiveness of private voluntary giving to changes in the price of giving. A good feel for the direction and the size of this response can help policy makers anticipate the effect of policy changes such as the granting of tax-exempt status to charities and the move towards the centralization of fund-raising activities in an institution like the United Way in the United States or the Community Chest of Singapore and the Community Chest of Hong Kong.

Taussig (1967) and Schwartz (1970), two pioneering studies in this direction, found voluntary contributions to respond only marginally to changes in the price of giving. Subsequent studies in the United States, however, have failed to produce a consensus on the magnitude of this effect. Several studies, including Feldstein (1975), Feldstein and Clotfelter (1976), Feldstein and Taylor (1976), Boskin and Feldstein (1977) and Brown (1987) have found charitable contributions to be highly responsive to changes in the price of giving, that is, a one percent reduction in the price of giving could result in as much as a three percent increase in contributions. In contrast, Reece (1979), Randolph (1995) and more recently, Andreoni and Scholz (1998) found this response to be closer to one percent. Estimates for Canada (see Hood, Martin and Osberg (1977), Glenday, Gupta and Pawlak (1986), Kitchen and Dalton (1990) and Kitchen (1992)) also show considerable diversity with estimates ranging from a mere 0.15 percent increase in contributions to as high as a 5 percent increase for a one percent reduction in the price of giving.

Almost all studies, including those carried out by Jones and Posnett (1991) for Britain and Weinblatt (1992) for Israel, however, have found that a one percent decline in the price of giving can enhance aggregate contributions by more than one percent. Recent studies on charitable contributions in Singapore by Wong, Chua and Vasoo (1998) and by Chua and Wong (1999) also reported that private voluntary contributions are highly responsive to changes in the price of giving. This responsiveness ranges from around one percent to as high as five percent, depending on the donor characteristics and the types of charities in question. Summarizing, the large body of work in this area points to the conclusion that a policy that reduces the price of giving can have strong beneficial effects on the welfare of the less fortunate. In this context, the policy to grant tax-exempt or, in the context of Singapore, IPC (Institution of Public Character) status to charities must have played an important role in the funding of these charities and whenever possible should be extended to those not currently enjoying this status. Private sector initiatives towards the centralization of fund-raising activities will also have a highly beneficial effect on the welfare of the less fortunate and it is to this that we will now turn.

5. CENTRALIZATION OF FUND RAISING AND THE COMMUNITY CHEST OF SINGAPORE

By centralizing the fund-raising activities of charities, economies of scale are reaped and a reduction in the price of giving through a reduction in the $(c_f + c_a)$ component may be realized. Centralization also accords additional savings since dissipative expenditures by member charities just to divert limited funds from each other is now unnecessary. As Rose-Ackerman (1982) argued, competition among charities for donations may push fundraising shares to very high levels. Thus a united charity (like the United Way) can help to economize on fundraising costs by reducing competition between the member charities, and donors may give more because the donations are now more efficiently spent. She also suggested that donors may have poor information about charities and therefore may delegate the difficult allocation task to someone else. Furthermore, since the united charity monitors the needs and performance of its members, donors may be convinced that their donations are used more efficiently in the provision of charitable services, and thus may also increase their giving. The centralization of fund-raising activities can also be highly beneficial to charities that do not have sufficient resources to engage in meaningful fund-raising exercises and at the same time are heavily dependent on a continued stream of unsolicited donations to remain viable.

In the context of Singapore, the activities of Children's Charities Association are an early example of centralizing fund-raising. But the scale of the Association's activities is nowhere close to that undertaken by the Community Chest of Singapore. The Community Chest of Singapore (CCS) was set up by the then Singapore Council of Social Service in 1983, and since then has played an important role in helping the less fortunate in Singapore. The Community Chest does not provide direct social services, but specializes in raising funds for over 50 charities that are its members. Donations to the Community Chest are tax-deductible, though not all CCS member organizations have the tax-exempt or IPC status. An individual who wishes to make a donation to a CCS member may either give to it directly, or alternatively donate to the Community Chest and earmark the sum for that particular agency. Funds that have not been earmarked are allocated by the Community Chest to its members according to various criteria, including need and the financial situation of the agencies. Member organizations of the Community Chest are generally not allowed to have independent fundraising activities, except for special fundraising events. Much of the contribution to Community Chest is through the SHARE (Social Help and Assistance Raised by Employees) program, under which a working person can voluntarily contribute to charity with a monthly pledge of a sum that is deducted from his salary. Most of the donations to the Community Chest are from individuals.

Although the beneficial effects of centralization are difficult to estimate, undoubtedly the Community Chest of Singapore has been highly successful in the mobilization of funds. Scale economies and a sound strategy for the dissemination of information (and this helps to reduce the price of giving through a reduction in the c_d component of price) concerning member activities have, in recent years, resulted in amounts raised that are in excess of $30 million annually. Playing a major role here is, of course, the SHARE program. By bringing the needs of the different charities under its wings to the prospective donor at his/her workplace, the program has significantly reduced the transaction cost (c_d) for these individuals. The Program's access to the payroll deduction system is a critical factor here. Besides increasing the level of contributions, the supportive role played by employers has also sharply increased participation.

Lest the benefits of centralization be carried too far, centralization of fund-raising has its setbacks. One major setback, despite the ability of the donor to earmark contributions for specific charities, is a lack of assurance that one's contribution will get to one's intended charities. Because of this inability to unambiguously direct one's gift towards one's intended charity, despite the Community Chest being a somewhat more efficient mechanism for fund-raising, donors have been prepared to pay higher prices so as to be able to direct their contributions to specific charities engaged in the delivery of services which they can directly relate to and identify with. While the price of giving tends to be pushed down by the saving in solicitation costs, it tends to be pushed up by the fact that when a donor gives to the united charity, he does not have control over how his donation would be allocated among member charities. Fisher (1977) argued that even when earmarking of gifts is possible, a donor's action to earmark his gift for specific charities might be offset by the fund allocation policy of the united charity. When donors perceive that they cannot affect the final distribution of their gifts, they may lower their donations to the combined charity. As pointed out by Bilodeau (1992), if the united charity is aware of this, it may want to guarantee that earmarked contributions will not be offset completely.

In her study on the per unit cost of fund-raising for 28 selected charities in Singapore, Chan (1998) found that despite the high per dollar cost of fund-raising for some charities, large amounts of donation continue to flow to these charities. The National Kidney Foundation has a per dollar cost of fund-raising between 23 to 33 cents and that for the Singapore Red Cross is between 20 to 25 cents. This compares with a figure generally below 20 cents for the Community Chest. Yet funds continue to flow to these charities, making it unnecessary for them to seek the assistance of a more efficient centralized fund-raising body. This, as Rose-Ackerman (1980) argued, may be a result of the reputation (or symbol of quality) achieved by these charities over the years and thus may appeal to an "easy-to-identify" group of donors.

6. THE INCOME EFFECT

In a dynamic economy, economic growth changes the income levels of individuals but needs also tend to increase in a more affluent society. In this context, a good understanding of how the level of voluntary giving may change with changes in disposable income can help institutions providing services to the less fortunate to more accurately predict future trends in giving and to anticipate gaps in required and actual funding as the economy evolves. Appropriate policies and programs can then be designed and put in place in anticipation of such future trends. If the needs of the less fortunate grow at the same rate as the rate of economic growth but the responsiveness of contributions to income changes is low, then a balanced budget situation can quickly degenerate into a deficit situation threatening the continued viability of the institution the result of which may be detrimental to the welfare of the less fortunate.

Like the empirical results on the price responsiveness of charitable contributions, the studies on the income responsiveness also reveal a mixed bag of estimates. Numerous studies for the United States as well as those carried out for Canada and the United Kingdom have suggested a low but positive responsiveness of voluntary giving to changes in disposable income. Weinblatt's (1992) study for Israel and Wong, Chua and Vasoo (1998) and Chua and Wong (1999) for Singapore provide additional support for the low responsiveness finding. In contrast, Reece (1979) and Reece and Zieschang (1985) have found that a one percent increase in disposable income can generate an increase in contribution in excess of one percent, a finding reinforced in Ribar and Wilhelm (1995). Randolph (1995), using an intertemporal approach and exploiting the difference between transitory and permanent income changes, argued in support of the latter findings. His analysis suggests that a transitory increase in income may temporarily reduce the price of giving under a progressive tax structure and if individuals consider present giving and future giving to be substitutes, then temporary exposure to this lower price may cause the individual to give much more than otherwise but at the same time causing the amount that they give in the absence of the transitory increase in income to fall. This will result in a downward bias for the estimate of the income responsiveness of contributions to permanent income changes while producing an upward bias for the permanent price effect. At this point, however, there does not seem to be a clear consensus on the income responsiveness of charitable giving. Andreoni and Scholz (1998) have recently reported a very low responsiveness of income, their estimates put the income responsiveness in the neighborhood of 0.3 to 0.4 of a percent increase for a 1 percent increase in income.

7. A MORE ACTIVE ROLE FOR THE PUBLIC SECTOR?

As discussed earlier, in an environment involving more than one donor, an individual donor will quickly realize that the consumption of the less fortunate does not depend only on what he gives but on what every other donor is giving as well. This leads to the free-rider problem, which results in the less fortunate not receiving enough aid. The fact that giving can be a costly activity (there is the donor's transaction cost of getting the dollar to the less fortunate (c_d), the cost of fund-raising (c_f) and the cost of administration (c_a)) and the price of giving can easily exceed unity will work towards aggravating the shortfall. Furthermore, if the income responsiveness of contributions is low, the absolute shortfall will widen with time in a growing economy. There is thus a compelling case for contemplating a wider role for the government.

This line of reasoning, however, requires closer scrutiny. Direct intervention by the government will make the government just another "individual", and if in fact individuals do take into consideration how much they think other individuals will give, direct provision by the government will induce some cutback by private donors bearing in mind that the intervention itself needs to be funded. Consider the following example. Two donors contribute a dollar each to the consumption of a less fortunate individual and this gives him a consumption level of $2. Suppose this is deemed insufficient and the government intervenes to supplement this level of provision to say $3. Suppose the intervention dollar is financed by a tax of 50 cents each on the two donors, then it is only natural for the two donors to, other things equal, scale back their respective direct contribution to 50 cents since they have already contributed 50 cents via the tax-cum-transfer mechanism. This will render the intervention totally ineffective, a policy ineffectiveness result referred to as the Ricardian Equivalence Theorem and made clear in Warr (1982). If, on the other hand, only one of the two individuals contributed an amount equal to two dollars, then the same tax-cum-transfer policy will alter the distribution of burden across private individuals but its effect on the consumption of the less fortunate is again dubious. Approaching the issue from the public choice perspective, Roberts (1984) showed that perfect crowding out is not a theoretical impossibility. These findings, when considered in isolation, suggest two extreme policy positions; either we tolerate under-provision or otherwise, the function of looking after the less fortunate should be completely left to the government. In two papers, however, Andreoni (1989, 1990) argued that perfect crowding out might not occur because giving a dollar through a tax-cum-transfer scheme is not a perfect substitute for giving a dollar directly to the less fortunate. In the latter case, the act of giving itself, either because one is able to see gratitude in the recipient or whether one is able to demonstrate solidarity with the recipient or the recipient's cause, generates a warm glow effect whereas the tax-cum-transfer policy do not. Because of this consideration, governmental intervention may not be entirely futile.

Many studies have provided regression-based evidence of some crowding-out. Abrams and Schmitz (1978; 1984), for instance, have found evidence of partial crowding-out in the USA. This finding is repeated in studies for the United Kingdom [See Jones (1983) and Steinberg (1985)], for Israel [see Weinblatt (1992)] and more recently for the case of Singapore [see Wong, Chua and Vasoo (1998)]. Using data from the United Kingdom, Posnett and Sandler (1986), however, failed to find such an effect.

As the empirical results indicate, the relationship between private voluntary giving and public sector provision may not be as straightforward as suggested earlier. Although an increase in government spending on social services may result in a reduction in private charitable donations, this crowding-out is more likely the greater is the substitutability between government provision and private voluntary giving. Cash transfers and untied government grants to the less fortunate are more or less perfect substitutes for private donations. In this case, crowding-out is likely. The same cannot be said of direct provision of social services by the government. Driessen (1985) and Schiff (1990), for instance, have suggested that government provision and private voluntary giving may, in effect, be complements. For example, increased governmental provision may help to advertise particular concerns and attract greater private sector involvement. In such a situation, private donations may increase at the same time. Likewise, Weisbrod (1988) noted that government spending may in fact encourage private donations if donors see this as a signal that particular activities or programs are deserving of private support.

Rose-Ackerman (1986) has also analyzed various situations in which government grants may either increase or reduce private giving. A large government grant may enable a charity to increase significantly the number of clients served and reap economies of scale. The resulting improvement in efficiency in producing charitable output can have a positive impact on donations. Government grants to charities may require them to move toward a given ideology or alter the nature of their outputs, and if donors agree with the government's ideology giving would again increase. Of course, if donors disagree with the government's ideology they may divert their giving to other charities. Lastly, in accepting grants from the government, charities also accept its monitoring of their activities. If donors lack information about the charities, they may interpret government support as a "seal of approval" of their quality and increase their giving.

Preliminary work on charitable contributions by charitable activity carried out by the present authors suggests that all these considerations may be important in determining how government provision influences private voluntary giving.

8. CONCLUDING REMARKS

The main concern addressed in this paper is one of ensuring that sufficient funds are directed to activities that will improve the welfare of the less fortunate. In this respect, empirical studies providing quantitative estimates of the price and income responsiveness of charitable contributions by individuals provide useful information on how changes in public policy, economic growth and other developments can influence the funding of these activities. Knowledge of these key parameters can also improve the ability of institutions engaged in the funding and delivery of social services to anticipate gaps in funding and to undertake measures in anticipation of these gaps. As is clear from the discussion, although individual contributions are sensitive to changes in price and disposable income, there is no clear consensus on the magnitude of the price or the income responsiveness of these contributions. Current research, using improved techniques and more revealing data sets, may yet produce a more coherent picture.

As is the experience of many other countries, the centralization of fund raising activities in Singapore through the formation of the Community Chest has produced beneficial effects for member charities. For some, their continued existence has depended on this centralized funding mechanism. How the role of the Community Chest will evolve will depend on the perception of costs and benefits associated with membership by charities that are currently not members of the Community Chest. The extent to which the fund allocation policy of the Community Chest mirrors social preferences is also an important consideration. Here, how much funds the Community Chest allocates to the different types of activities and how much it allocates to the individual member charities are both relevant.

There has been considerable evidence of some crowding-out of individual contributions by government grants. But governmental involvement in the financing of a charity also provides information to donors and would-be donors about the worthiness of the cause pursued by a charity and in this way government actions may positively influence private individual contributions.

The empirical literature that we have surveyed focused mainly on the economic influences on the level of giving. But as we have pointed out, there may be a need to take a broader view and consider the possibility of encouraging giving through a change of the social mindset by cultivating in each of us an awareness of our individual responsibilities towards others. Such issues require further analysis.

References

1. Abrams, B.A. and Schmitz, M.D. (1978), "The 'crowding-out' effect of governmental transfers on private charitable contributions", *Public Choice,* Vol. 33 No. 1, pp. 29-39.
2. Abrams, B.A. and Schmitz, M.D. (1984), "The crowding-out effect of governmental transfers on private charitable contributions: cross-section evidence", *National Tax Journal,* Vol. 37 No. 4, pp. 563-568.

3. Andreoni, J. (1989), "Giving with impure altruism: applications to charity and Ricardian Equivalence", *Journal of Political Economy*, Vol. 97: pp. 1447-1458.
4. Andreoni, J. (1990), "Impure altruism and donations to public goods: A theory of warm-glow giving", *Economic Journal*, Vol. 100, pp.464-477.
5. Andreoni, J. and Scholz, K. (1998), "An econometric analysis of charitable giving with interdependent preferences", *Economic Inquiry*, Vol. 36, pp. 410-428.
6. Becker, G.S. (1974), "A theory of social interactions", *Journal of Political Economy*, Vol.82, pp.1063-1093.
7. Bilodeau, M. (1992), "Voluntary contributions to united charities", *Journal of Public Economics*, Vol. 48 No. 1, June, pp. 119-133.
8. Boskin, M.J. and Feldstein, M. (1977), "Effects of the charitable deduction on contributions by low income and middle income households: evidence from the national survey of philanthropy", *Review of Economics and Statistics*, Vol. 59 No. 3, August, pp. 351-354.
9. Brown, E. (1987), "Tax incentives and charitable giving: evidence from new survey data". *Public Finance Quarterly*, Vol. 15 No. 4, October, pp. 386-396.
10. Chan, F.Y. (1998), "*An economic analysis of charitable organizations in Singapore*", Department of Economics and Statistics, Honours Thesis.
11. Chua, V.C.H. and Wong, C.M. (1999), "Tax incentives, individual characteristics and charitable giving in Singapore", *International Journal of Social Economics*, Vol.26, Issue 12, pp.1492-1504.
12. Clary, E.G. and Snyder, M. (1990), "A functional analysis of volunteers' motivations", in *The Nonprofit Sector (NGOs) in the United States and Abroad: Cross-Cultural Perspectives*, United Way Strategic Institute, Boston, Mass., pp.79-93.
13. Clotfelter, C.T. (1985), *Federal Tax Policy and Charitable Giving*, The University of Chicago Press, Chicago, IL, and London.
14. Collard, D.A. (1978), *Altruism and Economy: A Study in Non-selfish Economics*, Oxford: Martin Robertson.
15. Culyer, A.J.(1973), "Quids without quos – A praxeological approach", in *The Economics of Charity*, Institute of Economic Affairs, Surrey, England,pp.33-61.
16. Driessen, P.A. (1985), "Comment on 'the crowding-out' effect of governmental transfers on private charitable contributions", *National Tax Journal*, Vol. 38 No. 4, December, pp. 571-573.
17. Feldstein, M. (1975), "The income tax and charitable contributions: part I – aggregate and distributional effects", *National Tax Journal*, Vol. 28 No. 1, March, pp. 81-100.
18. Feldstein, M. and Clotfelter, C. (1976), "Tax incentives and charitable contributions in the United States", *Journal of Public Economics*, Vol. 5 No. 1-2, January-February, pp. 1-26.
19. Feldstein, M. and Taylor, A. (1997), "The income tax and charitable contributions", *Econometrica*, Vol. 44 No. 6, November, pp. 1201-1222.
20. Fisher, F.M. (1977), "On donor sovereignty and united charities", *American Economic Review*, Vol. 67 No. 4, September, pp. 632-638.
21. Eliot, G. (1976) *Middlemarch*, edited by W.J. Harvey, New York, NY : Penguin Books.
22. Glenday, G., Gupta, A.K. and Pawlak, H. (1986), "Tax incentives for personal charitable contributions", *Review of Economics and Statistics*, Vol. 68 No. 4, November, pp. 688-693.
23. Hood, R.D., Martin, S.A. and Osberg, L.S. (1977), "Economic determinants of individual charitable donations in Canada", *Canadian Journal of Economics*, Vol. 10 No. 4, November, pp. 653-669.

24. Ireland, T.R. (1973), "The calculus of philanthropy", in *The Economics of Charity*, Institute of Economic Affairs, Surrey, England, pp. 65-78.
25. Johnson, D.B. (1973), "The charity market: Theory and practice", in *The Economics of Charity*, Institute of Economic Affairs, Surrey, England, pp. 81-106.
26. Jones, P.R. (1983), "Aid to charities", *International Journal of Social Economics*, Vol. 10 No. 2, pp. 3-11.
27. Kapur, B.K. (1999), "A communitarian utility function and its social and economic implications", *Economics and Philosophy*, Vol. 15, pp. 43- 62.
28. Kant, I. (1963), *Lectures on Ethics*, translated by Louis Infield, New York: Harper & Row
29. Kant, I. (2000), *The Metaphysical Elements of Ethics*, translated by Thomas Kingsmill Abbott, (internet edition), http://www.vt.edu/vt98/academics/books/kant/ethics.
30. Kitchen, H. (1992), "Determinants of charitable donations in Canada: a comparison over time", *Applied Economics*, Vol. 24 No. 7, July, pp. 709-713.
31. Kitchen, H. and Dalton, R. (1990), "Determinants of charitable donations by families in Canada: a regional analysis", *Applied Economics*, Vol. 22 No. 3, March, pp. 285-299.
32. Mauss, M. (1925, 1967). *The Gift; Forms and Functions of Exchange in Archaic Societies*, translated by Ian Cunnison, New York: Norton.
33. Margolis, H. (1982), *Selfishness, Altruism, and Rationality: A Theory of Social Choice*, New York: Cambridge University Press.
34. Posnett, J. and Sandler, T. (1986), "Joint supply and the finance of charitable activity", *Public Finance Quarterly*, Vol. 14 No. 2, April, pp. 209-222.
35. Posnett, J. and Sandler, T. (1989), "Demand for charity donations in private non-profit markets: the case of the UK", *Journal of Public Economics*, Vol. 40 No. 2, November, pp. 187-220.
36. Randolph, W.C. (1995), "Dynamic income, progressive taxation, and the timing of charitable contributions", *Journal of Political Economy*, Vol. 103, No. 4, pp.709-738.
37. Reece, W.S. (1979), "Charitable contributions: New evidence on household behaviour", *American Economic Review*, Vol. 69 No. 1, March, pp. 142-151.
38. Reece, W.S. and Zieschang, K.D. (1985), "Consistent estimation of the impact of tax
39. deductibility on the level of charitable contributions", *Econometrica*, Vol. 53 No. 2, March, pp. 271-293.
40. Ribar, D.C. and Wilhelm, M.O. (1995), "Charitable contribution to international relief and development", *National Tax Journal*, Vol. 48 No.2, June, pp. 229-244.
41. Roberts, R.D. (1984), "A positive model of private charity and public transfers", *Journal of Political Economy*, Vol. 92 No. 1, February, pp. 136-148.
42. Rose-Ackerman, S. (1980), "United charities: An economic analysis", *Public Policy*, Vol. 28, pp. 323-350.
43. Rose-Ackerman, S. (1982), "Charitable giving and 'excessive' fundraising", *Quarterly Journal of Economics*, Vol. 97 No. 2, May, pp. 193-212.
44. Rose-Ackerman, S. (1986), "Do government grants to charity reduce private donations?", in Rose-Ackerman, S. (Ed.), *The Economics of Nonprofit Institutions: Studies in Structure and Policy*, Oxford University Press, New York, NY, pp. 312-329.
45. Schiff, J. (1985), "Does government spending crowd out charitable contributions?", *National Tax Journal*, Vol. 38 No. 4, pp. 535-546.
46. Schiff, J. (1990), *Charitable Giving and Government Policy*, Greenwood Press, Inc., Westport, Ct.
47. Schwartz, R.A. (1970), "Personal philanthropic contributions", *Journal of Political Economy*, Vol. 78 No. 6, November/December, pp. 1264-1291.

48. Steinberg, R. (1985), "Empirical relations between government spending and charitable donations", *Journal of Voluntary Action Research,* Vol. 14 Nos. 2-3, April-September, pp. 54-64.
49. Sugden, R. (1984), "Reciprocity: The supply of public goods through voluntary cooperation", *Economic Journal,* Vol. 94, Issue 376, pp.772-787.
50. Taussig, M.K. (1967), "Economic aspects of the personal income tax treatment of charitable contributions", *National Tax Journal,* Vol. 20 No. 1, March, pp. 1-19.
51. Warr, P.G. (1982), "Pareto optimal redistribution and private charity", *Journal of Public Economics,* Vol. 19 No. 1, October, pp. 131-138.
52. Weinblatt, J. (1992), "Do government transfers crowd out private transfers to non-profit organizations? The Israeli experience", *International Journal of Social Economics,* Vol. 19 No. 2, pp. 60-66.
53. Weisbrod, B.A. (1988), *The Non-profit Economy,* Harvard University Press, Cambridge, MA.
54. Weisbrod, B.A. and Dominguez, N.D. (1986), "Demand for collective goods in private non-profit markets: can fundraising expenditures help overcome free-rider behaviour?", *Journal of Public Economics,* Vol. 30 No. 1, June, pp. 83-95.
55. Wong, C.M., Chua, V.C.H. and Vasoo, S. (1998), "Contributions to charitable organizations in a developing country: The case of Singapore", *International Journal of Social Economics,* Vol. 25 No.1, pp. 25-42.

Chapter 10

Altruism In Wartime: Self, And Others

LIEW-GEOK LEONG

1. NOTIONS AND DEFINITIONS

There is little disagreement among philosophers, sociobiologists and economists about altruistic behaviour as observed, even measured, although individual motives may be questioned. Without controversy, one may define altruism as "intentional voluntary behaviour that benefits another and is not performed with the expectation of receiving external rewards or avoiding external punishments or aversive stimuli" (Eisenberg & Miller 51). One may also associate such actions with sympathy for, and empathy with, others. These actions are taken to be selfless rather than selfish, although it is conceivable that apparently altruistic actions may be motivated by some form of self-benefit to be associated with egoism (Batson 2), like the desire for fame or privileged attention.

While it is generally agreed that sympathy and empathy are often related to prosocial behaviour of which altruism is an example, there is considerable evidence to "support the notion that apparently altruistic behaviours are often mediated by non-sympathetic, pragmatic, or self-oriented considerations....for example, internalized moral values" (Eisenberg & Miller 54). In distinguishing between "sympathy" and "commitment," Sen argues that "while sympathy relates similar things to each other--namely, welfares of different persons--commitment relates choice to anticipated levels of welfare. One way of defining commitment is in terms of a person choosing an act that he believes will yield a lower level of personal welfare to him than an alternative that is also available to him" (Mansbridge, ed. 32).

The situation is made more complex by the way we perceive ourselves and our welfare. As Sen puts it, "We all have many identities, and being 'just me' is not the only way we see ourselves. Community, nationality, class, race, sex, union membership, the fellowship of oligopolists, revolutionary solidarity, and so on, all provide identities that can be, depending on the context, crucial to our view of ourselves, and thus to the way we view our welfare, goals or behavioural obligations" (Zamagni, ed. 86).

2. ALTRUISTIC BEHAVIOUR IN WARTIME: SYBIL KATHIGASU AND ELIZABETH CHOY

In the context of war, the study of altruistic behaviour by Samuel and Pearl Oliner, published as *The Altruistic Personality: Rescuers of Jews in Europe* (1988), found that "rescue behaviour was not, as a rule, an impulsive response to an immediate situation, but rather an ongoing activity, carried out over a period of weeks, months or years." Their study defines altruism in objective, measurable criteria:

> We characterise a behaviour as altruistic when (1) it is directed towards helping another, (2) it involves a high risk or sacrifice to the actor, (3) it is accompanied by no external reward, and (4) it is voluntary.
>
> (Oliner & Oliner 6)

The social-psychological orientation adopted by the Oliners assumes "that behaviour is best explained as the result of an interaction between personal and external social, or situational factors. We view an altruistic behaviour as the outcome of a decision-making process in which the internal characteristics of actors as well as the external environments in which they find themselves influence each other" (Oliner & Oliner 10).

It is within a corresponding framework that the altruism of two women, Sybil Kathigasu of Perak, and Elizabeth Choy of Singapore, may be studied. When war came to Ipoh, Malaya, in December 1941, soon after the Japanese bombed Singapore on 8 December, Sybil Kathigasu (née Daly) was in her early forties (and more than ten years older than the newly married Elizabeth Choy, née Yong), with two grown children and a youngest child about five years of age. She was an experienced midwife and nurse, and a doctor's wife. Fluent in Cantonese, the dominant dialect of Ipoh and its environs, this Eurasian woman could also make herself understood in several other Chinese dialects. In the "chaos and confusion" that followed the bombing of Ipoh on 15 December 1941, during which Dr Kathigasu was wounded in the leg by shrapnel, the Kathigasus were forced to evacuate Ipoh with their family, and made their way south to a one-street town called Papan, once the biggest centre of population in the tin-rich Kinta Valley, but now obscured by the shifting tide of prosperity, although with the influx of refugees from Ipoh, the population of Papan had increased two to threefold.

"We had not been in Papan a day when, the news of our arrival having spread in the town, patients began to come in" (29). But their income from Papan was too small as the Kathigasus gave the poor and those who had lost everything free treatment, and charged others whatever fees they could afford. Until they secured the services of a local resident to help them out, they were in no position to know if their patients were telling the truth. Shortly after, Dr Kathigasu was compelled to resume his Ipoh practice to supplement the small income secured from the Papan dispensary which his wife was left to run.

It was only a matter of time before the Kathigasus found themselves involved in anti-Japanese activities of a more dangerous sort than secretly listening to the BBC news on their wireless set, nicknamed Josephine. When the Japanese overran Malaya, many Malayan men had fled their homes for the jungle-clad hills to hide from the Japanese, who singled out the Chinese for special attention (because the overseas Chinese had collected funds to help the mainland war effort after the Japanese invasion of Manchuria in 1937). They became part of the Malayan People's Anti-Japanese Army (MPAJA), an underground organization led and run by Communists. But when asked if she could help sick and wounded guerillas by supplying them with medicines,

> It took me only a moment to make up my mind. I could not approve of some of the guerillas' methods, but this was war. They were fighting the common enemy, and any help I could give them was a contribution to final victory. (69)

Even though she knew that anyone the Japanese suspected of aiding the guerillas "could expect to be kept alive only until the Japs were persuaded that they had wrung from him by torture, everything he knew" (59), she agreed to help the Communists.

Clearly then, in circumstances of life and death, Kathigasu marginalised political ideology that she might regard the guerillas as "fighting to save us from the Japs." She found that they never preached communism outside their own ranks and she "never thought of them as

Communists at all, but simply as allies of Britain and America in the fight against the Axis." In a crisis situation such as that precipitated by war, Kathigasu made action and commitment possible by pragmatically simplifying the ideological issues and second, by prioritising the immediate. She corresponded with and sent money and medicines to the MPAJA H.Q. by special courier. The collaboration between this devout Roman Catholic and her Communist friends included visits paid by guerillas every night for treatment and surgery. Her loyalty to the anti-Japanese cause was accompanied by calculating resourcefulness. She agreed to serve on a Peace Committee as a representive of the people of Papan, because "this might give me greater scope for anti-Japanese activities while also serving to establish my 'loyalty'."

Kathigasu admired the Communists because they "were a thorn in the flesh to the Japanese," "avoided regular battle with the greatest skill," exhorted the people to resist Japanese rule where possible," lay low but came forth "when the coast was clear to kill a notorious informer, a brutal policeman or a particularly sycophantic supporter of the Japanese regime." Again, in ignoring ideology for the perceived responsibility of a nurse, she came to wonder in anguish, "...what was the reason for my imprisonment, torture and sentence but that I had carried out the duties of my profession to the best of my ability and as my conscience commanded me?" (218).

Sybil Kathigasu's altruism was an expression of ideological resistance as well as humanitarianism. As doctor and nurse/midwife, the Kathigasus were duty bound to help the sick and the wounded. Both saw it fit to go beyond the call of duty by risking their own lives and those of family members, though they were under no compulsion to do so. Dr Kathigasu came to Papan from Ipoh to operate on the leg of a guerilla in order to extract two bullets which had lodged themselves. It was this humanitarian and altruistic act above all else that led to their arrest, torture, and imprisonment until the Japanese surrender set them free.

In Kathigasu as in Choy, altruistic behaviour was clearly motivated by unshakeable and empowering religious faith, which was also tied to a faith in an Anglophile's belief in the superiority of Empire and its civilised values, of which Kathigasu's devotion to the BBC news is an example. Her absolute Roman Catholic faith pervades *No Dram of Mercy*. Early in the book, she recalls a religious epiphany she had in January 1942, when a gentle tap had awoken her from an exhausted sleep:

... I was dazzled by a vision of the Sacred Heart before me. Overwhelmed by a feeling of awe and love, I arose and knelt by my bed, murmuring:

'My Lord, and My God.'

And His voice said to me

'My child, you must be ready to pay the supreme sacrifice, and for the glory that is to come.'

'My Lord, I cannot ...' I whispered.

'You can, and will, for I the Lord command it. I will be with you and will give you strength.'

A great fear came over me as I answered:

'I will pay the supreme sacrifice, my Lord. I promise this in Thy name.'

As the last rays of His brightness were vanishing, my mother awoke.

'Who were you talking to, Bil?'

'I was dreaming, Mother,' I answered, for I did not want to frighten her by telling her the truth.

But I knew within myself that I must be willing to face death if my God willed it. He Himself had come to warn and strengthen me. And I was fortified through all the trials that lay ahead by the knowledge that all that was taking place was ultimately part of a divine pattern beyond our human comprehension. (40-41)

Unswerving faith stood her in good stead throughout her imprisonment and interrogation by the Japanese whom she taunted and rebutted with, among other defiant remarks, "Long live Malaya and the British"; when the Japanese sang their anthem, she joined in with "God Save the King." Her interrogator, Yoshimura, found her "the worst prisoner I have ever had" (178).

It is not surprising that in praying to Mary or Jesus, or St. Anthony, Kathigasu should act as one appointed by God to fulfil a divine mission: "Let me face death, if I must in the spirit of the Holy Martyrs." Her religious analogy is revealing. "I knew the Stations of the Cross and the Litanies by heart, and said the Rosary on my ten fingers; prayer was a great consolation and a source of strength" (228). More martyr than saint, Kathigasu was a true believer in God, King and Conscience. Her altruism led to consequences which damaged her health and eventually caused her death. Altruistically, she sabotaged the Japanese, and altruistically suffered for the subversion. The physical violence inflicted on her led to partial paralysis, and though she recovered sufficiently to undertake a pilgrimage to Lourdes in fulfillment of a vow she had made in prison, she succumbed to the septicoemia that had spread from a fractured jaw, and died in June, 1949.

As Richard Winstedt observes in his Foreword to *No Dram of Mercy*, "Passionately loyal to the British flag, she loved it partly, I think, because it sheltered her religion." This association between religion and Anglophile loyalty is also reflected in Elizabeth Choy's autobiography. Choy came from a devout Christian family in Kudat, Sabah, went to a Lutheran school in Sabah, and continued her education in Singapore at the Convent of the Holy Infant Jesus in Victoria Street. The overseas Chinese, outraged by Japanese incursions into China, had contributed to a China Relief Fund to help in the war effort against the invaders. The Chinese educated in particular regarded China as the "motherland," and their sentiments had been actively encouraged by the privately-run, politicised Chinese-medium schools. However, with her English and missionary education, Choy felt too detached from the Chinese cause to help.

At the beginning of Occupation, the Choys were managing a canteen at Woodbridge Hospital, which the Japanese took over and renamed Miyako Hospital, which treated the British at Changi Internment Camp. Soon the canteen, from its humble function of supplying food, "became a conduit of messages between the internment camp in Changi and the 'outside' world" (Zhou 65). As Choy recalls,

> When the British were interned, they lacked medicines, food and news of friends. Through the hospital canteen, friends of the internees were able to send them medicines, food, money, messages and so on, using an ambulance that used to run between the internment camp and the hospital. (34)

A secret Fund had been set up by the Anglican Bishop Wilson, to help buy food and medicines for the internees. When the Japanese discovered the underground courier service the Choys operated, Choy Koon Heng was arrested by the Kempeitai on 29 October 1943, and accused of "assisting espionage, sending wireless sets to the camp and sending money to the internees." A fortnight later, his wife followed; "my husband was very badly tortured, and myself too. In fact, neither of us ever dreamt for one minute that we would come out alive" (34). Choy thinks that the Japanese also suspected them of contributing to the Double Tenth Incident, whereby seven Japanese vessels were destroyed by a team of saboteurs, Force Z, although "all we did was to help those in distress to live through their internment."

Choy's incarceration lasted some six and a half months (until 26 May 1944), whereas her husband was not released until almost two years later, after the Japanese surrender on 12 September, 1945. Tortured more severely than his wife, he was also given the water treatment, as was Dr Kathigasu--the latter, several times.[1] Choy was confined to a small windowless room ventilated by a narrow air-vent, and twelve by fifteen feet in size, where she lived most of the time with more than twenty men. Like Kathigasu, she was beaten and tortured, and once in front of her husband, two leads were taken from a generator and applied to her body for fifteen minutes. In Choy Koon Heng's testimony, his wife "was yelling all the time" from the electric shocks.

To this day, Mrs Choy, who had never expected to get out of the Kempeitai Headquarters alive, remains fearful of all things electrical. In "Empathy and Protest: Two Roots of Heroic Altruism," Konarzewski relates the Oliners' study of the rescuers of the Jews to character education, and found that the rescuers "were significantly more religious in childhood and had more religious fathers (it is perhaps significant in this respect that both of Choy's grandfathers were church workers). Konarzewski puts forward a possible interpretation of this aspect by assuming that "early religious experience weakens in the child the feeling of dependence on others....[and] the feeling of dependence on the supernatural helps the young person to deny his or her dependence on mundane powers" (Oliner & Oliner, et. al. 27). There is no reason to doubt, from their autobiographical travails, that both Kathigasu and Choy had a very religious upbringing which inculcated in them a commitment to the spiritual, and interpreted the moral in religious rather than secular terms. The ethic of care and concern for others that they both practised was imbued with a spiritual dimension. Like Kathigasu, who had a fear of implicating others and being responsible for their torture and suffering, Choy, upon her release, refrained from talking to people on the street to protect them from suspicion.

In the hands of the Kempeitai, Choy prayed constantly for comfort:

> All through my trials in life, I have derived great strength and comfort from my knowledge of God. When I was taken by the *Kempei Tai*, and there was no one who could help me, my only source of strength and comfort was God. And he never failed me....Such words as "Cast your cares upon Me," or "the peace of God, which passeth all understanding," or "You shall have life eternal," never fail to give strength, courage and hope to all believers. (65)

Once, when she volunteered to scrub the prison corridor so as to straighten her knees and change her posture, Choy reached the cell where the Anglican

Bishop was, and secretly received holy communion from him (with some stale rice for bread, and water from the commode for wine), an act which gave her spiritual sustenance and fortitude. It is interesting to note in passing that both women (in unconscious enactment of their traditional domestic roles) volunteered to scrub and clean the floor in an attempt to make things more habitable for themselves and fellow inmates.

Whereas Kathigasu bore undying enmity towards her captors, never departing from calling them "Japs" rather than "Japanese," Choy, who did not suffer so severely at their hands, was capable of a detachment which made her believe, despite their abuse, "that in their hearts they could not be so cruel. I made myself believe that it was because of their military obligations that they became so cruel and heartless." Kathigasu's account is rendered incomplete by her untimely death on 4 June 1949, whereas Choy, with the benefit of survival, was to observe that the Japanese presence in Malaya and Singapore, perilous, nasty, brutish and short though it was, changed the political consciousness of a colonised people from ignorance and complacency to awareness. A Greater East Asia Co-Prosperity Sphere it was not, but it awakened thoughts of self-ownership and governance which Kathigasu did not live to see.

3. CONTRIBUTING MOTIVES AND FACTORS

Had these two women realised the painful, protracted and traumatic consequences of their actions, had they been blessed, literally, with foresight, would they have done what they did do? To put the question in its context, are altruists born, *and* made? In all likelihood, they would have acted as they did act. The overriding strength of the religious imperative would have been sanction enough for them. For context and situation would have demanded their staunch commitment.

In analysing the motivations of the 406 rescuers who were the subject of the Oliners' research, Smolenska and Reykowski distinguishes three major classes of motives (*allocentric*, when the rescuer's attention is focused on the persecuted person's situation; *normocentric*, when a norm of helping activates the rescuer; and *axiological*, when basic values such as justice, or the sanctity of human life are seen to have been violated). Interestingly however, the authors point to the inadequacy of motivational processes alone in action, and then conclude by underlining attributes associated with mettle rather than motive, like specific personal qualities that seemed to facilitate (or inhibit) helping action: one of them was ego strength, as manifested in a capability to withstand the stress related to dealing with the highly threatening and burdensome situations. Another personal quality was a kind of self-efficacy. Many, if not most, of the rescuers were people who apparently believed in their own ability to cope with difficult life problems. Such beliefs appeared to help them assume responsibilities that were perceived by many others as overwhelming (223).

Psychologically, the totality of motives and factors for behaving and acting altruistically is probably more complex than love of God, Empire and Conscience; for arguably, such love need not be accompanied by external action. Nevertheless, the specific context of war which confronted Kathigasu and Choy, simplified and sharpened the complexity of human motive and action, turning choice into necessity, necessity into virtue. In their pro-active commitment, their willingness to act on their beliefs for the welfare of fellow human beings without expectation of reward, their subordination of life-threatening risks to the greater need and welfare of others, and their courageous attitude to the punishments they endured, Kathigasu and Choy embodied altruism of the highest calibre.[2]

Notes

1. Sardonically dubbed by Chin Kee Onn, the "Tokio-wine treatment--pumping of water into the victim through the rectum, or draining water into his stomach by a hose, one end of which was stuck into his mouth and the other end attached to a tap which was turned on. When the stomach became bloated, someone jumped on it, and that caused water to squirt out through the ears, eyes, nose and mouth of the victim." See *Malaya Upside Down* (Singapore: Federal Pub., 1976), 117. Neither Kathigasu nor Choy was subject to such torture.
2. Kathigasu was awarded the George Medal, and Choy the OBE, after the war.

References

1. Batson, C Daniel. *The Altruism Question: Toward a Social-Psychological Answer.* Hillsdale, New Jersey: Lawrence Erlbaum Assoc., 1991.
2. Chin, Kee Onn. *Malaya Upside Down* Singapore: Federal Publ., 1976 [1946].
3. Choy, Elizabeth. "My Autobiography" [as told to Shirle Gordon]. *Intisari* 4 1 1974
4. Eisenberg, Nancy., and Paul A. Miller, "Empathy, Sympathy and Altruism: Empirical and Conceptual Links." In Stefano Zamagni, ed. *The Economics of Altruism.* Aldershot, Hampshire; Brookfield, Vermont: Edward Elgar, 1995. Pp.51-75.
5. Kathigasu, Sybil. *No Dram of Mercy.* Singapore: Oxford Univ. Press, 1983 [1954].
6. Konarzewski, Krzysztof. "Empathy and Protest: Two Roots of Heroic Altruism." In Pearl M Oliner, Samuel P Oliner, et al., eds. *Embracing the Other: Philosphical, Psychological, and Historical Perspectives on Altruism.* New York & London: New York Univ. Press, 1992.
7. Samuel P Oliner, Pearl M Oliner. *The Altruistic Personality: Rescuers of Jews in Nazi Europe.* New York: The Free Press; London: Collier Macmillan, 1988.

8. Sen, Amartya K. "Rational Fools: A Critique of the Behavioural Foundations of Economic Theory." In Jane J. Mansbridge, ed. *Beyond Self-Interest.* Chicago & London: Univ. of Chicago Press, 1990. Pp. 25-43.
9. __________. "Goals, Commitment and Identity." In Stefano Zamagni, ed. *The Economics of Altruism.* Aldershot, Hampshire; Brookfield, Vermont: Edward Elgar, 1995. Pp. 79-91.
10. Smolenska, M Zuzanna, & Janusz Reykowski. "Motivations of People Who Helped Jews Survive the Nazi Occupation." In Pearl M Oliner, Samuel P Oliner, et al., eds., *Embracing the Other: Philosophical, Psychological, and Historical Perspectives on Altruism.* New York & London: New York Univ. Press, 1992. Pp. 213-225.
11. Zhou, Mei. *Elizabeth Choy: More than a War Heroine.* Singapore: Landmark, 1995.

Chapter 11

The Classical Origins of Modern Altruism in Plato's *Dialogues*

ANTONIO L. RAPPA

When Bharata heard from his spies about his mother, the Rajahmani's evil deeds, he organised a search party for Rama. When they found him, Baratha was told that his elder stepbrother refused to return because it would go against dharma as a result of an earlier pronouncement of the Maha-Rajah. Prince Baratha was so impressed with his altruism that he made a vow to govern in Rama's place till tradition allowed King Rama's return.

Ramayana

1. THE DIALOGUES

Altruism exists in folklore, legends and epics as depicted in the story of Bharata in the *Ramayana*. This chapter examines the classical origins of modern altruism in the Platonic *Dialogues*. These dialogues represent important political conversations that have become keystones in western political philosophy, and the social and political sciences. It is indeed significant that we begin with Plato as he is considered a pre-eminent political philosopher, and the prototypal political theorist (John G. Gunnell); the master theorist of forms (Sheldon S. Wolin); and a kind of civic educator of a philosophy and wisdom that entails both tragedy and suffering for its proponents and recipients (J. Peter Euben).[1]

This chapter concentrates on the classical origins of modern altruism in Plato's *Dialogues* in terms of justice, friendship, temperance, wisdom, and valour. The chapter also keeps in view the importance of scholarship on altruism within western modernity such as Adam Smith's *Theory of Moral Sentiments* (1759), Thomas Nagel's *The Possibility of Altruism* (1970), and Howard Margolis' *Selfishness, Altruism, and Rationality* (1982). Nagel, for example, argues that there potentially exists an objectively discernible morality for all rational agents to behave altruistically in terms of "a willingness to act in consideration of the interests of other persons, without the need of ulterior motives".[2] In another piece, Gary Becker offers a masterful mixture of economics and sociobiology in examining altruism (Becker, 1976).[3] The "value" of altruism as an essential part of human nature is another area gradually being developed as seen in the work on social psychology and human development (Piliavin and Charng, 1990:29).[4] Thus we can see that the importance of theorizing is, as Plato maintained, about "ultimately learning to see the universe as it really is" (Kariel, 1972:93).[5]

Turning backwards in history from the modern period to the classical one, we are reminded that Socrates was the cerebral fountain of Plato's work (Taylor, 1998:21-41).[6] These works are primarily made up of conversations between an older master and his younger students which is similar to but distinct from the Indian philosophers Manu and Kautilya. Manu was generally perceived as a demi-god while Kautilya himself wielded political power. Plato on the other hand was neither a demi-god like Manu nor a king like Kautilya. Apart from noble birth and access to the intelligentsia of his day, Plato relied on logical argument, satire, irony, wit, and what has come to be called the "Socratic method" in the *Dialogues* (Brickhouse and Smith, 1994: 3-9; Taylor, 1998:41).[7] The Platonic dialogues are classical conversations about life that have "universal" implications for modern epistemological work. For example, Ann Congleton reminds us that the "*Dialogues* are a [new prose] form created by Plato to meet the needs of Socrates…that if reason is to play a part in human decisions it must be made active in individual human beings…through joint inquiry, to lead the person to become an active associate in discussion".[8] After all, as Alfred North

Whitehead stated aphoristically in *Process and Reality* (1929), the Western European philosophical tradition is a series of footnotes to Plato.

The Republic is known in Greek as δημοκρατία [dimokratia] and represents a series of dialogues that are divided into books. *The Republic* is arguably the most powerful of all Plato's political writings where the possibility of achieving the public good that is represented by the "just individual" and the "just state" is explored.[9] There are some similarities between the Greek and the Hindu social division of labour that provide a backdrop for the exploration of modern altruism in Plato. The Hindus divided society into several functional classes that were supposed to ensure a politically well-governed and an economically efficient society if each individual played their part and recognised the *dharma*, defined by the Oxford Dictionary as being the "right behaviour" or "virtue"; and in its Sanskrit form, "the law". Briefly, the concept of altruism did prevail within the social hierarchicalization of pre-Socratic times as seen, for example, in the Hindu and Buddhist genealogies.[10]

Centuries later in the time of the Greeks, it is interesting to find a similar socio-economic and political hierarchicalization. Hellenistic society, says Plato, is divided into at least three classes of people: the guardians, the agrarians, and the auxiliaries. At the highest level are the guardians whose rulers represent near-perfect human models of virtue and wisdom who would receive their training at the Academy (Pausanias, *Description of Greece*, XXIX; *The Republic*, 343-344).[11]

The guardians did not receive any special wages, or material benefits for holding public office. Even though these guardians made decisions on behalf of the other classes in society, their status as the highest bearers of public office (and hence, public service) meant that they had to be seen to be above the temptation of material benefit. Unlike the complex, modern city-state of Singapore where money is seen as the primary means of attracting and retaining top political and bureaucratic "talent", the ideal guardians did not pay themselves high salaries, nor used their mandated offices to periodically vote for themselves significant pay increases to make up for increases in the private sector. In Plato's *Republic*, however, the guardians were motivated by a genuine desire for public service that was not influenced by the opportunity costs of public service. The guardians had to achieve (through the Academy) four important characteristics: wisdom, valour, self-control (temperance), and justice. By achieving these four traits, these political leaders would not only be in a position to lead society, they will also be seen to be legitimately capable of leading society. The agrarians are citizens who make up the merchant and commercial class. This group also includes artisans and farmers. The third class, the auxiliaries, represents the modern equivalent of the police, military, and paramilitary forces. Plato argued that when all these people in their respective social groups behave in the manner in which they are expected without coercion from any side, society develops a sense of the virtuous (the public good) and justice is achieved by the state and society in question. How then does one discover "modern altruism" within the Socratic period in this broad framework of hierarchical society?

The following section illustrates with textual evidence the five ingredients that are necessary but not sufficient components of altruism: justice, friendship, temperance, wisdom, and valour. The final section of the chapter discusses the meaning of altruism *vis-à-vis* its significance in Plato's *Dialogues*.

2. JUSTICE

In Book I of the *Republic*, Socrates, Cephalus, Thrasymachus, and Polemarchus and other minor characters indulge in a lengthy debate about justice or δικαιοσύνη [*dikaiosyni*]. Their conversations reveal that the great Greek poets believed that justice was giving to each man what is proper (or rightful to him under the law) to him: "If, Socrates, we are to be guided at all by the analogy of the preceding instances, then justice is the art which gives *good* to friends and *evil* to enemies." Plato uses the concepts of "good" and "evil" to mean "deserving" in the sense that our enemies deserve to have "evil" befall them and our friends deserve "good" to be done to them. The good and bad referred to in this quotation do not refer to the larger Good (public good). Plato's use of "good" to friends and "evil" to enemies is best explained by the conversation on the conduct of diplomacy: the making of war with enemies and the making of alliances with friends. The dialogues also tell us that justice may be characterised as (1) a human trait that cannot exist in animals; (2) as acts that lead men to virtue (the larger public good); (3) about learning from the wise. The polity as a whole recognises these traits of justice and accepts that justice is about the delivery of laws made by the state to their subjects where transgressors are punished for their unjust acts (*Gorgias*, 469c).[12] Since the laws are made by the citizens for the good of the citizens, the citizens must themselves uphold the laws they have created. Citizens must obey the law set down by the government with the ultimate belief that a just person will become wise and good, and the unjust person evil and ignorant. We can see that this legalistic basis of justice provides a fairly rudimentary framework for a polity that is ruled by law. The dialogues suggest that altruism can only take place within a framework of justice where there are clear laws and regulations for all to see, recognise and obey. But justice is not the only ingredient that helps characterise western interpretations of altruism. We have to look at another ingredient in the origins of altruism, that is called "friendship" or φιλία [*filia*].

3. FRIENDSHIP

The concept of friendship in the Hellenistic world was as crucial as the kind of bonds that modern cosmopolitans experience. Friendship occurs at two levels, the level of the individual citizen, and at the level of the state. Friends are those who often share common interests and common values as argued by Chambers in 1936 in terms of Plato's "objective standard of value".[13] Like the characters in Plato's works, friends often derive pleasure from lengthy debates about life in the *polis*, and its ontological imperatives -- *what is*, as a polar opposite of *what ought* to be. The evidence about the importance of friendship may be found in the early platonic dialogue called *Lysis* (friendship). The dialogue in *Lysis* is between an old Socrates and two young boys of noble birth. Their conversation is important because it reveals to the modern reader the similarities and differences in the meaning of friendship: people who are friendly are predisposed to act out selfless deeds. Lysis is a young, intelligent, and beautiful noble youth who appears in contrast to the old, ugly yet wise Socrates who discusses the material world with him. Socrates says to Lysis and Menexenus (the other young boy):

"Yea, by the dog of Egypt, I should greatly prefer a real friend to all the gold of Darius, or even to Darius himself: I am such a lover of friends as that and when I see you and Lysis, at your early age, so easily possessed of this treasure, and so soon, he of you, and you of him, I am amazed and delighted, seeing that I myself, although I am now advanced in years, am so far from having made a similar acquisition, that I do not even know in what way a friend is acquired."

Socrates prefers real friendship, one that grows over time between two human beings rather than the great material wealth of King Darius' gold. At his advanced age, he quickly recognises the importance of friendship and encourages them to discover themselves in their youth. True friendship involves both friends loving each other as seen in another early dialogue, *Charmides*:

"We were saying that both were friends, if one only loved; but now, unless they both love, neither is a friend."

Socrates' advice here is about real friendship that is equally motivated on either side by either party. Both have a part to play in the building of the bonds of friendship. The concept of friendship is an important ingredient in altruism. What is the link between friendship and friendliness? "Friendship" is about bonds between at least two persons that are built over time. "Friendliness" on the other hand is a social predisposition that indicates a willingness to communicate with another person without first casting suspicion or doubt. Thus a friendly person is more likely to be predisposed towards acts of altruism than a misanthrope, although the former predisposition is not a guarantee that a friendly person would necessarily be altruistic. This is because friendship may only be extended to the boundaries of a small circle of friends, and to the total exclusion of strangers.

A person who is asocial, antisocial or unfriendly is less likely to partake in altruistic behaviour. A friendly person is also more likely than not to participate in the polis or the city state, and behave in a manner that draws him or her towards participation in the democratic requirements and responsibilities of citizens. An antisocial person is more likely than not to be self-centred and too much of an individual self-maximizer to devote time or energy towards voluntary and other activities that require the selfless participation of citizens. Indeed, within the polis, part of the reason for Plato's lamentation was the fact that citizens in his time became increasingly self-serving and materialistic that they cared less for the state than for themselves. A state or polis that is composed of asocial, careless, and thoughtless citizens will ultimately fall to the clutches of political decay.

4. TEMPERANCE

What exactly is temperance? In *Charmides*, Plato defines it, not unusually, in terms of human nature. Temperance or μετριοπάθεια [*metriopatheia*] involves having a modest and balanced spirit and possessing self-control. While the idea of temperance appears marginal to the concept of altruism when compared to friendship and altruism in *Lysis*, it becomes clear when we read *Charmides* that temperance serves an important function, and that temperance represents another necessary (though not sufficient) ingredient in the creation of altruism:

Charmides blushed, and the blush heightened his beauty, for modesty is becoming in youth; he then said very ingenuously, that he really could not at once answer, either yes, or no, to the question which I had asked: "For, said he, if I affirm that I am not temperate, that would be a strange thing for me to say of myself, and also I should give the lie to Critias, and many others who think as he tells you, that I am temperate: but, on the other hand, if I say that I am, I shall have to praise myself, which would be ill manners; and therefore I do not know how to answer you."

The modesty of youth and the self-control exerted by the young boy is in itself an illustration of self-control. Plato is himself being modest and perhaps a little coy when he suggests that he would prefer to let others who know him say that he is temperate, rather than he himself which would be immodest. But Plato is teaching us another lesson here. He is making it quite clear that those who preach or even boast of their own modesty ought to be less believed than those who have their temperance revealed by others. This perhaps does not appear to be important in private actions and within the private realm, but certainly plays an important part in the public realm, and especially for those who partake of, and hold, public office. Temperance is itself a virtue that only others can observe in ourselves. Plato warns us that self-praise in effect is no praise at all, and that the polis ought to be careful about those who boast of their own abilities, or worst, those who secretly desire power but orchestrate political situations in order to create an image of modesty and temperance, when in fact such a virtue is missing (*Gorgias*, 453b-455c; 455d-460a). Those who desire political power and self-aggrandisement are those who are most likely to fall prey to flattery.

In order, then ... what, in your opinion, is Temperance? At first he hesitated, and was very unwilling to answer: then he said that he thought temperance was doing things orderly and quietly, such things for example as walking in the streets, and talking, or anything else of that nature. In a word, he said, I should answer that, in my opinion, temperance is quietness.

As we have seen in the earlier quote, Plato's idea of temperance was more than merely being "quiet". Rather, Plato teaches us that the idea of temperance is part of being "noble and good" where the use of the words "noble" and "good" refer to dignity in action, and circumspection in thought. How is temperance affiliated to the concept of altruism? Clearly, the idea of temperance as instructed by Plato is about self-control and the ability to do things in an orderly and organised fashion. Charmides' maturity, even as a young and beautiful boy, is itself a remarkable example of self-control, and "quiet temperance", speaking only when questioned, questioning only in a modest way to his older and wiser counterpart. In other words, Charmides is the ideal example of a youth who is well brought up and who knows his place in society in terms of his own age with respect to others. Charmides' *silence* in the group discussion reveals more about the meaning of temperance than the *speeches* of his peers with the master. Thus Charmides evokes a clear potential for selflessness and with that in mind, the potential for altruistic behaviour. Charmides' knowledge of his station in society, his position among his peers, and where he stands in conversation with his peers and the master reflects a precocious maturity and a degree of self-control. Charmides is not out to seek inordinate attention for himself from his peers or adulation and praise from the Master. He is a temperate person because he has control over his speech and his self.

However, one might ask at this juncture whether a temperate person may also be selfish, and then go on to argue that a selfish person could not possibly be altruistic? Here, it is important to remember that temperance is only one of several ingredients in altruism.

Furthermore, it is less crucial for the argument in this chapter that a temperate person could potentially be a selfish one. Rather, a temperate person is also one who is temperate in terms of desire and want. On the other hand, there is a tendency for a selfish person to be less than temperate, and less than "balanced" in desire or επιθυμία [*epithymia*] and want θέλω [*thelo*] (*Gorgias*, 499c-522e). This however, does not imply that a temperate person cannot deteriorate into a selfish one – therefore losing his temperate nature entirely -- but that would be an entirely different argument and result in the "pitfalls of dichotomising behaviour into nonaltruistic versus altruistic behaviour" (Monroe, 1994:863).[14]

We have now covered two early dialogues where two ingredients of altruism are grounded, firstly the idea of friendship in *Lysis*, and the idea of temperament in *Charmides*. We will now turn to another ingredient called wisdom.

5. WISDOM

Plato's genius is seen in his incisive comments about the nature of human beings in their ordinary conversations about life in and around the *polis* and in his ability to draw upon congenital characteristics with wit and irony. In *Philebus* Plato's principal character, Socrates, is confronted with the problem of pleasure over wisdom or σοφία [sofia]. A pleasurable life, Socrates believes, provides one kind of satisfaction, while a life of wisdom provides satisfaction of a different sort. Socrates says in *Philebus* that the satisfaction derived from wisdom is greater than the satisfaction derived from pleasure. This is because pleasure does not last, but wisdom can provide both pleasure and an assurance that it will last a lifetime. Plato writes, "wisdom and intelligence and memory, and their kindred, right opinion and true reasoning, are better and more desirable than pleasure...[and] are the most advantageous of all things". In the case of wisdom as pleasure, when a youth discovers the joys of solving enigmatic situations, he seeks another enigma with a greater intensity of difficulty. When a child is at an inquiring age, he will search for the answers to all his questions from all and sundry, till he turns to books for more information that cannot be garnered from the human beings that he knows or meets. In *Phædrus* for example, there is a story of a cave dedicated to Zeus where the oracle preached to simple-minded men who lacked the intelligence of gifted youth. Wisdom, Plato is saying, ought to grow with time. And the youth of today "are not satisfied with examining if things are actually this way or that way" *(Phædrus,* 275b-c*)*. Plato's own way of learning was of course from the experiences and language of those he knew. *The Republic* itself tells us that Plato advised citizens to be lovers of knowledge and lovers of wisdom in order to lead fulfilling lives. But how does wisdom relate to altruism? Clearly, Plato reveals to us in the Republic and elsewhere that wisdom will lead to the accumulation of greater knowledge about other citizens and their lives. The knowledge of others leads to the ability to compare ourselves with others' experiences. The experience of wisdom leads to understanding of others.[15] Understanding others' experiences, opinions, and points of view increases the potential for altruistic behaviour because of empathy and a shared sense of humanity that connects all human beings across time (differences between human generations) and space (differences between culture, location, and tradition).

6. VALOUR

Book V of *The Republic* (on Matrimony and Philosophy) defines valour or ανδρεία [andreia] in terms of bravery that is "operationalised" in three main ways: (1) valour in terms of providing protection for one's own family; (2) valour in defending the state against the enemies of the state; (3) the recognition of valour and acts of bravery by the *polis*. The brave ought to be given the correct honours and respect within the *polis*. If the brave are rewarded by the *polis*, then this will motivate them to strive for the highest goals, "Let no one whom he has a mind to kiss refuse to be kissed by him while the expedition lasts. So that if there be a lover in the army, whether his love be youth or maiden, he may be more eager to win the prize of valour" (*The Republic* 468c). Acts of valour were celebrated by poets in their odes and songs. The Greek historians say that, "a monument [was erected] for all the Athenians whose fate it was to fall in battle, whether at sea or on land, for their valour...on the field of battle". The ancient Greeks loved the idea of erecting monuments and cenotaphs in honour of the brave as a permanent symbol of military achievement. Valour was considered a military virtue as well as a civic one. This was because it was in the nature of "proto-nationalist" Athenian campaigns and Hellenistic warfare in which it was considered honourable to die on the field of battle and in defence of the *polis*. For example, the *Symposium* speculates that the best army would be one composed of pairs of lovers, each striving to serve and protect the other.[16] But valour was also a civic virtue because it meant that such service to the *polis* would not only ensure protection but also the survival of the city state and the confederation. In one conversation, the great poet Homer says that at special public occasions where sacrifices are made the brave and valorous ought to be honoured with "with hymns and those other distinctions which we were mentioning".[17] Valour is therefore an important ingredient of altruism because to die on the field of battle in order to protect one's family, and by extension the *polis*, against the enemies of the state is to make the ultimate sacrifice -- to die so that others may live. This is a pre-eminent illustration of altruism, although not all altruistic acts have to go to such extreme ends in order to be considered altruistic. The notion of altruism as the ultimate sacrifice is however a powerful model of martyrdom which serves as a motivational point for other citizens. The role of the martyr has been portrayed throughout Greek history and includes Theseus the adventurer, Solon the law-giver, Aristide the just, Pericles the father of

Athens, Pelopidas Hippoclus, Phocion the second-in-command to Chabrias, Philopoemen, and Pyrrhus.

7. DISCUSSION

7.1 Plato's Pre-eminence

In the first paragraph, Plato's importance as a political philosopher and pre-eminent political theorist was briefly illustrated through the perception of three major political theorists in the modern age (Wolin, Gunnell, and Euben). We also noted the paraphrase from Whitehead with regard to the Western European philosophical tradition. As the pre-eminent political theorist, Plato's *Dialogues* suggest that justice, friendship, temperance, wisdom, and valour are five necessary and jointly sufficient ingredients of altruism. While there is no single semantic equivalent, the word "altruism" appears in the classical Greek lexicon, it is clear that the origins of altruism were clearly established in the early, middle, and later *Dialogues*.

According to Plato, life is about the discovery of knowledge through mortal minds which are inferior to the minds of the gods. The gods of course represent the ideals that man cannot achieve. However, this does not mean that the discovery and achievement of ideals are impossible. Perfectionism is a feature of a superhuman. It would take a man much greater effort and much more time to achieve, if ever, the superhuman feats of the gods. This is why heroes play a crucial role in life narratives and the collective memory. If we can accept such an ontology then we can see how the five ingredients have come together in the modern period into the concept of "altruism" from the French, *altruisme*, and the Italian, *altrui*.[18]

7.2 Altruism as a Range of Possibilities

Altruism does not exist in "isolation" and is better understood in terms of a range of possibilities. At one end are simple acts done without desiring anything in return. This may be voluntary work at a crèche, an old folks home, or giving counsel and advice to prison inmates. At the other end of the range of altruistic possibilities is the ultimate sacrifice of giving up one's life in order to protect one's family, a friend, a stranger, and the *polis*. Indeed, this has been clearly recorded in the military history of civilisation, and of war and peace (Thucydides' *History of the Peloponnesian Wars* and in Book I of Plato's *The Laws*).

Altruism is one way in which harmony and unity may be developed in an anarchic world of disorder and instability and to promote the spreading of truth as seen in Plato's "Allegory of the Cave" (*The Republic*, 514a-521b). The modern world as we know it today has changed significantly since classical Greece in technological, social, economic, and psychological complexity. Yet, the contemporary problems of modern human beings are not too different from that of Plato's classical descriptions of the human condition in classical Greece. Both classical and modern human beings are afflicted by greed, avarice, hunger, poverty, war, famine, flood, drought, and death. Altruism represents one way in which modern human beings can minimize the causes of suffering as seen in the problem that results in ignorance of human nature (*The Republic*, 334e).

Altruistic acts are likely to lead to the easing pain and suffering. The concept of altruism is also part of a larger comprehensive programme where in a world where human beings are confronted by their own physical, and metaphysical limitations, and need ideals that are good and just. This according to Plato will create a good and just society where, as he reminds us in *The Republic*, 335d, that it is impossible for "good men to make other men bad by virtue". The word "virtue" here refers to good deeds, those acts that make men good. Good deeds and good acts cannot make other men bad.

While no classical Greek word exists for the modern equivalent of "altruism", one cannot say that altruistic behaviour did not happen in those days. For example, a friend who helps another friend selflessly is performing an altruistic act inasmuch as a friendly stranger performs a similar deed for a complete stranger, previously unknown to him. This was documented in the insurmountable act of selflessness by King Cordus who desired to save Athens by giving up his life when he was told of the Oracle's prophecy. In modern times there are many acts of valour that have also saved others' lives such as the story of the posthumously decorated soldier who saves his fellow platoon-mates when he destroys an enemy bunker and dies in the course of its destruction. Another example of altruism would be the impoverished young person who believing firmly in the ideals of social justice, and possessing the knowledge of the great disparities of wealth that capitalism creates, gives her last dollar to a person-in-need whom she has never met nor is likely to ever meet again in the hope that it might alleviate the needy person's pain.

7.3 Altruism as an Antonym of Selfishness

There is a cautionary tale in *The Republic* where modern readers are forewarned of what happens when people stop being altruistic and begin behaving selfishly. Selfishness is non-altruistic as Plato observes in the case of the gluttons:

"However, I have not had a fine banquet, but it's my own fault, not yours. For in my opinion, I am just like the gluttons who grab at whatever is set before them to get a taste of it, before they have in proper measure enjoyed what went before. Before finding out what we were considering at first -- what the just is -- I let go of that and pursued the consideration of whether it is vice and lack of learning, or wisdom and virtue. [*The Republic*, 354b]"

The gluttons are those dispossessed of civility, and concerned with their own greed, denying their own senses to other kinds of dishes that moderation in taste would allow. Plato argues that a higher (abstract) attribute – in this case what it is to be "just" – cannot be attained if one's basic desires are not controlled. The glutton as can be seen, do not possess temperance and cannot see the importance of learning and acquiring the virtue of the just. The symbolic representation of the Athenians as gluttons in a decaying Athens is Plato's moral outcry against their uncivil and corrupt behaviour, and a personal satire against the very people that he himself knew and were his own blood relations.[19] In the quote above it is clear that none of the ingredients of altruism are present, there is no justice, friendship, temperance, wisdom, or valour. In fact, Plato reiterates that selfishness is a vice, "and lack of learning, or wisdom and virtue."

7.4 Plato's Method

Passage 354b of *The Republic* illustrates Plato's comparison of "vice and lack of learning" with "wisdom and virtue" as a simple dualistic device that engages the human mind because Plato believed that human beings tend to think in opposites. This dualistic mode of thought -- good-bad, right-wrong, heaven-hell, black-white, man-woman -- suggests a simplistic notion of what it means to be human, and provides an easy way of "understanding" humanity (*Gorgias*, 468e-473e; 510b-522e). Plato understood that human beings possessed the ability to do good and the ability to do bad; this was why he constructed a radical system of abstract universalism (an ideal) in his

Dialogues. He hoped that the love he had for his country transposed into political philosophy would save the city from ruin. He failed. But in his failure he provided great illumination for future generations that studied his work. One of the small and interesting slivers of advice that may be drawn out of his work is, as we have seen, in the examination of the origins of altruism. It would be mere speculation to consider that if Plato had focussed more energy on the virtue of altruism, Athens may have been saved. However, the facts indicate that he did leave a legacy that considered the importance of friendship, wisdom and experience, valour, temperance, and justice. While not all these concepts were completely detailed, it is now important to endeavour to tie these together into a coherent form *vis-à-vis* the role of the individual citizen and his responsibility to the City.

Human beings can only be made perfect if they become one with the City, that is to say, *the polis*. If the City is perfect then its citizens and civilisation will flourish automatically. But in order for the City to be perfect, the City must have perfect social, political and economic structures as ideals. These ideals can only be created with perfect citizens with a shared sense of morality, a shared responsibility towards justice, and a common understanding of the law of the Republic as we see in 351a, "if justice is indeed both [a] wisdom and [a] virtue, I believe it will easily come to light that it is also mightier than injustice, since injustice is lack of learning". For Plato, gaining knowledge is an obvious choice – we recall his dualism – the good citizen will have to choose between what is considered moral and what is considered immoral. What is considered moral is the good and what is considered immoral is not. The division between the moral and immoral may be understood by the choices that good citizens make within the Republic. The good will arise because the majority of the citizens will make it their conscious choice. These citizens will be guided by their own knowledge of the events that constitute their political, social, economic, and cultural milieu.

Altruism may not have had a classical Greek equivalent but it certainly was practiced by the Athenians and the Spartans. For example, the modern word marathon represents the approximate distance that a Greek soldier had to run from Marathon to Athens in 490 BC to let the citizens know that the Greeks had won a major battle against the Persians. The Greek soldier died after delivering the news. It is also celebrated in Greek myth such as the slaying of the Minotaur by Theseus son of Poseidon; Ajax and Melenaus sons of Nestor in the *Iliad*; and the most celebrated case of Pericles.

8. CONCLUSION

Plato believed that unity was the essence of the ideal City in *The Republic* where citizens felt joy, pain, and sorrow. It was the citizen's responsibility to strive for goodness and such goodness could be achieved through justice, friendship, temperance, wisdom, and valour.[20] The citizen striving for goodness needs the friendship of others in the search for self-fulfilment. A citizen is considered good if he genuinely accepts and carries out his duties and responsibilities in the *polis*.

Plato must have known that his ideal forms were too lofty. He predicted that questionable guardians of the past would evolve into questionable leaders of the present, and that the perfect City might not been achieved. Indeed, and sadly, this was the case for Plato's Athens. J. Peter Euben reminds us that the very characters that were represented in the Platonic dialogues as friends would later become arch enemies in real life in their search for power; those who represented just and virtuous citizens of the day such as *Polemarchus* and *Niceratus* were themselves "murdered for their fortunes" by Plato's relatives in an oligarchic struggle for material wealth, moving, as it were, back to the future. Man is by nature fallible, and it is altruism that helps redeem us all. Human beings today are indoctrinated into believing that science, rationality, and technology are the answers to the problems of modernity. Mankind ought to be moving towards greater civic consciousness through altruism as a salve and another way out of the problem of modern technology and rationalism.

Many scholars today tend to think of altruism as illusory and ill-founded. This might have contributed to the dearth of writing on the origins of altruism in Plato's *Dialogues*.[21] Ironically, many politicians today advocate the practical value of altruism as "a good" in terms of voluntarism, and as way of binding and bonding citizens towards common goals and interests in nation-building and state-building. Plato's classical ideas about human nature continue to remain valid like the good deeds of Prince Baratha, and the obedience of Crown Prince Rama in the *Ramayana* that preceded the Greek classics.

Plato's *Dialogues* are seminal insights into the meaning of life, and the importance of understanding ourselves through understanding the ingredients of character. This chapter illustrated the origins of altruism in the dialogues and the important role that it played in shaping the good and virtuous life of citizens. The chapter began by establishing the importance of Plato's work when viewed from the perspectives of three modern political theorists. We then established the five jointly sufficient ingredients of altruism: justice, friendship, temperance, wisdom, and valour.

Plato argued that human experience was imperfect and dependent on perfection, and on ideals (Benn, 1902:40).[22] Human beings need and depend upon ideal forms not only to discover their own imperfections but also to help them achieve "a life of perpetual approximation towards Ideal eternity," (Roberts, 1902:387),[23] and on the same metaphysical plane as the Creator (Rogers, 1936:75).[24] We already know that "the Good" is made up of all the virtues (Lodge, 1922:52; Demos, 1937: 247).[25] But "the Good" is also an ideal where there is no pain and anxiety, and perfect self-actualisation. It is only through participation in the *polis* that the citizen can achieve the ideal Platonic form. Therefore, the conclusion to this chapter is that altruism is integral to the Platonic interpretation of the ideal human within the ideal community (Lodge, 1946:654; Randall, Jr., 1967:322).[26]

Notes

1. See John G. Gunnell, *Political Theory: Tradition and Interpretation* (Cambridge, Mass.: Winthrop Publishers, 1979):136-37; Sheldon S. Wolin, "Norm and Form: The Constitutionalization of Democracy," in J. Peter Euben, John R. Wallach, and Josiah Ober (eds.), *Athenian Political Thought and the Reconstruction of American Democracy* (Ithaca and London: Cornell University Press, 1994):49-50; and J. Peter Euben, "Plato's Republic: The Justice of Tragedy" in his book, *The Tragedy of Political Theory: The Road Not Taken* (Princeton: Princeton University Press, 1990):273.
2. Thomas Nagel, *The Possibility of Altruism* (Oxford: Clarendon Press, 1970).
3. Garry Becker, "Altruism, Egotism, and Genetic Fitness: Economics and Sociobiology", in *The Economic Approach to Human Behaviour* (Chicago: University of Chicago Press, 1976).
4. Jane Allyn Piliavin, Hong-Wen Charng, "Altruism: A Review of Recent Theory and Research", *Annual Review of Sociology*, 16, 27, 1990:65.
5. Henry S. Kariel, *Saving Appearances: The Reestablishment of Political Science*, (Belmont and North Scituate: Duxbury Press, 1972).

6. Christopher C. W. Taylor, "Socratic Literature and the Socratic Problem", and "Plato's Socrates", in *Socrates* (Oxford and New York: Oxford University Press, 1998):21-41.
7. Thomas C. Brickhouse, and Nicholas D. Smith, "Does Socrates Have A Method?" in *Plato's Socrates* (New York: Oxford University Press, 1994). Christopher C. W. Taylor, *Socrates* (Oxford and New York: Oxford University Press, 1998).
8. Ann Congleton, "Two Kinds of Lawlessness: Plato's *Crito,*" *Political Theory* 2, 4, 1974:432.
9. Raphael Demos, "Plato's Idea of the Good", *The Philosophical Review*, 46, 3 (May) 1937:245.
10. See for example, Richard King, *Indian Philosophy: An Introduction to Hindu and Buddhist Thought* (Edinburgh : Edinburgh University Press, 1999).
11. *Pausanias' Description of Greece*, trans. by W.H.S. Jones (London: Heinemann, 1918). See also, D. H. Fowler, *The Mathematics of Plato's Academy* (Oxford: Clarendon Press, and New York: Oxford University Press, 1987).
12. Irving M. Zeitlin. *Plato's Vision: The Classical Origins of Social and Political Thought* Englewood Cliffs: Prentice Hall, 1993):39-42.
13. L. P. Chambers, "Plato's Objective Standard of Value " *The Journal of Philosophy*, 33, 22 (October), 1936:596.
14. Kristen Renwick Monroe, "A Fat Lady in a Corset: Altruism and Social Theory", *American Journal of Political Science*, 38:4 (November, 1994): 861-893. See also, Kristen Renwick Monroe's award-winning, *The Heart of Altruism: Perceptions of A Common Humanity* (Princeton: Princeton University Press, 1998).
15. While in Plato's time, this tended to be limited to the Greek confederation, there was a sufficiently diverse range of characters to account for virtually every single human trait that we know of today, and hence the viability of the large range of Platonic dialogues as universal lessons for human civilisation. See Thomas C. Brickhouse and Nicholas D. Smith *Plato's Socrates* (New York : Oxford University Press, 1994):155-165.
16. See for example, Crane Brinton, *A History of Western Morals*. New York: Paragon House, 1990:178-9.
17. *The Republic*, 468e.
18. The Concise Oxford English Dictionary, 5th edition, 1963:35.
19. See for instance, Rupert Clendon Lodge, "Reality and the Moral Judgment in Plato (I)", *The Philosophical Review*, 29, 4. (July) 1920:355.
20. For the Aristotelian counterpoint, see Patrick Coby, "Aristotle's Three Cities and the Problem of Faction", *Journal of Politics* 50, 4, 1988:896-919.
21. See for example, June Annas, "Plato and Aristotle on Friendship and Altruism", *Mind* (New Series), 86, 344, 1977:532.
22. A. W. Benn, "The Later Ontology of Plato", *Mind*, New Series, 11, 41 (January), 1902:31-53.
23. Eric J. Roberts, "Plato's View of the Soul", *Mind*, New Series, 14, 55 (July), 1905:371-389.
24. A. K. Rogers, "Plato's Theory of Forms", *The Philosophical Review*, 45, 1, (January), 1936:61-78.
25. Rupert Clendon Lodge, "The Genesis of the Moral Judgment in Plato", *International Journal of Ethics*, 33, 1, 1922:34-54; Raphael Demos, "Plato's Idea of the Good", *The Philosophical Review*, 46, 3. (May), 1937:245-275.
26. Rupert C. Lodge, "Plato and Progress", *The Philosophical Review*, 55, 6, (November), 1946:651-667; John Herman Randall, Jr., "Plato's Treatment of the Theme of the Good

Life and his Criticism of the Spartan Ideal", *Journal of the History of Ideas*, 28:3 (July – September) 1967:307-324.

References

1. Annas, June. 1977. "Plato and Aristotle on Friendship and Altruism", *Mind (New Series)*, 86, 344:532-554.
2. Barker, Ernest. 1906. *The Political Thought of Plato and Aristotle*. London.
3. Benn, A. W. 1902. "The Later Ontology of Plato", *Mind*, New Series, 11, 41 (January):31-53.
4. Becker, Garry. 1976. "Altruism, Egotism, and Genetic Fitness: Economics and Sociobiology", in *The Economic Approach to Human Behaviour*, Chicago: University of Chicago Press.
5. Brickhouse, Thomas C., and Nicholas D. Smith. 1994. *Plato's Socrates*. New York: Oxford University Press.
6. Buckley, Terry. 1996. *Aspects of Greek History, 750-323 B.C.* London and New York: Routledge.
7. Chambers, L. P. 1936. "Plato's Objective Standard of Value" *The Journal of Philosophy*, 33, 22 (Oct):596-605.
8. Demois, Raphael. 1937. "Plato's Idea of the Good", *The Philosophical Review*, 46, 3 (May):245-275.
9. Euben, J. Peter. 1990. "Plato's Republic: The Justice of Tragedy" in his book, *The Tragedy of Political Theory: The Road Not Taken*. Princeton: Princeton University Press.
10. Fowler, D. H. 1987. *The Mathematics of Plato's Academy*. Oxford: Clarendon Press, and New York: Oxford University Press.
11. Gunnell, John G. 1979. *Political Theory: Tradition and Interpretation*. Cambridge, Mass.: Winthrop Publishers.
12. _______. 1982. "Interpretation and the History of Political Theory." *American Political Science Review*, 76:2:317-327.
13. Kariel, Henry S. 1972. *Saving Appearances: The Reestablishment of Political Science*. Belmont and North Scituate: Duxbury Press.
14. King, Richard. 1999. *Indian Philosophy: An Introduction to Hindu and Buddhist Thought*. Edinburgh : Edinburgh University Press.
15. Lodge, Rupert Clendon. 1920. "Reality and the Moral Judgment in Plato (I)". *The Philosophical Review*, 29, 4 (July):355-373
16. _______. 1922. "The Genesis of the Moral Judgment in Plato", *International Journal of Ethics*, 33, 1:34-54.
17. _______. 1946. "Plato and Progress", *The Philosophical Review*, 55, 6, (November):651-667.
18. Monroe, Kristen Renwick. 1994. "A Fat Lady in a Corset: Altruism and Social Theory", *American Journal of Political Science*, 38:4 (November): 861-893.
19. _______. 1998. *The Heart of Altruism: Perceptions of A Common Humanity* Princeton: Princeton University Press.
20. Nagel, Thomas. 1970. *The Possibility of Altruism*. Oxford: Clarendon Press.
21. Pausanias. [2nd Century, A.D.]1918. *Pausanias' Description of Greece*, trans. by W.H.S. Jones. London: Heinemann.
22. Piliavin, Jane A., and Hong-Wen Charng. 1990. "Altruism: A Review of Recent Theory and Research", *Annual Review of Sociology*, 16, 27-65.

23. Plato. 1903. *The Four Socratic Dialogues of Plato*. Translated by Benjamin Jowett. Oxford: The Clarendon Press.
24. ______. 1979. *Gorgias*. Translated by Terrence Irwin. Oxford: Clarendon Press and New York: Oxford University Press.
25. ______. *The Laws*. 1988. Translated by Thomas L. Pangle. Chicago: University of Chicago Press.
26. ______. *Protagoras*. 1991. Translated by C. C. W. Taylor. Oxford: Clarendon Press; and New York: Oxford University Press.
27. Randall, Jr., John Herman. 1967. "Plato's Treatment of the Theme of the Good Life and his Criticism of the Spartan Ideal", *Journal of the History of Ideas*, 28:3 (July – September):307-324.
28. Roberts, Eric J. 1905. "Plato's View of the Soul", *Mind, (New Series)*, 14, 55 (July):371-389.
29. Rogers, A.K. 1936. "Plato's Theory of Forms", *The Philosophical Review*, 45, 1, (January):61-78.
30. Stalley, R. F. 1983. *An Introduction to Plato's Laws*. Oxford.
31. Taylor, Christopher C. W. 1998. *Socrates*. Oxford and New York: Oxford University Press.
32. Vlastos, Gregory. 1973. *Platonic Studies*. Princeton: Princeton University Press.
33. Whitehead, Alfred North. 1929. *Process and Reality*. New York: Macmillan.
34. Wolfe, Alan. 1998. "What is Altruism?" in Walter W. Powell and Elizabeth W. Clemens (eds.), *Private Action and the Public Good*. New Haven: Yale University Press.
35. Wolin, Sheldon S. 1994. "Norm and Form: The Constitutionalization of Democracy," in J. Peter Euben, John R. Wallach, and Josiah Ober. Editors. *Athenian Political Thought and the Reconstruction of American Democracy*. Ithaca and London: Cornell University Press.
36. Zeitlin, Irving M. 1993. *Plato's Vision: The Classical Origins of Social and Political Thought* Englewood Cliffs: Prentice Hall.
37. Connolly, William E.[1988]1993. *Political Theory and Modernity*, Ithaca and London:Cornell University Press,pp.141-2

Chapter 12

Conclusion

BASANT K. KAPUR

The chapters in this volume provide, as the reader will readily appreciate, an 'intellectual feast'. There is much to learn, and to reflect upon, from the varied insights and perspectives provided by authors from diverse disciplinary backgrounds. It is not possible to summarize all this richness within the confines of a single chapter. My aim, therefore, is more modest: to tie together what appear to be some of the central strands in the preceding discussion, with a view to providing an organizing frame of reference for further systematic thinking on the subject. In so doing, I will also take the liberty of introducing some of my own reflections, based on my reading and study over the past decade or so. This Chapter is, accordingly, somewhat interpretive in character, and designed, as just indicated, to stimulate further contemplation and study by readers with an actual or potential interest in the deep, multi-faceted subject of altruism.

The issues on which we focus are the definition of altruism, the altruistic personality, altruism and self-cultivation, the metaphysical dimension, and related issues. It turns out that there is a fairly vast literature on these issues, which we will attempt to piece together: I hope that the reader will thus not only bear with the diverse quotations which are adduced below, but also find them provocative and stimulating.

1. THE DEFINITION OF ALTRUISM

Various definitions have been proposed in earlier chapters, including:

'I take the term "altruism" to refer to a concern for the well-being of others' (Kim-Chong Chong, this volume).

'Altruism refers to an act performed voluntarily to help someone else when there is no expectation of receiving a reward in any form (Schroeder, Penner, Dovidio and Piliavin, 1995)' (Elizabeth Nair, this volume).

'We say that one acts altruistically when one feels and acts as if the welfare of others were an end in itself' (Wei-Bin Zhang, this volume).

The third definition is in a sense intermediate between the first two: the second definition excludes any psychic reward as a motivation, while the first – although this may not be the author's intention - allows for any kind of psychic reward, including self-regarding ones (e.g. the desire for publicity, social approval, and the like). The third, it would appear, would allow, broadly, for other-regarding psychic rewards, but not self-regarding ones.

The issue is complicated by the subject of empathy, discussed by both Elizabeth Nair (*op. cit.*) and Anthony Chang (this volume). Chang views empathy – the vicarious experiencing or sharing of the observed emotional state of another – as a motivation for pro-social (helping) acts and behaviour. Nair accepts that this is entirely possible, but argues that in the case of some individuals 'empathic joy' – 'personal pleasure derived from feedback that the victim has been helped by the intervention' – is 'egoistic in that we all like to feel good'. She further contends that even pro-social behaviour motivated by the desire to alleviate one's empathy-induced 'sense of discomfort' at another's misfortune is self-regarding in nature, although one might question this: the capacity to feel such discomfort is, one might argue, a sign that the individual is *not* totally selfish.

The example of empathic joy given by Nair suggests that it is not always possible to separate the reasons for pro-social behaviour into neat compartments of other- and self- regarding motivations respectively: there may be some overlap between the two. To conclude, then, I would suggest that, in principle, pro-social behaviour that is motivated *primarily* by other-regarding considerations should be viewed as altruistic, while that motivated primarily by self-regarding considerations should be viewed as egoistically-inspired, while at the same time recognizing that the distinction may, in some situations, not be entirely clear-cut.

In support of this, one might consider an insight of Immanuel Kant (*Lectures on Ethics*, quoted in David Collard (1981, p. 176)): 'Commencing good from obligation through habit we can end by doing it from inclination, and to this extent love can be commanded'. This, too, indicates that other-regarding psychic motivations should be accepted within a definition of altruism. Indeed, more broadly, there could well be a self-reinforcing process at work. Not only can love and empathy be sources of altruistic acts and behaviour, they can be further deepened by the latter. Such deepening can be a natural, and entirely 'human', consequence of pro-social behaviour, leading in turn to the development of an altruistic orientation towards life generally, or of an altruistic personality. We turn to this subject next.

2. THE ALTRUISTIC PERSONALITY

Chong (*op. cit.*) advances Mencius' thesis that 'humanity is such that there are certain spontaneous ethical predispositions which manifest themselves in appropriate situations', and which give rise to altruistic acts. Similarly, Anthony Chang focuses in detail on the nature of empathy, and its relationship to pro-social behaviour. These insights raise the broader issue of whether it is possible to characterize a personality type or types who are regularly and spontaneously altruistic. There is, in fact, an interesting, deep, and instructive literature on this subject, which we briefly review here.

Consider first J. Philippe Rushton's (1980 p. 84; cited in Frank (1988)) characterization of the 'altruistic personality':

'This person is more motivated to engage in altruistic acts. He or she has internalized higher and more universal standards of justice, social responsibility, and modes of moral reasoning, judgment, and knowledge, and/or he or she is more empathic to the feelings and sufferings of others and able to see the world from their emotional and motivational perspective...the consistently altruistic person is likely to have an integrated personality, strong feelings of personal efficacy and well-being, and what generally might be called "integrity"...(In addition, altruists) behave consistently more honestly, persistently, and with greater self-control than do nonaltruists.'

This is a rich and pregnant definition, with various deep implications, of which we highlight two in this section:

(1) We first note the mention of 'universality' in it. This resonates with insights from various philosophical traditions. Consider, for example, a Confucian or Neo-Confucian perspective:

'The enlargement of the self, with its eventual union with Heaven as the most generalized universality, travels the concrete path of forming communions with a series of expanded social groups' (Wei-Ming Tu (1985, p. 134)).

Tu makes it clear that this process of 'enlargement of the self' does not connote a process of egoistic aggrandisement, but the reverse: '(t)he cultivation of the self..requires an unceasing struggle to eliminate selfish and egoistic desires' (Ibid., p. 137). In a very interesting passage, Tu also points out the dangers of not reaching out continually to progressively wider social groups:

'if (for example) we are incapable of establishing meaningful relationships with people not connected by blood or marriage, our familialism degenerates into nepotism, which is yet another form of structural limitation. Like self-centredness, nepotism restricts us to a small circle. In the short term, self-imposed isolationism or protectionism may give us a false sense of security but eventually, it will numb our sensitivity, diminish our creative power, and corrupt our Heaven-ordained nature. As a result, we will not be able to protect the well-being of our families or maintain our own integrity. Just as egoism is detrimental to the self, nepotism brings misfortune to the family' (1989, emphasis added[1]).

(2) The suggestion, then, is that the 'enlargement of the self', and its 'eventual union with Heaven as the most generalized universality', are intimately associated with 'the cultivation of the self'. Again, parallels can be found with other philosophical/spiritual traditions: indeed, as we suggest below, there are deep commonalities on this entire subject across both Western and Eastern traditions. To quote an eminent Christian philosopher, Reinhold Niebuhr (1948, pp. 63-4):

' "He that findeth his life shall lose it: and he that loseth his life for my sake, shall find it"...This paradox..calls attention to the fact that egoism is self-defeating, while self-sacrifice actually leads to a higher form of self-realization. Thus self-love is never justified, but self-realization is the *unintended but inevitable* consequence of unselfish action' (emphasis added).

Tu has also argued that 'the self must overcome egoism to become authentically human' (1989, p. 115). We may indeed view 'self-realization' as, *inter alia,* entailing the development of the qualities identified by

Rushton above. A more detailed discussion of this is warranted, which we proceed to next.

3. THE RELATIONSHIP BETWEEN ALTRUISM AND SELF-CULTIVATION

Let us recall again Rushton's finding that 'the consistently altruistic person' is likely to have 'an integrated personality', and to 'behave consistently more honestly, persistently, and with greater self-control than do non-altruists'.

What does it mean *not* to have an integrated personality? Consider an insight of Aristotle, as exposited by Sir Ernest Barker (1959, p. 243): 'In individual men the reason which should control their being is involved in other elements of appetite and passion'.[2] Similarly, various philosophies and religions conceive of man as divided into a higher self and a lower self. Altruism then, by inducing people to care for others, even when, on occasions, it entails subordinating one's instinctual selfish desires to the concern for others, may be viewed as a means of helping human beings to evolve from their lower to their higher selves, thereby 'cultivating' themselves and, *inter alia*, achieving greater self-control (i.e., greater control over their 'appetites and passions') and a more integrated personality.[3]

Interestingly enough, a very similar view was expressed by Aristotle, and, as Antonio Rappa argues in his chapter, even earlier by Plato. Aristotle regarded involvement in the affairs of the state and other associations *in a spirit of 'justice and friendship'* as virtually indispensable to the development of a person's ability to act rationally in a wide variety of situations:

'(I)n any human soul reason is always adulterated: it is always mixed with passion. But the State in its ideal form is the vehicle of *pure* reason: the law of the State is reason without passion' (Barker, p. 243).

'The commanding forces within us are a chance congeries, united by the fact of their co-existence within a single personality, but not by any causal tie of reason. Political science in its widest sense teaches us to assimilate, because it teaches us to unify, these commanding forces, as all issuing from the single compulsion of the one end of human striving – happiness, or the

Good. And because such a union gives for the first time a clue for self-guidance – because it enables a man to determine himself rationally in the light of a principle – it lifts him to a higher stage of moral life. Progress in political science is not so much to know more as to be better – not an increase of knowledge, but of goodness through knowledge. It means self-knowledge, and *with that self-control*' (*Ibid.*, p. 242, emphasis added).

In sum, Aristotle's views may be expressed in two propositions: (a) Participation in the activities of the State – and of other associations[4] - is a virtually indispensable means of achieving increased self-control. As quoted, 'Progress in political science..means self-knowledge, and with that self-control'. The argument here can be interpreted to the effect that participation in State and other activities continually confronts the individual with moral and other challenges, and his introspective examination of his – rational as well as 'knee-jerk' - responses to these challenges increases his self-awareness and, thence, his self-control.[5] An individual living an isolated life is not likely to be, or become, conscious of all his latent impulses (because situations in which all of those impulses are 'activated' would not often arise in his life), and is therefore, by not being 'forced' to confront those impulses, not likely to ever realize his full moral potential. (b) To be fully effective, participation in State and other activities has to be geared to the pursuit of justice and friendship – to the extent, indeed, of regarding each friend as 'another self' (Barker, p. 236). In other words, such participation should not be motivated by the pursuit of self-interest. The essential reason for this is that the 'elements of appetite and passion' that Aristotle speaks of, or the 'dark and turgid impulses' that Niebuhr speaks of, are inherently self-regarding in nature. Pursuit of self-interest in State and other activities, while it may lead to a certain – or even a considerable – amount of rationality in a limited domain of the individual's endeavour, is by its very nature likely to instinctually confirm him in his self-regarding impulses and tendencies in many other domains, and thus preclude him from moving to the 'perfect freedom' (see Section IV below) which complete rational self-control confers. Self-regarding appetites, passions, and impulses exist in the non-rational part of an individual's being, and it is only when unselfish intentions and tendencies are internalized by the individual over an extended period of practice and endeavour that the former will be gradually neutralized.[6]

On a related note, if, as one thinker has observed, a hallmark of a civilized person is the capacity to delay gratification, altruism may be viewed as a valuable civilizing influence. It may also – if I may digress slightly - be an essential building-block of society: for example, what happens to society, and to the upbringing of individuals, when, as James Collier (1991, pp. 252-3, 255) remarks, parents put their own interests first:

'Between the high divorce rates, the rising number of children born to unwed mothers, and the widespread institutionalizing of young children (in day-care centers, and so forth), we have seen in America an abandonment of parental responsibility which is unmatched in human history...It is probable that we are now raising a generation that will be less well-socialized, more self-centered, and probably somewhat more impoverished in its cognitive functions than previous generations. The damage, I submit, has already been done, and the results are abundantly evident in the rates for crime, alcoholism, drug use, and disaffiliation we are seeing in our young...*so long as Americans continue to put the interests of themselves over the needs of their children* we are going to create a social system which each year will be less pleasant to live in' (emphasis added).

The discussion in this Section also has rather fundamental implications regarding Economic Theory. The two fundamental postulates normally taken to define Economic Man are '*self-interested goals* and *rational choice of means*' (Hirshleifer (1985), p. 54, emphases in original). We now see that, empirically, these two postulates may well be incompatible with each other, especially in situations involving choice over time, in which self-control is important: the selfish individual may not be able to 'rationally' maximize his long-term well-being, giving in instead to short-term attractions, while the altruistic individual may well be more successful in this regard. There is in fact considerable evidence of inconsistency in people's intertemporal choice behaviour.[7] In his important work, Robert Frank (1988) has therefore stressed the role of emotions and altruism in helping to address the self-control problem.[8]

4. THE METAPHYSICAL DIMENSION

Some references to the metaphysical dimension have been made above, in the quotations from Tu and Niebuhr, and in the discussion of the higher and lower selves of man. It is invoked most explicitly in Liew-Geok

Leong's chapter in this volume, where she shows how the spiritual faith of Sybil Kathigasu and Elizabeth Choy endowed them with the courage and fortitude to undertake extraordinary personal risks, and to undergo very severe physical suffering, as a consequence of helping others during the Japanese Occupation in Malaysia and Singapore. In this Section, we undertake a more systematic discussion of the metaphysical dimension, and its relationship to altruism.

Consider, firstly, two statements by Christian philosophers:

'Each part is related or ordained to God as the End of everything, but this ordination of each being to God implies a corresponding ordination of the parts to one another...*it is not possible to love our neighbour if we don't love God*; and we do not love ourselves really if we do not love our neighbour (De Torre (1980), pp. 223, 226; emphasis in original).

'God is, therefore, love. The conscious impulse of unity between life and life is the most adequate symbol of his nature....An all-embracing love is enjoined because God's love is like that' (Niebuhr (1948), pp. 48, 59[9])

As documented in detail in Kapur (1995, Chapter 1), very similar views are expressed in other great religions and philosophies – Islam, Hinduism, Buddhism, and Confucianism. To provide just two quotations, from Islam and Hinduism:

'The structural edifice of social life (in Islam) is pervaded by very deep and sincere feelings of love, goodness and brotherhood. The whole social life is a true picture of co-operation and mutual help...The Holy Prophet said.. "None of you is a true believer in Islam until and unless he loves for his fellow men what he loves for himself" ' (Rahman (1980), pp. 381-2)

'Love..is identifying yourself with all beings in the world. When we accept that all the world is the One Supreme Self, we must love all beings literally as ourselves' (Swami Parthasarathy (1988), p. 146)

The commonalities across religions and philosophies are indeed striking, and suggest that courses in Comparative Religion which focus on these commonalities, without suggesting that all religions are identical, could perform a valuable educational function if offered in schools and universities. This is not to suggest, among other things, that altruism *has* to be grounded in a metaphysical view of man.[10] The latter view does seem, to me, to provide an essential unifying and completing focus for the understanding of altruism, but this is an issue which each individual will have to decide for himself after a study of the relevant writings. To provide one example of the considerations he would have to reflect upon: is it possible that empathy has an underlying metaphysical basis, or is it simply a socio-psychological phenomenon?

A misconception that deserves comment is the notion, sometimes held, that a wide-ranging altruism entails the loss of one's individual identity through an 'undifferentiated oneness' with others. On this issue, Aristotle's observations on the role of the State do in fact carry wider implications. 'Man is naturally born with a disposition to virtue: the work of the State is to train the disposition in a habit of regular action…the State..is an association of friends mutually provoking one another to virtue' (Barker, p. 271). Indeed, 'the true end of the State must be, not to make its members one, but *to raise them to the fullness of their being*, by encouraging the highest activities of a good life' (p. 405, emphasis added[11]). Ironically enough, man moves closest to 'perfect freedom' when 'reason, the highest element of the soul and the peculiar differentia of man, has become conscious of itself and has learned to use its powers' (p. 427). Or, as Tu above has put it, we become 'authentically human' only when we have 'enlarged our selves'.

5. RELATED ISSUES

(a) It is important that we do not over-simplify our characterization of altruism. A 'concern for the well-being of others' (Chong) can very well be an intelligent and discriminating concern, rather than an uncritical one. This point is well brought out by Wei-Bin Zhang's chapter on the welfare state, and is epitomized by the Chinese saying, 'Give a man a fish, and he will eat for a day; teach him to fish and he will eat every day.' Professor C.L. Ten's discussion of an altruism tempered by a respect for pluralistic accounts of the good also points to the need for an intelligent and discriminating concern for others.

(b) Similarly, we should recognize that human beings are not 'black or white' entities, but are characterized by mixtures of altruistic and selfish motives. Consciously or unconsciously, they calculate trade-offs, such as the trade-off between risk and altruism, as Michael Collins emphasizes in his chapter. Even a highly altruistic person may well compare the costs of an altruistic act to himself with the benefits to others.

(c) This volume has adopted the conventional definition of altruism as denoting a concern for others. However, on a more speculative note, we might ask whether it is possible to broaden the definition of altruism – to include *anything* done for its own sake, rather than for the prospect of a reward for oneself – and whether this can be a basis of, among other things, scientific and artistic creativity (for example, valuing truth, or advancing the frontiers of knowledge, for their own sake). Certainly this would be consistent with Frank's view of emotions or intrinsic interests as means of overcoming the self-control problem. It is well-known, for example, that one of the most notable characteristics of great scientists and scholars is their intrinsic 'passion' for their work, rather than their desire for material rewards *per se*.

In concluding this chapter, we may state the fundamental insight of this volume: altruism is a rich, fundamental, and multi-faceted phenomenon, that has deep implications across the entire range of disciplines in the humanities and social sciences – which reflect the fundamental role it plays in human life generally. Just as its importance extends across diverse disciplines, so also are diverse disciplinary perspectives required to provide a fuller understanding of it. Each discipline illuminates important aspects of it, and enriches other disciplines' study of it. If this volume has stimulated the reader to further deep thought on the subject of altruism, it would have served its purpose.

Notes

1. The thesis advanced here is clearly congruent with Chong's contention that particularistic concerns can, and indeed should, if properly developed, serve as a basis for non-particularistic concerns.
2. Niebuhr (*op. cit.*, p. 26) expresses a similar view: 'There has been little suggestion in modern culture of the demonic force in human life, ..or of the dark and turgid impulses, imbedded in the unconscious of the individual and defying and mocking his conscious control and his rational moral pretensions'.
3. In relation to A.T. Nuyen's chapter, may I suggest here that it is not 'subjectivity' *per se* that is linked to altruism, but the higher self of man.
4. The State may in fact simply be 'described as an association of associations' (including the family) (Barker, p. 237).
5. '(A)ctive thought on the deepest of moral questions is necessary to the political life' (Barker, p. 290).
6. As Tu above puts it, self-cultivation requires an 'unceasing struggle to eliminate selfish and egoistic desires'.

7. For a detailed discussion, see Kapur (1995, Section 3.3).
8. Specifically, Frank refers to the tendency, on which experimental psychology furnishes ample evidence, for current rewards or penalties to appear much more vivid in people's imagination than future ones. People (and animals) have a 'psychological reward mechanism' that assigns 'disproportionate weight to near-term rewards', thus creating a self-control or impulse-control problem (Frank, pp. 82-3). He then goes on to argue that 'a person who cares only about material rewards' is likely to succumb to this self-control problem, and make ill-advised short-term choices, whereas people with certain ingrained emotions and values may, on that account, have psychological reinforcements against the self-control problem.
9. Niebuhr also makes the following beautiful observation: 'all human life is informed with an inchoate sense of responsibility toward the ultimate law of life – the law of love'.
10. The qualifier 'among other things' is inserted to indicate that metaphysics deals not solely with altruism, but with other issues as well – man's relation to the Divine, what it means to cultivate a genuine spiritual consciousness, and the like.
11. It follows that the unity of the State should not be achieved through coercive means, but rather voluntarily. 'It is Aristotle's aim to insist, first of all, that the State *does* indeed cohere through a moral purpose, and in a moral life – but in that way and that sense only. Its unity is spiritual, and only spiritual' (*Ibid.*, p. 404, emphasis in original).

References

1. Barker, Sir E., *The Political Thought of Plato and Aristotle*, New York: Dover, 1959.
2. Chang, P.M.A., 'Empathy and Helping', this volume.
3. Chong K.C., 'Mencius and the Possibility of Altruism in Early Chinese Philosophy', this volume.
4. Collard, D.A., *Altruism and Economy: A Study in Non-Selfish Economics*, Oxford: Martin Robertson, 1981.
5. Collier, J.L., *The Rise of Selfishness in America*, New York: Oxford University Press, 1991.
6. Collins, M., 'Altruism, Risk, and Sibling Rivalry', this volume.
7. De Torre, J.M., *Christian Philosophy*, Manila: Vera-Reyes, Inc., 1980.
8. Frank, R.H., *Passions Within Reason: The Strategic Role of the Emotions*, New York: W.W. Norton and Co., 1988.
9. Hirshleifer, J., 'The Expanding Domain of Economics', *American Economic Review*, 75 (6), December 1985, 53-68.
10. Kapur, B.K., *Communitarian Ethics and Economics*, Aldershot: Avebury, 1995.
11. Leong, L.G., 'Altruism in Wartime: Self, and Others', this volume.
12. Nair, E., 'Altruism or Social Exchange?', this volume.
13. Niebuhr, R., *An Interpretation of Christian Ethics*, 4th ed., London: SCM Press Ltd., 1948.
14. Nuyen, A.T., 'Altruism as the Condition for Subjectivity', this volume.
15. Rahman, A., *Islam: Ideology and the Way of Life*, Singapore: Pustaka Nasional Pte Ltd, 1980.
16. Rappa, A., 'The Classical Origins of Modern Altruism in Plato's *Dialogues*', this volume.
17. Rushton, J.P., *Altruism, Socialization, and Society*, Englewood Cliffs, New Jersey: Prentice-Hall, Inc., 1980.
18. Parthasarathy, S.A., 'Commentary on *Kaivalyopanishad*', in Brown, K. (ed.), *The Essential Teachings of Hinduism*, London: Rider, 1988.

19. Ten, C.L., 'Altruism and Its Limits', this volume.
20. Tu, W.M., 'Neo-Confucian Religiosity and Human-Relatedness', in Tu, W.M., *Confucian Thought: Selfhood as Creative Transformation*, Albany, New York: State University of New York Press, 1985, pp. 131–48.
21. Tu, W.M., *Centrality and Commonality: An Essay on Confucian Religiousness*, Albany, New York: State University of New York Press, 1989.
22. Zhang, W.B., 'Economic Consequences of Altruism: A Two-Group Growth Model of the Welfare Economy', this volume.

Index

D

E

F

G

O

P

R

S

MIX
Papier aus verantwortungsvollen Quellen
Paper from responsible sources
FSC® C105338

If you have any concerns about our products,
you can contact us on
ProductSafety@springernature.com

In case Publisher is established outside the EU,
the EU authorized representative is:
Springer Nature Customer Service Center GmbH
Europaplatz 3, 69115 Heidelberg, Germany

Printed by Libri Plureos GmbH
in Hamburg, Germany